W9-AYW-379

Comprehensive K-6 Teacher Guidebook

EAN#: 978-0-936785-81-3
ISBN#: 0-936785-81-0
TL#: HWTG2021WC

Published by Concerned Communications, LLC
P.O. Box 1000 • Siloam Springs, AR 72761

Authors: **Carol Ann Retzer and Eva Hoshino**
Layout: **Mark Decker**
Illustrations: **Rob Harrell**
Colorists: **Josh and Aimee Ray**

Printed in the United States of America

For more information about **A Reason For Spelling®, A Reason For Science®,**
A Reason For Guided Reading®, and **A Reason For Handwriting®,** visit our website.

www.AReasonFor.com

Table of Contents

A Reason For Handwriting

Kindergarten Worktext

Featuring Creation & Sharing

General Guidelines for Teaching
Beginning Writers

**Kindergarten is a year of beginnings —
of new discoveries and excitement!**

It's also a year of challenge as a teacher faces tough questions like: "How much do I 'push' a student?" "When do I encourage my student to begin reading… or writing?" "Is there a measurable academic level a child must reach before the end of the year?"

Although individual readiness questions defy simple answers, educators *have* discovered certain trends. Many children can read and write by age five, yet research suggests it's unwise to push them. If given more time to explore their world, to broaden their base of readiness, most children "pick up" reading and writing quickly when the time is right, soon catching (and often passing) their peers. And this extra time can be crucial, since a child's attitude toward learning often develops during the first few months of school!

The **A Reason For Handwriting**® curriculum is organized to give a variety of options for meeting individual needs. The following sections explore some of these options, and offer valuable tips for working with beginning writers.

Two Presentation Options
One option is to let children begin writing in their Student Worktexts as soon as alphabet presentation begins. The teacher introduces a single letter at a time, careful not to push the child beyond their abilities. Students complete the lesson pages and project pages as directed.

A second option is to introduce all the letters of the alphabet *before* giving children the Student Worktexts. Nature-enrichment activities (see lesson plans pages 20-50) are presented as each letter is introduced and taught. After each letter has been presented and visually introduced, students may begin writing in their Worktexts. Some teachers delay this step until second semester, allowing even more time for motor-skills development.

The approach used depends on the overall readiness of the child. Regardless of which option is chosen, Alphabet Wall Sheets and Student Desk Cards can enhance the learning process. These visual reminders can be displayed around the room, laminated as flashcards, attached to student desktops, or inserted into student folders.

Those First Few Days
Since Manuscript strokes are primarily circles and lines, exercises that emphasize these shapes are very important. Such activities also minimize the stress of introducing writing by making it FUN!

Begin by blowing soap bubbles. Describe the bubbles — shiny, colorful, round — to help students remember the shape. Next, Sky Write some bubbles. (See page 9.) First demonstrate, then have the students imitate your hand motion. (If you face the class, make sure your circle goes in the *opposite* direction so that the students will see it correctly!) Watch carefully to make sure each student understands circle shape and direction.

Now have students draw bubbles in different colors and sizes, using unlined paper and crayons or felt-tip markers. Stress the importance of beginning at the two o'clock position, going up and around. Place your hand over a student's hand to encourage correct letter formation.

When students have perfected bubbles, move on to sticks (straight lines). Verbalize the stroke as you Sky Write it. Say, "Begin at the top and go straight down." Students should make several pages of sticks on unlined paper.

After students have practiced "bubbles and sticks" on unlined paper, switch to lined paper[1]. Have students make a page of bubbles, then a page of sticks, then another page of bubbles, etc. Conclude with an activity that combines bubbles and sticks to reinforce what has been learned. Ask them to draw pictures using bubbles and sticks (such as a teepee, a bunch of grapes, etc.).

Don't eliminate these simple exercises! The extra time you spend now will pay off later in good letter formation. Practice Lessons provide a final check to make certain every student has understood these essential skills.

Letter Presentation

Alphabet letters are introduced in letter formation groups (circle, curve, downstroke) instead of alphabetically. This helps students master the strokes as they are presented, giving them a feeling of success.

Due to high usage, lowercase letters are presented first. Capital letters are presented next, combined with their lowercase match. Since capitals are also in letter formation groups, the introduction order is slightly different from the lowercase letters.

While this method of introduction is highly effective for teaching handwriting alone, some teachers may wish to vary letter order to coincide with a phonics program. Student Worktext pages are perforated to accommodate this need. They may be removed, filed, and then passed out as needed to accommodate any letter order.

[1] *Page 241 is a blank practice page you may photocopy as needed. Black Line Masters are the only pages in this curriculum that may be legally photocopied, and permission is granted only for classrooms or individual homeschools using A Reason For Handwriting®.*

Forming Manuscript Letters

It's vital to demonstrate the strokes for each letter before students begin writing. Students must *picture* the letter correctly in their minds before they can *write* it correctly. As students begin to write, carefully check their work. Positive praise will greatly enhance student progress.

Gently correct any formation errors. For instance, beginners often tend to write in all capital letters. This must be corrected immediately to avoid future problems. Also, remind students that most Manuscript letters are made without lifting the pencil. (The exceptions are k, x, y — and the letters which require a dot or cross like i, j, f, and t.) Using continuous line formation now will simplify the transition to Cursive writing later.

Correct letter formation cannot be over emphasized! Promoting proper handwriting from the start is better than trying to correct bad handwriting habits!

Pre-Writing
Readiness Activities

Before students begin formal handwriting instruction, they need to participate in a wide variety of experiences using small and large motor-skills. They should also be exposed to specific visual readiness activities. The following activities will greatly enhance students' writing skills as they begin to use pencil and paper.

Visual Readiness

During daily discussions, write the key word or words of the subject on the board. This helps students become familiar with correct direction and sequence of strokes, and provides visual imagery of finished letters and words. When this activity is done regularly, students will unconsciously begin to comprehend correct letter form.

In addition, students also enjoy activities that focus on the alphabet without writing it — saying and recognizing the letters of the alphabet, and identifying names (especially their own), and words that begin with a specific letter.

Eye/Hand Coordination Activities

There are a number of eye/hand coordination activities that will greatly enhance a student's pre-writing skills. Some of these include:

- Putting together puzzles
- Building with snap cubes or blocks
- Cutting out pictures and shapes
- Threading beads
- Lacing and tying shoes
- Threading sewing cards
- Finger painting letters and shapes
- Tracing letters and shapes in sand
- Bouncing and catching a ball
- Drawing on the board or large paper
- Matching designs with pattern blocks
- Copying simple shapes and patterns

Motor-Skills Readiness

When students are ready to begin writing, allow them to copy large letters on the board or a large sheet of unlined paper. This allows you to model the correct letter formation without imposing the confines of letter size and lines. Next, give them felt-tip pens or crayons to write in a smaller space **(still unlined)**.

As students demonstrate interest and readiness, show them the correct way to write their name, beginning with the capital letter, followed by lowercase letters. **(Note: Many students have learned to write their name in all capitals. This exercise helps you correct this counter-productive habit.)**

In all these exercises, ***make the process fun!*** Make a game of correct letter formation. Help students "discover" that most letters are written from top to bottom and left to right. Praise student progress and reinforce attempts to follow the correct form.

Readiness Checklist

The student should:

- Have a desire to write.
- Be able to recognize the letters of the alphabet.
- Be able to distinguish left from right.
- Display a dominant hand.

Tips for Letter Positioning
Using the Treehouse

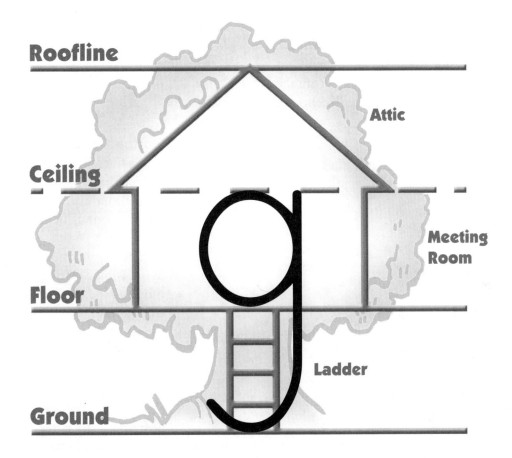

Since young writers often have difficulty when learning new letters, **A Reason For Handwriting**® offers a tool to help with letter formation. We call it the **Treehouse**.

Primary elements of the **Treehouse** include the **Roofline**, the **Ceiling**, the **Floor**, and the **Ground**. (The **Treehouse** illustration is used throughout the Kindergarten, Manuscript A, and Manuscript B Worktexts.)

Students quickly grasp the placement of each new letter when it is expressed in terms of the **Treehouse**. (Examples: "The capital R begins with a stroke from the **Roofline** straight down to the **Floor**…" or, "The lowercase p starts with a stroke from the **Ceiling** down to the **Ground**…")

These descriptions can also be helpful when remediating specific problem areas. (Examples: "Make sure the lowercase c stays inside the meeting room," or "Shouldn't the tail of your g go all the way to the **Ground**?")

Specific letter descriptions using the **Treehouse** can be found in the Appendix of this Teacher Guidebook, beginning on page 226.

In addition, a Black Line Master of the **Treehouse** is provided on page 240. This will allow you to introduce each new letter using the **Treehouse** as a visual tool.

Essential Steps for
Introducing New Letters

As each new letter of the alphabet is introduced, stress the letter's name, sound, and sequence of strokes. Also, help students understand where the letter is positioned on the line using the Treehouse.

To Maximize The Learning Experience, Students Should:

See the letter
Hear the letter
Move with the shape of the letter
Write the letter on paper

Here is the suggested sequence for introducing new letters:

Step 1: The teacher names the letter. Example: "Today we're going to learn about the letter A."

Step 2: The teacher describes the letter's sound or sounds. Example: "You can hear the [ay] sound in the word ape; or the 'a' may sound like [æh] as in apple, or [aw] as in want."

Step 3: The teacher describes the strokes and demonstrates how the letter is made. Example: "The letter 'a' begins just like an 'o' but it has a line added to the side. Be sure to write the entire letter without raising your pencil from the paper." (See "Detailed Descriptions," pages 226-230.)

In addition to these first critical steps, the following steps help students form a "mind picture" of each letter — greatly enhancing their chances for success!

Step 4: The teacher and students Sky Write the letter together. Using the pointer finger of your writing hand, outline the letter in the air, slightly above eye level. Say the letter's sound, or describe the strokes as you Sky Write. The student should imitate your movements as closely as possible. (Watch for anything that might indicate the student is having trouble.)

Step 5: The teacher and child Palm Write the letter together. Using the pointer finger of your writing hand, outline the letter on your opposite palm, describing the letter aloud as you form it. The student should imitate your movements as closely as possible. (You may also wish to Palm Write directly on the palm if the child is having trouble.)

Step 6: The students begin practicing the letter on paper.

If students need additional practice visualizing letters, the following activities may be helpful.

Have the students write the letter with finger paints on large sheets of paper.

Have the students write the letter in sand, salt, or cornmeal. Shoebox lids, cookie trays, or other shallow boxes work well for this.

Alternate Forms of
Handwriting Practice

Sky Writing

Sky Writing is a helpful way to practice the formation of individual letters. Demonstrate the letter formation with your pointer finger by "writing" in the air. Describe the letter as you demonstrate. For example, when making the capital A say, "Down, down, across." For the lowercase b say, "Down, up, around."

Now practice the letter with your students. Go over the letter several times, Sky Writing together. After practicing, ask the students to close their eyes and make the stroke(s) of the letter from memory.

When the students open their eyes, have them "write" the letter on the palm of their left hand with the pointer finger of their right hand (reverse if a student is left-handed). Practice this several times, with the student repeating the stroke descriptions aloud.

Back Writing

Students really enjoy this simple game! After you have introduced three or four new letters, ask the student to stand with his/her back turned. Then use your pointer finger to "write" the letter on his/her back. Use big, definite strokes. Then, have the student guess which letter was outlined.

Once students understand the concept, they can take turns "writing" and guessing letters.

Proper Positioning

Paper Position

Right and left-handed students should learn the same principle of paper placement. Students should place their paper at the same angle as the arm they use for writing (see illustrations). Demonstrate how the page can easily be moved up as the writing nears the bottom of the page. (Note: These paper positioning principles apply to both Cursive and Manuscript writing.)

Special attention should be given to left-handed students. Correct paper placement (see above) and pencil position will help the student write without a "hooked hand" position, or an exaggerated head tilt.

Body Position

A good writing position provides comfort and balance. Encourage students to:

- Sit comfortably back in the seat, facing the desk squarely.

- Place both feet flat on the floor.

- Lean slightly forward, but without letting the body touch the edge of the desk.

- Rest both forearms on the desk.

- Hold the paper in place with the free hand.

Pencil Position

Students should hold the pencil between the thumb and index finger, letting it rest lightly on the middle finger. The thumb should be about half an inch above the sharpened pencil point.

Kindergarten
Lesson Planning

The following information is included for each of the lesson plans:

Letter Description

Letter Description provides a specific description of the way the focus letter is formed. (See also "Detailed Descriptions," page 226). For extra practice, encourage students to trace the letter in the Treehouse at the beginning of each lesson. Remind them to follow the arrows carefully.

Letter Sounds

Letter Sounds provide the sound of the focus letter as used in common words. Depending on your phonics program, you may choose to introduce only one sound for each letter (corresponding to the initial sound of the illustration word), or you may wish to include all the sounds listed.

Resource Information

Resource Information provides specific background information about the animal or object used in each lesson, with comments designed to interest students.[1] (Be sure to check this section well in advance so you have plenty of time to compile the recommended resources you wish to use.[2])

Work Page Directions

Work Page Directions provide instructions for completing a project on the back of each letter page.[3] These hands-on activities not only reinforce the lesson, but also expand students' knowledge, understanding, and appreciation of God's World. Project pages are designed to be removed from the Worktext, completed by the student, and sent home weekly or collected into an individual student alphabet book.

Additional Resources

Additional Resources can be found in the Appendix of this Guidebook. Since not all students are visual learners, you should plan to include some alternate activities each week to maximize their learning experience. Suggested activities include Sky Writing, Palm Writing, Back Writing, and specific verbal descriptions for letters.

---

[1] *Even though they are not proper nouns, some resource words (Eagle, Hippo, Dolphin, etc.) are written with capital letters to enhance practice.*

[2] *Examples: a book of colorful butterflies; slices of apples showing different varieties; etc.*

[3] *Some activities require special materials like yarn, construction paper, glue, glitter, etc. Be sure to gather these in advance.*

Please
Read This First!

Before beginning formal handwriting instruction, please review "General Guidelines" (Teacher Guidebook, page 4), and "Readiness Activities" (Teacher Guidebook, page 6). These pages provide important tips on working with beginning writers.

Also, review with students "Let's Start at the Beginning" (Student Worktext, page 3), and correct formation of letters in "The Alphabet" (Student Worktext, page 4). This will help introduce students to **A Reason For Handwriting**®.

PRACTICE LESSONS

To The Teacher

Student Worktexts have been designed to help beginning writers practice and review basic writing skills. They also provide a tool to help evaluate individual student mastery. (Please note that all Student Worktext pages are perforated, and may be removed as desired.)

(See Student Worktext, page 7)

Lesson Focus
Following dotted-lines

Directions
"Follow the path with your pencil to help each animal find its food."

Teaching Tip
The Student Worktext frequently uses dotted lines to enhance instruction. This first page gives students practice in following a dotted line.

Extended Teaching
If the student has difficulty following the dotted line, allow additional time to practice small motor skills. Activities such as assembling puzzles, stringing beads, or building with blocks are good eye/hand coordination exercises that help build such skills.

(See Student Worktext, page 8)

Lesson Focus
Making circles[1]

Directions
"Trace each bubble. Be sure to follow the arrows." Monitor students to make certain they are using the counter-clockwise stroke. Students may wish to decorate this page by adding more bubbles with different colored crayons.

Teaching Tip
Before the students begin this page, spend time Sky Writing circles (see page 9) with the class. Emphasize the counter-clockwise formation. Describe the movement: "Start at the two o'clock position and go *up around*, *down around*, *up*." Praise students for correct direction of strokes.

Extended Teaching
Students will enjoy blowing bubbles and describing them. Remind students that circles should be round like bubbles. Any time the circle letters seem to be losing their shape, get out the bubbles! It's a great reminder.

[1] *Note: All circles in these Practice Lessons (bubbles, grapes, etc.) are the same size as the capital O and lowercase o.*

Lesson 3

(See Student Worktext, page 9)

Lesson Focus
Making circles

Directions
"Trace each grape. Be sure to follow the arrows." Monitor students to make sure they are following the arrows (moving counter-clockwise) as they trace the "grapes."

Teaching Tip
Circles are used in forming many letters in the Manuscript alphabet. Most circle letters (c, o, a, d, g, q) are written with a counter-clockwise stroke.

Extended Teaching
If students need more practice making counter-clockwise circles, have them draw more "grapes" on the page. (Space is provided.) They may wish to outline the grapes using a purple, light green, or dark blue crayon. If possible, give students the experience of tasting several different colors of grapes.

Lesson 4

(See Student Worktext, page 10)

Lesson Focus
Making downstroke lines (straight and slanted)

Directions
"Trace the straight and slanted lines. Follow the pattern to finish each line. Be sure to use the start dots." Monitor students to make sure they complete all the lines on the page.

Teaching Tip
The downstroke is the most common stroke in letter formation. Emphasize the top to bottom motion. This is *vital* as many preschoolers have learned to write bottom to top! Sky Write downstrokes in sets of three as you verbalize the movement: *"down . . . down . . . down."* Repeat and have students verbalize with you.

Extended Teaching
Stand in front of the class and drop a ball. Ask students which direction the ball fell — up or down? Then respond, "Our lines need to go down too!" Have students identify straight or slanted lines in the room (wall corners, window edges, the flagpole, pencils, etc.). Buy some stick pretzels and have students use them to make straight line pictures (a box, a picture frame, a house, or simple geometric designs).

(See Student Worktext, page 11)

Lesson Focus
Making circles (large and small)

Directions
"Trace the circles following the arrows. Be sure to use the start dots." Monitor students to make certain they are using the start dots, and that they are following the counter-clockwise arrows.

Teaching Tip
Sky Write circles with the students, describing the strokes aloud. As you model Sky Writing, be sure to turn your shoulder and writing arm so you can write in the same direction as the students. This avoids confusing them with "mirror" writing.

Extended Teaching
Take a "circle walk" around the school, asking students to look for objects that are circles. Find these shapes together: clocks, balls, lights, circles on the playground, doorknobs, etc. When you return to the classroom, have students draw pictures of the circles they've seen. Encourage them to use counter-clockwise strokes.

(See Student Worktext, page 12)

Lesson Focus
Writing circles and downstrokes

Directions
"Trace the circles and lines, then follow the same pattern to finish the page."

Teaching Tip
Demonstrate good posture, paper position, and pencil holding (page 10). Remind students that it's much easier to write neatly if their paper is placed at the same angle as their writing arm.

Extended Teaching
Encourage students to draw pictures using only straight lines and circles (a bicycle, a watch, a computer, an ice cream cone, etc.).

Practice **Lesson 7**

(See Student Worktext, page 13)

Lesson Focus
Making slanted lines

Directions
"Trace the slanted lines, then follow the same pattern to finish each line." Monitor students as they finish the pattern of zigzag lines. Make certain they are using start dots, and that they finish filling in all the lines.

Teaching Tip
Sky Write a zigzag pattern, verbalizing *"down, up; down, up."* Encourage students to practice this pattern on the board or on large, unlined paper.

Extended Teaching
Discuss what things might be drawn using only slanted lines (a steeple, a tent, a roof, a teepee, etc.). If they desire, allow students to draw these objects on unlined paper.

Practice **Lesson 8**

(See Student Worktext, page 14)

Lesson Focus
Making circles

Directions
"Trace each bubble. Be sure to follow the arrows." Monitor students to make sure they are following the arrows (moving counter-clockwise) as they trace the "bubbles."

Teaching Tip
Students may wish to draw seaweed or seashells around the fish to finish the page. Also, watch for students having difficulty with direction of stroke. Now is the time to encourage more practice to help overcome incorrect habits.

Extended Teaching
Ask students to make a circle with the index finger and thumb of their non-writing hand (an "okay" sign). Now have them trace this "circle" using the pointer finger of their writing hand. Have students take turns describing this counter-clockwise circle stroke. These descriptions will help students imprint the circle stroke in their minds.

Scope & Sequence - Kindergarten

Skills/letters emphasized in the Kindergarten Student Worktext are found in the following lessons.

Manuscript Terms

CAPITAL GROUPS
Circle (C, G, O, Q)
Curve (J, S, U)
Downstroke (B, D, E, F, H, I, J, K, L, M, N, P, R T, U)
Forward curve (B, D, P, R)
Slantstroke (A, K, M, N, V, W, X, Y, Z)
Two-stroke (B, D, K, M, N, P, Q, R, T, X)
Three stroke (A, E, F, H, I)

LOWERCASE GROUPS
Circle (a, b, c, d, e, g, o, p, q)
Curve (h, m, n, r, s, u)
Downstroke (b, f, h, i, j, k, l, m, n, p, r, t,u)
Slantstroke (k, v, w, x, y, z)
Tail (g, j, p, q, y)
Tall (b, d, f, h, k, l, t)
Two stroke (f, i, j, k, t, x, y)

Mechanics
(page numbers)

Explanation of letter placement on line: 3
Pencil position and paper placement: 4
Alphabet model with arrows: 4
Letter to parents explaining program with letter model: 5, 6
Following a line: 7
Downstroke: 10, 12, 13
Circle: 8, 9, 11, 12, 14
Slantstroke: 13

General Skills

LETTER PRACTICE

Capital Letters
Circle: 27, 28, 29, 30
Curve: 37, 38, 39
Downstroke: 31, 32, 33, 34, 35, 36, 37, 38, 40, 41, 42, 43, 44, 45, 47
Forward curve: 40, 41, 42, 43
Slantstroke: 44, 45, 46, 47, 48, 49, 50, 51, 52
Two stroke: 30, 32, 40, 41, 42, 43, 44, 45, 47, 51
Three stroke: 33, 34, 35, 36, 46

Lowercase Letters
Circle: 1, 2, 3, 4, 5, 6, 8, 9, 14
Curve: 10, 11, 12, 13, 17, 18
Downstroke: 7, 8, 9, 10, 11, 12, 13, 15, 16, 17, 19, 20, 21
Slantstroke: 21, 22, 23, 24, 25, 26
Tail: 5, 6, 9, 16, 25
Tall: 4, 7, 8, 10, 19, 20, 21
Two stroke: 15, 16, 19, 20, 21, 24, 25

Review
(page numbers)

Cane-stroke: f: 60; j: 59
Capital and lower case letter review: 91, 92, 107, 108, 121, 122, 137, 138
Circle letters: o, c, a: 27; d, g, q: 28; e: 59; c, a, o, d, e, g: 139
Curve letters: r, n, m: 44; r, m, n, h, u, s: 140
Downstroke letters: b, p, h: 43; r, n, m: 44; f, t, u: 60; d, b, r: 75; r, m, n, h, u: 140; i, t, l, b, h, f: 142
Lower case alphabet: 77, 78
Mixed-stroke: e, j, s: 59; f, t, u: 60; s, f, z: 76
Slantstroke: k, v, w: 73; x y, z: 74; k, v, w, x, y, z: 141
Tail letters: g, j, p, q, y: 143
Tall letters: b, d, f, h, k, l: 144

Practice Letters

A
Capital: 46
Lowercase: 3, 46

B
Capital: 41
Lowercase: 8, 41

C
Capital: 28
Lowercase: 2, 28

D
Capital: 43
Lowercase: 4, 43

E
Capital: 33
Lowercase: 14, 33

F
Capital: 34
Lowercase: 20, 34

G
Capital: 29
Lowercase: 5, 29

H
Capital: 35
Lowercase: 10, 35

I
Capital: 36
Lowercase: 15, 36

J
Capital: 37
Lowercase: 16, 37

K
Capital: 47
Lowercase: 21, 47

L
Capital: 31
Lowercase: 7, 31

M
Capital: 45
Lowercase: 13, 45

N
Capital: 44
Lowercase: 12, 44

O
Capital: 27
Lowercase: 1, 27

P
Capital: 40
Lowercase: 9, 40

Q
Capital: 30
Lowercase: 6, 30

R
Capital: 42
Lowercase: 11, 42

S
Capital: 39
Lowercase: 18, 39

T
Capital: 32
Lowercase: 19, 32

U
Capital: 38
Lowercase: 17, 38

V
Capital: 48
Lowercase: 22, 48

W
Capital: 49
Lowercase: 23, 49

X
Capital: 51
Lowercase: 24, 51

Y
Capital: 50
Lowercase: 25, 50

Z
Capital: 52
Lowercase: 26, 52

GENERAL LESSONS

To The Teacher

Before beginning the general lessons, review the mechanics of handwriting. (See **Proper Positioning**, page 10.)

As students work through the following pages, remember to take time to acknowledge and praise their progress. Positive verbal reinforcement will greatly enhance the learning process.

Lesson 1
octopus

Lesson 2
cat

Lesson Focus
The lowercase
letter o

See Student Worktext pages 15-16

Lesson Focus
The lowercase
letter c

See Student Worktext pages 17-18

Letter Description[1]
"The lowercase o is like the bubbles we drew and the grapes we traced. Start at the two o'clock position and go *up around*, *down around*, *up*.[2] Make sure your o touches the Ceiling and Floor of the meeting room!"

Letter Sounds
[o] as in octopus, [ō] as in oat, [ü] as in food

Resource Information
"The octopus is an animal that lives in the ocean. It has a soft, rounded body, and eight arms called tentacles. Even though its body is soft, its beak is strong enough to crush shells. It can also swim very fast! Most octopuses are small — about the size of a large man's fist."

"God gave the octopus a very special way to protect itself. When an enemy comes near, it squirts a dark liquid into the water so the enemy can't see it! When an octopus gets excited, it can change colors — blue, green, orange, gray, purple, red, white, or even striped!"

Work Page Directions
"Outline the octopus carefully, then color it whatever color you choose. Color the ocean water blue, and add some green seaweed so the octopus will feel at home!"

Letter Description
"The lowercase c curls up like a sleepy cat. Start at the two o'clock position and go *up around*, *down around*, *up* — but don't go all the way up or your cat will become a bubble! Be sure your c touches the Ceiling and the Floor."

Letter Sounds
[k] as in cat, [s] as in cent

Resource Information
"The cat is a popular house pet. Even though cats are very smart, they like to have their own way — so they may take longer to train than a dog."

"Do you know how cats talk? They *meow*. A cat may meow for attention, or to let you know when it wants to go out or come in. Happy cats purr. Angry cats hiss."

"Although cats don't like to take baths, they are very clean. At least once a day, a cat will lick its paw, then wash its face and head. Cats remind us we need to wash often — but with soap and water, not a wet paw!"

Work Page Directions
"What color would you like your cat to be? Color this cat that color, then draw and color a nice, warm rug for the cat to sit on."

---

[1] *Letter Descriptions throughout this Guidebook are based on the Treehouse (page 7).*
[2] *Italicized words include visual/verbal cues. Emphasize these words with corresponding hand motions.*

Lesson Focus

The lowercase letter a

See Student Worktext pages 19-20

Letter Description

"The lowercase a begins like the letter o, but has a downstroke added to the side. It goes *up around*, *down around*, *up* — then *straight down*. Don't pick up your pencil until you've finished, and make sure it touches the Ceiling and the Floor."

Letter Sounds

[a] as in alligator, [ā] as in ape, [ä] as in far

Resource Information

"Alligators look something like giant lizards, but with thicker bodies and tails. They are usually dark olive or dull gray. This helps them hide in the muddy waters where they live. Alligators have many sharp teeth."

"God designed the alligator's head so that the alligator can lie completely under the water with just its eyes and nose sticking out. An alligator swims by sweeping its tail from side to side. It can also move very quickly for short distances on land."

"A mother alligator lays about 50 eggs at a time in a wet, grassy nest. Baby alligators are about nine inches long when they are hatched. In the winter, alligators bury themselves in the mud, hide in deep holes, or simply rest under the water."

Work Page Directions

"Outline the alligator with a dark green crayon. Color some murky brown water around him. You can also add stalks of green swamp grass so the alligator can hide better."

Lesson Focus

The lowercase letter d

See Student Worktext pages 21-22

Letter Description

"The lowercase d is like an a except the stick goes *straight up* to the Roofline, then back *down* to the Floor. Don't lift your pencil, and make sure the circle touches the Ceiling and the Floor."

Letter Sounds

[d] as in dog

Resource Information

"There are many kinds of dogs — big dogs, little dogs, dogs with long tails or no tail at all! Dogs come in many colors, shapes, and sizes. How many kinds of dogs can you name?"

"Dogs are friendly, obedient animals and are very faithful friends. How do you know when a dog is happy?" (It wags its tail, gives happy barks, licks you, etc.)

"Dogs can be taught to obey commands because they are smart and want to please. Dogs were the first animals to be tamed by people."

Show the students pictures of different kinds of dogs. If time permits, encourage students to tell about their dog or a friend's. Ask them to share its name, color, size, etc.

Work Page Directions

"Color the dog to look like *your* dog or like a dog you'd like to have. Doesn't your dog need a toy? Draw and color something a dog would like to play with or chew on."

goat

quail

Lesson Focus
The lowercase letter g

See Student Worktext pages 23-24

Lesson Focus
The lowercase letter q

See Student Worktext pages 25-26

Letter Description
"The lowercase g starts at the two o'clock position, goes *up around*, *down around*, *up around* to the Ceiling, then *down* to the Ground with a monkey tail to the left. Don't lift your pencil, and make sure the circle touches the Ceiling and Floor."

Letter Sounds
[g] as in goat, [j] as in giraffe

Resource Information
"A male goat is called a buck. A female goat is called a doe. A young goat is called a kid. Can you name another female animal that is called a doe?" (a deer)

"There are several kinds of goats that are raised on farms. Nubian goats have long, floppy ears. Angora and Cashmere goats have very soft hair. Toggenburg and Alpine goats give rich, healthful milk."

"There are also wild mountain goats that live on rocky hillsides. They can easily run up and down the mountain side. They often have large, curly horns."

Work Page Directions
"Goats are usually white, black, brown, or gray — or a combination of these colors. Make your goat one of these colors, then draw or glue on some grass for the goat to eat."

Letter Description
"The lowercase q is similar to the g, except the tail curls in the opposite direction. Start at the two o'clock position, go *up around*, *down around*, *up around* to the Ceiling, then *down* to the Ground with a monkey tail to the right."

Letter Sounds
[kw] as in quail

Resource Information
"Quail are very pretty birds. Have you ever seen a quail run across the road with its family? A family of quail is called a covey [kuh¹-vee]. There can be as many as 18 babies in one covey!"

"God gave the quail a good way to protect itself. It has speckled brown feathers, and can easily hide in bushes or tall grass. When a quail holds very still, it is very hard to see."

Work Page Directions
"Color your quail to make it look speckled. Remember, a quail is mostly different shades of brown and tan. Now draw a bush or some dry grass for your quail to hide in. Maybe you can even find a feather to glue on your quail!"

See Student Worktext pages 27-28

Lesson Focus

A review of lowercase letters
o, c, a, d, g, q

Lesson Focus

The lowercase letter l

See Student Worktext pages 29-30

Letter Description

"The lowercase l is one of the easiest letters to make. Begin at the Roofline, and go *straight down* to the Floor — top to bottom. That's it!"

Letter Sounds

[l] as in lion

Resource Information

"The lion is a kind of cat — but much, much *bigger*! It is very fierce, and has a loud roar."

"Lions live in a group called a pride. If a lion has been away from the pride, the other lions rub his cheeks in greeting when he returns. How do *you* greet your friends?" (shake hands; say hello; give them a hug; etc.)

"The picture in your book is a male lion. Only the male has a ruff of fur around his head. Do you know what that fur is called? (a mane) The male lion is the only kind of cat that has a mane. His mane makes him look even bigger and stronger!"

Work Page Directions

"Color the body and face of your lion brownish gold. Make his eyes green. To make a fluffy mane for your lion, cut pieces of yarn and glue them to his head."

Lesson Description

This is the first of the review lessons. Before students begin this page, Sky Write each of these letters (see page 9), reviewing letter formation. Praise students to help reinforce the correct counter-clockwise stroke of each letter.

Lesson Directions

"This is our first review lesson. Beside each animal is the letter that begins its name. Trace the letter, then finish the line by writing that letter several times. Be sure to use the start dots."

Lesson 8 — bear

Lesson Focus
The lowercase letter b

See Student Worktext pages 31-32

Letter Description
"The lowercase b starts at the Roofline. Go *straight down* to the Floor, then *circle up around* right, and back *down around* to the line. Be sure the circle touches the Ceiling and Floor, and don't lift your pencil until you finish the letter."

Letter Sounds
[b] as in bear

Resource Information
"When you hear 'bear,' what comes to mind? A polar bear? A teddy bear? Smokey the bear?"

"Real bears look friendly, but can be very dangerous in the wild. They have small eyes and can't see very well. But they do have a good sense of smell."

"Bears spend most of the winter in a deep sleep called *hibernation*. Just before they hibernate, bears eat enough food to keep them alive for several months. While hibernating, a female bear may give birth to one or two cubs. They are very tiny, but when spring comes, the cubs grow very fast!"

"Even though bears can be dangerous, they are generally quite peaceful. They try to keep out of fights, and will run away from danger. These are good habits we can learn from the bears."

Work Page Directions
"Color your bear either dark brown or black. This bear looks as if he smells something good to eat. Bears eat lots of things, but they especially like berries! If you wish, you may draw a bush full of berries for your bear to eat."

Lesson 9 — penguin

Lesson Focus
The lowercase letter p

See Student Worktext pages 33-34

Letter Description
"The lowercase p starts with a stroke from the Ceiling *straight down* to the Ground, then back *up* and *circle around* to the right. Be sure your circle touches the Ceiling and Floor, and don't lift your pencil until you're finished."

Letter Sounds
[p] as in penguin

Resource Information
"The penguin is a very interesting bird. When it wants to go somewhere, it doesn't fly — it walks! Although penguins walk very slowly, their webbed feet and flippers help them swim very fast."

"It is very cold where penguins live. Sometimes they live right on the ice! But God has given them special feathers to help keep them warm."

"Penguins live in large groups called colonies. The male penguin cares for the eggs and the baby chicks. Sometimes the father penguin will move the eggs by carrying them on his feet! Male penguins often huddle together in groups to help keep the eggs warm."

Work Page Directions
"Color your penguin black and white. What color do you think his beak and feet should be?" (yellow or orange) "If you wish, you may draw some water for the penguin to swim in."

Lesson 10
hippo

Lesson Focus
The lowercase letter h

See Student Worktext pages 35-36

Letter Description
"The lowercase h looks a lot like a chair. It starts at the Roofline and goes *straight down* to the Floor, then back *up* to the Ceiling, *circle over*, and back *down* to the Floor."

Letter Sounds
[h] as in hippo

Resource Information
"Have you ever seen a hippopotamus in a zoo? Like many of the largest land animals, the hippo comes from Africa. Can you name some other large animals that live in Africa?" (elephant, giraffe, etc.)

"Hippos may look clumsy and slow, but when they want to, they can run as fast as *you* can! Hippos are also very good swimmers. They stay near the rivers and spend most of their day in the water. Sometimes when a hippo is swimming, all you can see are its ears and eyes sticking out of the water!

"Baby hippos are called calves. What other animal has a baby called a calf? (a cow) A hippo calf often rides on its mother's back when she is in the water."

Work Page Directions
"A hippo has thick, brownish-gray skin. Color your hippo that color. If you wish, you may draw a hippo calf, too."

Lesson 11
rabbit

Lesson Focus
The lowercase letter r

See Student Worktext pages 37-38

Letter Description
"The lowercase r is a short letter that stays between the lines. It begins with a stroke from the Ceiling to the Floor, then goes back up and circles over to the two o'clock position."

Letter Sounds
[r] as in rabbit

Resource Information
"Have you ever touched a rabbit? Rabbits are soft and furry. Some people call the wild rabbit a *cottontail* because it has a fluffy, white tail."

"Although rabbits are cute, sometimes farmers don't like them because they nibble on the tender young plants in gardens and fields."

"When a rabbit is frightened, it can jump as far as 10 feet! If it is being chased, a rabbit will often run in a zigzag pattern to escape its enemy."

Work Page Directions
"Color the inside of your rabbit's ears pink. Color its nose black or pink. Make your rabbit's fur soft brown, gray, white, or even spotted. When you finish coloring your rabbit, glue a cotton ball on its tail. Now your rabbit is a *real* cottontail!"

Lesson 12
newt

Lesson 13
mouse

Lesson Focus
The lowercase letter n

See Student Worktext pages 39-40

Lesson Focus
The lowercase letter m

See Student Worktext pages 41-42

Letter Description
"This lowercase n is a lot like the letter r. Start at the Ceiling and go *straight down* to the Floor, then *up/around* and back *down* to the Floor. Remember the n has only one hump."

Letter Sounds
[n] as in newt

Resource Information
"A newt is a type of salamander. Like the frog, it is an amphibian — a creature which is able to live on both land and under water."

"Newts hatch from eggs laid on plant leaves under water. They breathe through gills, but as they grow, they develop lungs and spend more time on land."

"A newt eats insects and worms. The best known newt in the United States is the red-spotted newt. It is about four inches long.

"Is the newt the same as a lizard?" (No. A lizard is a reptile, not an amphibian.) "Also, if a newt loses a leg, it will grow another one!"

Work Page Directions
"Make this a red-spotted newt. Color it black with red spots. (Hint: It's easier to draw and color the spots first, then fill in the background.) What an unusual creature!"

Letter Description
"The lowercase m is like an n, but with two humps. It begins at the Ceiling and goes *straight down* to the Floor, then *circle up, around, down* to the Floor (pause), then *up, around, down* to the Floor again. Isn't the m fun to write?"

Letter Sounds
[m] as in mouse

Resource Information
"Mice usually live in the fields and the forests. They eat seeds, plants, and grain. A mouse can hear very well, but it can't see as well as you can."

"Some people keep mice as pets. Pet mice are often white with pink eyes. Other mice are usually gray or brown. Scientists sometimes use white mice in special experiments to learn about what makes people sick, and how to help people get well again."

"Mice like to make their homes where it is dark and warm. That is why some mice live under a house or in an attic or a basement. A mouse will shred tissue or cloth to make itself a soft nest."

Work Page Directions
"Mice are usually white, gray, or brown. You can glue a piece of corn on the page for your mouse to eat. Draw a dark hole on your page so your mouse can scamper away quickly if it sees a cat!"

See Student Worktext pages 43-44

Lesson Focus
A review of lowercase letters
b, p, h, r, n, m

Lesson Description
This is the second review lesson. Before students begin this page, Sky Write each of these letters (see page 9) reviewing letter formation. Praise students to help reinforce the correct counter-clockwise stroke of each letter.

Lesson Directions
"Beside each animal is the letter that begins its name. Trace the letter, then finish the line by writing that letter several times. Be sure to use the start dots."

elephant

Lesson Focus
The lowercase letter e

See Student Worktext pages 45-46

Lesson Description
"The lowercase e starts with a short line in the middle of the meeting room (from left to right), then circle *up, around, down, around, up* and end at the four o'clock position. Make sure your circle touches the Ceiling and the Floor."

Letter Sounds
[e] as in elephant, [ē] as in eat

Resource Information
"The elephant is the largest land animal. Elephants have floppy ears, long trunks, and wrinkled, gray skin. African elephants have large ears; Indian elephants have much smaller ears."

"God gave the elephant a wonderful tool to use. Can you guess what it is? It's the elephant's trunk! An adult elephant may have a trunk that is six feet long. The trunk is so powerful that the elephant can push over small trees with it, and so flexible that it can pick a single leaf!"

"Elephants eat plants — lots of plants! A single elephant can eat as much as 300 pounds of plant food a day, and drink up to 50 gallons of water."

Work Page Directions
"This is an African elephant. It has large ears and powerful upper teeth called tusks. Color your elephant dusty gray, but leave the tusks white. You may wish to draw a peanut on the page."

iguana

jaguar

Lesson Focus
The lowercase letter i

See Student Worktext pages 47-48

Lesson Focus
The lowercase letter j

See Student Worktext pages 49-50

Letter Description
"The lowercase letter i is easy to write! Start at the Ceiling and go *straight down* to the Floor. Lift your pencil, then place a dot in the middle of the attic. That's it!"

Letter Sounds
[i] as in iguana, [ī] as in ice

Resource Information
"The iguana is a large green lizard with a long tail that is fringed in black. It lives in tropical climates and eats fruits, flower buds, and young leaves. The most common iguana moves slowly and is very shy, so it is easily caught. Iguanas have long, sharp claws to help them climb trees. They like to rest on branches that hang out over the water. Then if something frightens the iguana, it can drop into the water. Iguanas are very good swimmers."

"The female iguana will dig a burrow in a sunny area, lay her eggs inside, cover them, then leave them alone. When they hatch the young dig out of the burrow."

"There are many kinds of iguanas. One kind, the marine iguana, likes to swim in the surf! This iguana lives by the ocean and eats seaweed."

Work Page Directions
"Draw some leaves around the iguana, and color them green. Now if you color your iguana green, it will be easy for it to hide."

Letter Description
"The lowercase j begins just like the i. Go *straight down* the ladder to the Ground and *curve up* left like a monkey's tail. When you finish the letter, pick up your pencil and place a small dot in the middle of the attic."

Letter Sounds
[j] as in jaguar

Resource Information
"The jaguar is a large and powerful wild cat. It has beautiful golden fur with brown and black spots. The black spots are mainly on its head, legs, and stomach. Why do you think God gave the jaguar spots?" (Spots help the jaguar hide by blending in with its surroundings.)

"Jaguars live in forests and scrubland areas where there are many places to hide. They come out at night to hunt other animals."

"Have you ever seen a jaguar? Jaguars come from Mexico, and Central and South America. The Maya Indians from that part of the world believed the jaguar had great strength and courage."

Work Page Directions
"Outline the jaguar with a yellow or gold crayon. Color the fur that color. Now color the spots brown or black so your jaguar can hide easily."

Lesson 17
umbrellabird

Lesson Focus
The lowercase
letter u

See Student Worktext pages 51-52

Letter Description
"The lowercase u begins at the Ceiling. Go *straight down* toward the Floor, *curve around* and back *up* to the Ceiling, then *straight down* to end at the Floor. Don't lift your pencil until you've finished."

Letter Sounds
[u] as in umbrellabird, [ü] as in rule, [ū] as in use

Resource Information
"The umbrellabird lives in the tropical rain forests of Central and South America. It has a tuft of forward-facing feathers on its head that form a crest, and a flap of skin covered with feathers hanging down from its neck. The crest and flap look something like an umbrella with a long handle. That's how the umbrellabird got its name!"

"The umbrellabird has a chunky body, a wide bill, and a big head. Its feathers are black, and its feet and bill are gray. The umbrellabird is about the size of a crow."

"Like many rain forest creatures, the umbrellabird's numbers are decreasing each year as its habitat is destroyed."

Work Page Directions
"This umbrellabird looks ready for the rain, don't you think? Color it lightly black, with gray feet and a gray bill. If you wish, you may draw some raindrops coming down around the umbrellabird."

Lesson 18
snail

Lesson Focus
The lowercase
letter s

See Student Worktext pages 53-54

Letter Descriptions
"Begin the s at the two o'clock position, *curve up* to the left, then *curve right* though the meeting room, then *curve down* to the left, stopping at the eight o'clock position." (Note: Make an s-s-s sound as you Sky Write the letter.)

Letter Sounds
[s] as in snail

Resource Information
"A snail is a very interesting creature because it carries its house on its back! The snail's house looks like a coiled seashell. Some snails have beautiful, brightly-colored shells. Most garden snails usually have plain brown shells."

"Sometimes you can find land snails in damp, shady places like a garden or flowerbed. Other snails live in lakes and ponds, or even in the ocean."

"The snail creeps along on one foot. As it moves, you can see the feelers on its head — and its tiny eyes, too! It even has a tiny mouth with tiny teeth."

Work Page Directions
"Is your snail a land snail, or a sea snail? Color your snail to look like the one you choose, then glue yarn to follow the coil of its shell."

See Student Worktext pages 55-56   See Student Worktext pages 57-58

Lesson Focus
The lowercase letter t

Lesson Focus
The lowercase letter f

Letter Description
"The lowercase t starts with a stroke from the Roofline *straight down* to the Floor. Lift your pencil, and then make a cross stroke at the Ceiling from left to right."

Letter Description
"The lowercase f is a tall letter. It starts in the attic with a canestroke. *Circle up, around*, then *straight down* to the Floor. Lift your pencil and make a cross stroke at the Ceiling."

Letter Sounds
[t] as in turtle

Letter Sounds
[f] as in frog

Resource Information
"God gave the turtle a wonderful way to protect itself. When it senses danger, it just pulls its head, legs, and tail safely inside its shell!"

"The female turtle digs a hole in the ground and lays eggs. Then she covers the eggs and goes away. The sun keeps the eggs nice and warm, and they soon hatch into baby turtles. The babies never see their mother."

"We think of turtles as moving slowly but steadily — but not all turtles are this way. Water turtles can swim very fast!"

"Turtles come in many different colors and sizes. Some are black, brown, or dark green. Others are bright orange, red, or yellow. Some have dark bodies and shells with bright spots of color."

Resource Information
"How do frogs move around? They hop or leap with their strong back legs. Many frogs can leap as much as 20 times their body length!"

"Many frogs spend part of their lives on land and part in the water. Their long legs make them good swimmers. Frogs live in many kinds of places. Some frogs even live in trees."

"God gave frogs very special eyes. A frog's eyes bulge out to help the frog see in almost any direction. A frog can see insects anywhere around him. When a bug comes close — ZAP! — the frog scoops it in with his long, sticky tongue! Frogs eat many insects that are pests to us."

Work Page Directions
"Choose the color or colors that you want your turtle to be. If you wish, you can draw some green leafy plants for your turtle to munch on!"

Work Page Directions
"Frogs often blend in with their surroundings. This frog should be green — just like the leaves on the limb where he's sitting. Color his eyes red or orange. If you wish, you may draw some bugs for the frog to eat, too."

Review

See Student Worktext pages 59-60

Lesson Focus
A review of lowercase letters
e, j, s, f, t, u

Lesson Description
This is the third review lesson. Before students begin this page, Sky Write each of these letters (see page 9) reviewing letter formation. Praise students to help reinforce the correct counter-clockwise stroke of each letter.

Lesson Directions
"Beside each animal is the letter that begins its name. Trace the letter, then finish the line by writing that letter several times. Be sure to use the start dots."

Lesson 21
kangaroo

See Student Worktext pages 61-62

Letter Focus
The lowercase letter k

Letter Description
"The lowercase k starts with a stroke from the Roofline *straight down* to the Floor. Lift your pencil. Now start at the Ceiling and *slant left*, *slant right*, and end at the Floor."

Letter Sounds
[k] as in kangaroo

Resource Information
"What is it that makes a kangaroo so different from other animals? It has a pouch! Do you know what its pouch is used for?" (protecting its baby)

"Baby kangaroos are called joeys. They are as tiny as baby mice when they are born. Joeys stay warm and cozy in their mother's pouch for several weeks. Finally, when they are old enough, they come out and begin to bounce around and play. But the joeys jump back inside the warm pouch at night, or when there is danger."

Work Page Directions
"Kangaroos are usually reddish brown or light gray. Choose one of these colors for your kangaroo mother, and make the baby joey a slightly lighter shade."

vulture

walrus

See Student Worktext pages 63-64

Lesson Focus
The lowercase letter v

Letter Description
"The lowercase v stays completely inside the meeting room. It starts at the Ceiling and slants *down right* to the Floor, then slants *up right* to the Ceiling. Make sure you don't lift your pencil until you are finished."

Letter Sounds
[v] as in vulture

Resource Information
"Vultures are large birds with dark feathers on their bodies and no feathers on their heads. The most common vulture is the turkey vulture, often called a turkey buzzard. The world's largest land bird, the California condor, is also a vulture."

"Vultures rarely hunt on their own, but instead look for animals that are already dead. When they find dead animals, they eat them. This is actually helpful as the dead animals would otherwise decay, smell bad, and spread disease."

"Vultures remind us not to judge a person's usefulness by their outward appearance. We each have a special way we can help in this world."

Work Page Directions
"Color the vulture's head red, its beak yellow, and its feathers black or brown. If you wish, you may draw a rock ledge where the vulture can safely lay its eggs. Draw one, two, or three eggs."

See Student Worktext pages 65-66

Lesson Focus
The lowercase letter w

Letter Description
"The lowercase w is made with one long stroke. Starting at the Ceiling, slant *down right* to the Floor, slant *up right* to the Ceiling, slant *down* back to the Floor, and slant *up* to finish at the Ceiling."

Letter Sounds
[w] as in walrus

Resource Information
"A walrus is the only type of seal that has tusks. Can you remember the other animal we've studied that has tusks?" (the elephant) "The walrus' tusks are a special kind of upper teeth that grow downward."

"Why does a walrus have tusks? God gave it these special tools to help it climb on the ice, and to pry shellfish from the ocean floor."

"The walrus spends a lot of its time in the water looking for food. This walrus looks like it could really eat a *lot* of food, doesn't it?"

Work Page Directions
"The walrus is dark brown, its moustache is light brown, and its tusks are white." (optional) "Break a toothpick in half, then glue one half of the toothpick on each of your walrus' tusks."

Lesson 24
fox

Lesson Focus

The lowercase letter x

See Student Worktext pages 67-68

Letter Description

"Both strokes in the lowercase x start at the Ceiling and end at the Floor. The first stroke slants *down right* to the Floor. The second slants *down left* to the Floor, crossing the first stroke exactly in the middle of the meeting room."

Letter Sounds

[ks] as in fox[1]

Resource Information

"Did you know that the fox is really a type of wild dog? Foxes have bushy tails, large pointed ears, and long noses. Some foxes are reddish brown and others are gray. Their fur is very soft and long."

"A fox has very good hearing. It can hear a mouse 'squeak' from far away. A young fox is called a pup or cub. Foxes live in dens which may be in a cave, among rocks, or in a hollow log or tree."

"Jesus talked about the foxes in Scripture. He said that the foxes have holes, and the birds have nests — but He had nowhere to live." (See Matthew 8:20.)

Work Page Directions

"Would you like to make this a red fox or a gray fox? Either one is okay. If you wish, you may also draw some soft grass for the fox to sit in. Color the grass green."

[1] No animal name *starts* with X, so this example uses a word that *ends* with the X sound.

Lesson 25
yak

Lesson Focus

The lowercase letter y

See Student Worktext pages 69-70

Letter Description

"The first stroke of the lowercase y slants *down right* from the Ceiling to the Floor. The second stroke slants *down left* from the Ceiling to the Ground — touching the first stroke at the Floor."

Letter Sounds

[y] as in yak

Resource Information

"The yak lives in a far away country called Tibet. Tibet has very high mountains, and the yak is a very useful animal to the people who live there. They use the yak as a pack animal. It can carry very heavy loads. People and mail can travel by yak into places that cars could never go."

"There are no cows in Tibet, so people also get milk from the yak. The yak's soft hair is often used to make warm coats."

"Does the yak look slow? Don't be fooled! A yak can run swiftly down icy slopes, and swim across strong flowing rivers. Watch for a yak next time you visit a zoo."

Work Page Directions

"Color your yak light black or dark brown. Draw some short grass below the yak, and color it a light brown or tan."

Lesson 26

zebra

Lesson Focus
The lowercase
letter z

See Student Worktext pages 71-72

Letter Description

"The lowercase z is the last letter of the alphabet. When you make this z, you've finished the whole lowercase alphabet! Start at the Ceiling, make a line straight *right*, slant *down left* to the Floor, then finish with a line straight *right*."

Letter Sounds

[z] as in zebra

Resource Information

"A zebra looks a lot like a horse — but unlike the horse, a zebra is very wild and hard to tame. Zebras live on the grassy plains of Africa. They usually stay together in large herds. Like horses, zebras can run very fast."

"What makes a zebra look different from a horse?" (its stripes) "Why do you think God gave zebras striped coats?" (to help them hide in the tall grass)

Work Page Directions

"You'll have to be very careful as you color your zebra! Make the background — its stomach, face, etc. — black or dark brown, and leave the stripes white. If you wish, you may draw some grass for your zebra to eat."

Review

See Student Worktext pages 73-74

Lesson Focus
A review of
lowercase letters
k, v, w, x, y, z

Lesson Description

This is the fourth review lesson. Before students begin this page, Sky Write each of these letters, (see page 9) reviewing its formation. Praise students to reinforce correct formation of each letter in this group.

Lesson Directions

"Beside each animal is the letter that begins its name. Trace the letter, then finish the line by writing that letter several times. Be sure to use the start dots."

See Student Worktext pages 75-76

Lesson Focus

A review of lowercase letters d, b, r, s, f, z

Lesson Description

This is the first comprehensive review lesson. These letters are a sampling taken from earlier lowercase lessons. Before you begin this page, review the correct formation for each letter.

Lesson Directions

"Here are some letters that we studied earlier this year. Beside each animal is the letter that begins its name. Trace the letter, then finish the line by writing that letter several times. Be sure to use the start dots."

Review

See Student Worktext pages 77-78

Lesson Focus

Comprehensive lowercase letter review

Lesson Description

This is a comprehensive review of all lowercase letters. Students may trace each sample letter for practice, then using the start dots, they must write each letter correctly in the space to the right of each sample. Carefully monitor students for correct strokes and direction.

Lesson Directions

"Write the entire lowercase alphabet. Remember to go the correct direction as you make each letter. Be sure to use the start dots."

Lesson Focus
The capital ○

See Student Worktext pages 79-80

Letter Description
"The capital ○ is just like the lowercase o — only bigger! *Circle up, around, down around, up around,* and back to the start. Be sure it touches the Roofline and the Floor."

Letter Sounds
[o] as in odd, [ō] as in oat, [ü] as in food, [ou] as in owl

Resource Information
"Whooo, whooo, whooo knows the bird that makes this sound? Have you ever heard an owl hoot at night?"

"Owls have great big eyes that make them look very wise. Although they can see very well during the day, they can see even better at night. They sit in a tree, on a fence or a pole and watch for small animals on the ground. When they see one, they swoop down, kill it, and eat it. Farmers like to have owls living nearby because they eat lots of mice."

Work Page Directions
"Color the owl's feet and beak yellow. Color its face tan, and its feathers brown. Don't forget to color the tree branch, too!

"To make feathers for your owl, you can tear tissue paper or construction paper into small oval pieces, and glue them on its body. If you overlap these paper feathers, it will make your owl look fluffy!"

Lesson Focus
The capital ⊂

See Student Worktext pages 81-82

Letter Description
"The capital letter ⊂ is made exactly like the lowercase c — only bigger! Go *up around, down around, up*. Make sure your capital ⊂ touches the Roofline at the top, and the Floor at the bottom."

Letter Sounds
[k] as in cloud, [s] as in cent

Resource Information
"Did you know that clouds are very useful? People who predict the weather watch the clouds to know what tomorrow's weather will be."

"There are several different types of clouds. Some tell us that good weather is coming, and others tell us to watch out for storms."

"The clouds in this picture are called *cumulus* [kyoomˡ-yuh-luhs] clouds. They are light and fluffy on top, with a flat base at the bottom. You usually see cumulus clouds when the weather is warm and sunny. Be sure to look for cumulus clouds the next time you plan a picnic or go for a bike ride!"

Work Page Directions
"First, outline your clouds with orange, red, or gold. Color the sky a pretty blue. If you wish, you may draw a bird flying through the clouds."

Lesson 29
Goose

Lesson Focus
The capital G

See Student Worktext pages 83-84

Letter Description
"The capital G is similar to the capital C, but continue to *circle up* to the Ceiling, then make a line *straight left*. Don't lift your pencil."

Letter Sounds
[g] as in goose, [j] as in giraffe

Resource Information
"What animal is similar to a goose? (a duck, a swan, etc.) All these water birds have webbed feet that make them good swimmers. Geese are larger than most ducks, but are a little smaller than swans."

"Geese eat grain and vegetables. Sometimes they also eat insects and small water creatures."

"Geese live up to 30 years and a pair of geese stay together for life! The female goose makes a nest in a hollow in the ground. She makes it soft by lining it with feathers from her breast. Then she lays three to six white eggs."

"The male goose is called a gander. Ganders are very good fathers. They help the mother while the babies are being hatched and raised."

Work Page Directions
"Many geese are white, so you may leave your goose uncolored — except for its beak and feet. White geese have orange feet and beaks. Or you may color your goose to look like the Canadian goose at the top of page 83. Canadian geese have black feet and beaks."

Lesson 30
Quartz

Lesson Focus
The capital Q

See Student Worktext pages 85-86

Letter Description
"The capital Q is made exactly like a capital O, except it has a short slanting line in the bottom right corner. Be sure your circle touches the Roofline and the Floor." (Remind students that the Q is always followed by a u.)

Letter Sounds
[kw] as in quartz

Resource Information
"Quartz is the most common mineral. It is the main ingredient of sand, so it is used in making sandpaper and glass. A special kind of quartz is even used in some clocks and watches. If you look closely at a handful of sand, you can see tiny pieces of quartz. They look like little pieces of broken glass, or tiny clear rocks."

"Quartz crystals are large pieces of quartz. Depending on where you live, you may have seen them sticking out of a creek bank or along a lake shore. Quartz crystals come in several beautiful colors. Some of the most common are clear, smoky, rose, purple, and yellow."

Work Page Directions
"What color do you want your quartz to be? Choose a gray, rose red, purple, or yellow crayon to color your quartz. After you have carefully colored the crystals, glue on glitter to make it sparkle."

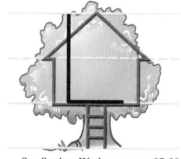

Lesson Focus
The capital L

See Student Worktext pages 87-88

Letter Description
"The capital L starts at the Roofline and goes *straight down* to the Floor. *Turn right* when you reach the Floor to make a leg for it to stand on. Don't pick up your pencil."

Letter Sounds
[l] as in leaf

Resource Information
"Leaves are a very important part of a plant. God made them food factories! Each leaf gets energy from the sun. It combines that energy with good things from the soil to create food for the plant."

"Three basic kinds of leaves are broad leaves, narrow leaves, and needles. Broad leaves are very wide and are found on trees like oaks and maples. Narrow leaves are slender and are found on trees like willows, and on plants like grass. Needles are very thin, and are found on evergreen trees like pine and spruce."

(optional) Collect specimens of these three kinds of leaves, glue them on construction paper, and label them to make leaf posters.

Work Page Directions
"Maple leaves change color in the fall. In some parts of the country, fall leaves make whole hillsides turn red, yellow, or gold. Color your fall leaf red or yellow. You may wish to use watercolors to paint your leaf. Good fall colors are red, yellow, and gold. You can even mix in some brown or light green for more shades."

Lesson Focus
The capital T

See Student Worktext pages 89-90

Letter Description
"The capital T starts with a stroke from the Roofline *straight down* to the Floor. Lift your pencil, then *make a cross* at the Roofline from left to right."

Letter Sounds
[t] as in tree

Resource Information
"Trees are the largest plants. They are very good for many things. Can you think of some?" (lumber, nuts, fruit, shade, etc.)

"Every state has a state tree. Do you know the official tree for our state? It is the _____ tree!" (Be sure to check an encyclopedia or online for this information in advance.)

"There are many different kinds of trees. You can tell many kinds of trees by their shapes or their leaves."

(optional) Take a nature walk to identify trees.

Work Page Directions
"Color the shade tree green, and make the trunk brown. If you wish, you can add a green lawn under the tree, or draw some birds or clouds in the sky."

See Student Worktext pages 91-92

Lesson Focus
A review of capital letters

O, G, L, Q, C, T

Lesson Description
This is the first capital letter review. Before students begin this page, Sky Write each of these letters (see page 9) reviewing letter formation. Praise students to help reinforce the correct counter-clockwise stroke of each letter.

Lesson Directions[1]
"Draw a line from each capital letter to its lowercase letter." (page 91)

"Write a capital letter to match each lowercase letter. Be sure to use the start dots." (page 92)

[1] Note: Instructions for individual pages may be given at different times.

Lesson 33
Eagle

Lesson Focus
The capital E

See Student Worktext pages 93-94

Letter Description
"The capital E has three strokes. Start at the Roofline, go *straight down* to the Floor, then *straight right*. Return to the starting point and make two short strokes to the right — one at the Roofline, and a shorter one at the Ceiling."

Letter Sounds
[e] as in elephant, [e] as in eagle

Resource Information
"The eagle is one of the largest, most powerful birds in the world. Up close the eagle looks fierce and proud."

"The bald eagle is the symbol of the United States. There is even a picture of this eagle on some of our money!" (coins and bills) The bald eagle is not *really* bald. It only looks that way from a distance because of the white feathers on its head."

"Bald eagles build their nests at the top of tall trees near water. The eagles will return to the same nest each year, adding fresh leaves each time. Over time, the nest gets bigger and bigger."

Work Page Directions
"Outline the feathers of your bald eagle with black, then color its feathers dark brown. Color the eagle's beak yellow. Make sure you don't color its head, because its head feathers are white!"

Lesson 34
Fish

Lesson Focus
The capital F

See Student Worktext pages 95-96

Letter Description
"The capital F is like an E without the bottom stroke. Start at the Roofline and go straight down to the Floor. Return to the starting point and make two short strokes to the right — one at the Roofline, and a shorter one at the Ceiling."

Letter Sounds
[f] as in fish

Resource Information
"God made many sizes, colors, and kinds of fish. One funny-looking fish can blow itself up like a balloon! Another one eats its babies! Another one has both eyes on one side of its body!"

"Some fish live in fresh water — lakes, rivers, and streams. Others live in the salty water of the oceans."

"In order to breathe under water, fish have gills. Since you live on land, isn't it good that you have a nose instead of gills? God gave every creature just what it needs to stay alive."

Work Page Directions
"Tropical fish come in many bright colors. Color your fish as brightly as you can! Be sure to color the water around it blue."

(optional) "Glue some Cheerios® to your page to make bubbles rising from your fish's mouth."

Lesson 35
Horse

Lesson Focus
The capital H

See Student Worktext pages 97-98

Letter Description
"The capital H has three strokes. The first stroke starts at the Roofline and goes straight down to the Floor. Make the second stroke parallel to the first. The third stroke connects the first two at the Ceiling."

Letter Sounds
[h] as in horse

Resource Information
"The horse is a very useful animal. Horses can be trained to obey commands they hear, like a word or a whistle, as well as 'touch' commands (like moving the reins)."

"Some people use horses for farming, or rounding up cattle. Many horses are ridden just for fun. Others are trained to jump or to race."

"A baby horse is called a foal. It can stand shortly after birth, and in just a few hours it can be running around! The mother horse is called a mare."

"Horses have good memories. They remember if someone has been unkind to them."

Work Page Directions
"Horses are black, brown, reddish-brown (also called 'bay'), gray, gold (called 'palomino'), white, and sometimes even spotted! Color your horse the color you choose."

Lesson Focus
The capital I

See Student Worktext pages 99-100

Letter Description
"The capital I has three strokes. It begins at the Roofline and goes straight down to the Floor. Finish with a short line from left to right across the top, then across the bottom."

Letter Sounds
[i] as in it, [i] as in I (The name you call yourself.)

Resource Information
"The letter I is a word all by itself! When you talk about yourself, you say things like, 'I like to help others,' or 'I will smile at someone today.' Can you think of other ways to use the word I?"

Ask students to complete the statement, "I can _____." Encourage them to think of good things and positive actions.

Work Page Directions
"Finish this picture so it looks like you! Make sure you're smiling, and don't forget to draw your nose and ears. If you don't know what color your eyes and hair are, look in the mirror or ask a friend. If your hair is longer than the picture shows, then draw some more!"

Lesson Focus
The capital J

See Student Worktext pages 101-102

Letter Description
"The capital J begins at the Roofline and goes *straight down* to the middle of the meeting room, *curves down left* touching the Floor, then *curves up* back to the middle of the meeting room."

Letter Sounds
[j] as in jellyfish

Resource Information
"A jellyfish is not made of jelly, and it is not a fish! It is a delicate sea creature with the shape of a bell. Its body is mostly water, and filled with a clear jelly-like substance between two layers of cells. A jellyfish can be as small as a pea, or bigger than you!"

"The jellyfish has a 'mouth' that hangs down from the middle of its body like the clapper of a bell. It also has long frilly parts (called arms) and trailing tentacles. The tentacles carry a poison which can paralyze small sea creatures, or give *you* a painful sting!"

"Jellyfish come in many sizes, shapes, and colors. When a jellyfish swims, it looks like an umbrella opening and closing. This motion squeezes out water to help it move and stay afloat."

Work Page Directions
"The jellyfish is difficult to see in the ocean since it blends in with the water. Color your jellyfish very lightly. Use a pale blue or pink. Glue sand to the bottom of the page for the ocean bottom."

Lesson Focus
The capital U

See Student Worktext pages 103-104

Letter Description
"The capital U is just like the lowercase u, only bigger! Start at the Roofline and go *straight down* toward the Floor, *curve around* and *back up* to the roof, then *straight down* to end at the Floor."

Letter Sounds
[u] as in up, [ū] as in universe

Resource Information
"God made the entire universe. The universe includes everything on the earth, and everything in the heavens — the planets, the stars, and more. The universe is so big that no one but God knows its real size!"

"But even in this huge universe, God knows every person in it. Isn't it wonderful that He cares about you and me?"

(optional) "Would you like to learn the names of the planets? Starting nearest the sun, they are Mercury, Venus, Earth, Mars, Jupiter, Saturn, Uranus, and Neptune."

Work Page Directions
"Can you see Earth in this picture? (planet at far left) Color its oceans blue, and its land either brown or green. The planet with the ring around it is Saturn. Color Saturn orange and its ring yellow or gold. In the third circle draw a smiling face as a reminder that *you* are part of God's universe, too!"

Lesson Focus
The capital S

See Student Worktext pages 105-106

Letter Description
"The capital S is just like the lowercase s, only bigger! Start just below the Roofline, then *curve up left*, then *down around right* at the Ceiling, then *down around left* touching the Floor, then *curve up* and stop just above the Floor."

Letter Sounds
[s] as in sun

Resource Information
"Without the heat and light from the sun, there would be no life on Earth! Our planet would be cold and dark and still. Aren't you thankful God made the warm sun!"

"Earth and all the other planets travel around the sun. This movement is what causes the Earth's seasons: spring, summer, fall, and winter."

"Your body needs some sunshine every day. It helps make your bones strong. Try to play outside in the sun whenever you can!"

Work Page Directions
"During the day the sun looks bright yellow-orange, but at sunrise or sunset it can be many other colors. If you want to make a sunrise or sunset, use pink, orange, or purple for the sun's rays. If you want a noonday sun picture, then color your sun bright yellow or orange."

See Student Worktext pages 107-108

Lesson Focus
A review of capital letters

F, H, I, J, U, E

Lesson Description
This is the second capital letter review. Before students begin this page, Sky Write each of these letters, (see pg. 9) reviewing letter formation. Praise students to help reinforce the correct counter-clockwise stroke of each letter.

Lesson Directions
(page 107) "Draw a line from each capital letter to its lowercase letter."

(page 108) "Write a capital letter to match each lowercase letter. Be sure to use the start dots."

Lesson Focus
The capital P

See Student Worktext pages 109-110

Letter Description
"The capital P begins with a stroke from the Roofline to the Floor. Return to the starting point and circle around and down to the Ceiling."

Letter Sounds
[p] as in pumpkin

Resource Information
"Pumpkins are large, round, and orange. How do you eat a pumpkin? Some people make pumpkin pie! Did you know there's *another* part of the pumpkin you can eat, too? You can eat the seeds!"

(optional) Cut a pumpkin open and show the stringy part inside. Carefully remove the seeds and wash them. Have students count the seeds.

After counting the seeds, wash them thoroughly, and soak them in salty water. Spread them on a cookie sheet and roast them at 250° for 45 to 60 minutes. The seeds will puff up a bit as they roast. Cracking and eating these pumpkin seeds at lunchtime will provide a new taste adventure!

Work Page Directions
"Outline the pumpkin with an orange crayon, then color the pumpkin with light strokes. Finish by coloring the stem and leaf green."

Lesson 41
Butterfly

Lesson 42
Rainbow

Lesson Focus
The capital B

See Student Worktext pages 111-112

Letter Description
"The capital B has two strokes. Start at the Roofline and go straight down to the Floor. Lift your pencil and return to the start. Then *circle down around right* connecting at the Ceiling, then *down around right* connecting at the Floor."

Letter Sounds
[b] as in butterfly

Resource Information
"The life cycle of the butterfly is very interesting! A butterfly egg hatches into a worm-like caterpillar. The caterpillar stuffs itself on leaves for several days. It grows so big it splits its skin! This may happen several times."

"Finally, the caterpillar spins a cozy little nest for itself called a cocoon. It curls up inside. You can't see anything happening, but the caterpillar is turning into a butterfly inside that cocoon."

"After a few weeks, a beautiful butterfly will come out of the cocoon, and fly away!"

Work Page Directions
Show students colored pictures of several varieties of butterflies from an encyclopedia, or online, or butterfly book. Point out the butterflies that are common to your area. "Be sure to color the wings of your butterfly so they match each other."

Lesson Focus
The capital R

See Student Worktext pages 113-114

Letter Description
"The capital R begins with a stroke from the Roofline *straight down* to the Floor. Return to the starting point, and *curve around and down* to the Ceiling, then *angle right* down to the Floor."

Letter Sounds
[r] as in rainbow

Resource Information
"We often see a rainbow in the sky when the sun is behind us and the rain is falling in front of us. Can you name the colors of the rainbow?" (The six primary colors — from inside to outside — are violet, blue, green, yellow, orange, and red.)

"The story of the very first rainbow comes from Scripture. Do you remember how it goes?" (If time allows, read the story aloud from Genesis 9:12-17.)

"The shape a rainbow makes is called an arch. If you look closely, you can see a similar arch in the lowercase r!"

Work Page Directions
Consider letting students use watercolors to paint their rainbows. Watercolors tend to blend slightly, giving the picture a softer look.

Lesson 43
Dolphin

See Student Worktext pages 115-116

Lesson Focus
The capital D

Letter Description
"The capital D has two strokes. Start at the Roofline and go *straight down* to the Floor. Back at the starting point, go *out* and *around right*, and *back down* to the Floor."

Letter Sounds
[d] as in dolphin

Resource Information
"Dolphin is a small whale-like mammal with a pointed snout. Dolphins are found in all oceans of the world and even in some rivers. If you've seen a 'dolphin show,' the star was probably the 'bottle-nosed dolphin.' Like dogs and chimpanzees, dolphins are very smart and easy to train."

"Dolphins communicate with each other with clicks and whistles. Dolphins also have a natural sonar system that helps them locate objects under water. The dolphin will make sounds and listen for the sound to be reflected off the object."

"Dolphins live in groups called pods. Marine biologists tell us that when a dolphin is old or sick, the other dolphins in the pod help it. Like the dolphins, we must learn to help each other, too."

Work Page Directions
"Color your dolphin gray or very light blue. If you wish, you can draw a ball or ring in the water for your dolphin to play with — or maybe a small fish for it to eat!"

Lesson 44
Nest

See Student Worktext pages 117-118

Lesson Focus
The capital N

Letter Description
"The capital N starts with a stroke from the Roofline *straight down* to the Floor. Return to the starting point and *angle down right* to the Floor, then *straight up* to the Roofline."

Letter Sounds
[n] as in nest

Resource Information
"It's lots of fun to find a bird's nest in a tree or bush. It's even more exciting if the nest has eggs or baby birds in it! But be sure not to touch them, or the mother may be frightened away!"

"Most birds build nests to hold their eggs and shelter their young. Some nests are just a few stones or bits of grass by the water. Other nests are a hole inside a tree. Some nests are even made of mud! The most common building materials for nests are straw, twigs, and feathers."

(optional) Use an encyclopedia, library book, or on-line resource to show colored photographs or drawings of several kinds of nests. Talk about specific birds that live in your region.

Work Page Directions
"Color your picture to make it look like the nest of a bird that might live near your home. Make sure the eggs are the right kind for your nest."

Lesson 45
Monkey

See Student Worktext pages 119-120

Lesson Focus
The capital M

See Student Worktext pages 121-122

Lesson Focus
A review of capital letters

P, M, N, B, D, R

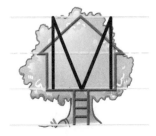

Letter Description
"The capital M starts with a stroke from the Roofline *straight down* to the Floor. Return to the starting point, then *angle down* to the Floor, *angle up* to the Roofline, then *straight down* to the Floor."

Letter Sounds
[m] as in monkey

Resource Information
"The monkey is an active animal that loves to climb trees and swing from branches. The monkey's fingers and toes help it hold on as it climbs and swings."

"Monkeys often live together in family groups. Female monkeys usually have only one baby at a time, and the mother will carry the baby everywhere she goes. At first the baby will cling to the mother's underside, then as it grows older it may even ride on her back!"

"Some monkeys eat leaves and grass, but smaller monkeys eat fruit and small insects, too. Monkeys in the zoo like bananas and other fruit as well."

"What color are the monkeys you have seen? Monkeys come in gray, brown, red, and all the shades in between. Some even have white fur around their face that looks like a beard!"

Work Page Directions
"Decide what color you want your monkey to be. Use lighter shades on the monkey's hands, feet, and face. Use darker shades on its body. Don't forget to color the tree limb that the monkey is sitting on!"

Lesson Description
This is the third capital letter review. Before students begin this page, Sky Write each of these letters (see pg. 9) reviewing letter formation. Praise students to help reinforce the correct counter-clockwise stroke of each letter.

Lesson Directions
(page 121) "Draw a line from each capital letter to its lowercase letter."

(page 122) "Write a capital letter to match each lowercase letter. Be sure to use the start dots."

Lesson 46
Apple

See Student Worktext pages 123-124

Lesson Focus
The capital A

Letter Description
"The capital A has three strokes. Start at the Roofline and *slant down left* to the Floor. Return to the starting point and *slant down right* to the Floor. The third stroke connects the first two at the Ceiling."

Letter Sounds
[a] as in apple, [ā] as in ape, [ä] as in want

Resource Information
"There are many different kinds of apples, but almost all of them are a shade of red, green, or yellow. What are some ways we might describe an apple?" (skin outside, white inside, crunchy, seeds in the middle, woody stem, etc.)

"Did you know that God made something special inside every apple? There's a star inside!" Note: Cut through the middle of an apple at the "equator" and the seed section should show a star shape.

(optional) "How many seeds do you think are in an apple?" Cut open at least three apples and count the seeds in each. Add all the seeds, then divide by three to get the average.

Work Page Directions
"Color your apple the same color as the kind of apple you like best. Color just the bottom edge of each slice since the centers are white. Or if you wish, you may color the centers a very light yellow." (optional) "When you have finished coloring the apple, glue two apple seeds on the edge of your apple slices."

Lesson 47
Koala

See Student Worktext pages 125-126

Lesson Focus
The capital K

Letter Description
"The capital K begins with a stroke *straight down* from the Roofline to the Floor. Start the second stroke at the Roofline, *slant left* to touch the first line at the Ceiling, then *slant right* down to the Floor."

Letter Sounds
[k] as in koala

Resource Information
"The koala is a small tree-climbing animal that lives in Australia — the country where kangaroos are from. The koala has something else in common with the kangaroo. They both have a pouch where they carry their babies! A baby koala stays in its mother's pouch for several months. When it is older, it begins to ride around on its mother's back."

"The koala only eats the leaves and buds from one kind of tree. The tree is called a eucalyptus [you-kah-lip¹-tuss]. In the United States, eucalyptus trees are found in California. But there are no wild koalas there to eat them!"

Work Page Directions
"Color your koala brown, and make his nose black. There are plenty of eucalyptus leaves for your koala to eat. Color the leaves green, and the tree limb light brown."

Lesson Focus
The capital V

See Student Worktext pages 127-128

Letter Description
"The capital V is just like the lowercase v, only bigger! The stroke is just the same, except it starts and ends at the Roofline: *slant down right*, *slant up*. Make sure you don't lift your pencil until you're finished."

Letter Sounds
[v] as in volcano

Resource Information
"A volcano is usually a cone-shaped mountain. When a volcano explodes, or *erupts*, melted rocks and fire are thrown hundreds of feet into the air. Ashes can fill the air for hundreds of miles. Melted rock, called *lava*, flows down the side of the mountain."

"Scientists' knowledge of volcanoes is limited, but they are learning more each day. One thing that everyone who deals with volcanoes knows is that there is tremendous power there."

If there is a volcano near your area, describe it to the class. Check an encyclopedia or on-line resource for pictures of volcanoes. Your local library may even have a film available on this fascinating subject.

Work Page Directions
"Color the mountain brown and the exploding fire red, yellow, and orange. The streams of lava flowing down the mountain should be red-orange."
(optional) "You may glue small stones above the volcano to show the rocks flying out of the earth."

Lesson Focus
The capital W

See Student Worktext pages 129-130

Letter Description
"The capital W is just like the lowercase w, only bigger! Start at the Roofline and *slant down* to the Floor, *slant up* to the Roofline, *slant down*, *slant up*. Don't lift your pencil until you are finished!"

Letter Sounds
[w] as in watermelon

Resource Information
"Have you ever seen a watermelon growing on a vine in a field? The vine can be very long and have several watermelons on it."

"Some watermelons are solid green on the outside, and some are striped green and white. Inside most watermelons are bright red, but some kinds are bright yellow!"

(optional) If the season is right, serve your students slices of watermelon at lunch. For a math activity, have them save the seeds and count them. Ask who got the most seeds? Who got the fewest? See if any two children got the same number of seeds.

Work Page Directions
"The watermelon in your picture is a striped watermelon. Use your darkest green crayon, and color every other stripe. Color the stripes in between light green. Don't forget to color the inside of the watermelon slice bright red, and the seeds black or brown!"

Lesson 50
Yucca

Lesson Focus
The capital Y

See Student Worktext pages 131-132

Letter Description
"Begin the capital Y by making a lowercase v in the attic. Make sure it touches the Roofline and the Ceiling. The second stroke goes from the bottom of the v straight down to the Floor."

Letter Sounds
[y] as in yucca

Resource Information
"The yucca is a plant that grows in the desert where there is lots of sand and not much water. But God designed the yucca so it can stay green all year."

"When the yucca blooms, it has white bell-shaped flowers. The yucca blossoms open up at night, and they smell very nice."

Work Page Directions
"Color the leaves on your yucca green and the stems brown. Don't color the blossoms because they are white! If you wish, you can draw some sand dunes in the background and color them light brown."

(optional) "Would you like to make your page into a desert scene? Thinly spread glue on your page and sprinkle it with clean sand. You can also glue on some pieces of popcorn to make yucca blossoms!"

Lesson 51
Ibex

Lesson Focus
The capital X

See Student Worktext pages 133-134

Letter Description
"The capital X is just like the lowercase x, only bigger! Make sure that both strokes go from the Roofline to the Floor, and that they cross at the Ceiling."

Letter Sounds
[x] as in ibex [1]

Resource Information
"The ibex is a type of mountain goat that lives in the very high mountains of Europe and Asia. The male ibex has long horns that curve backward. The horns of the ibex are rough to the touch, not smooth like the tusks of the elephant or walrus."

Work Page Directions
"Color your ibex gray or brown. If you wish, you may draw some mountains behind your ibex, so it will have a place to live."

[1] No animal name *starts* with X, so this example uses a word that *ends* with the X sound.

Lesson 52
Zebu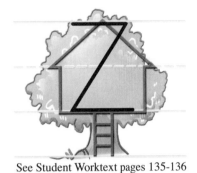

Lesson Focus
The capital Z

See Student Worktext pages 135-136

Letter Description

"The capital Z is just like the lowercase z, only bigger! Use the same zigzag stroke — *straight right*, *slant down left*, *straight right*. Remember to make your Z touch the Roofline and the Floor."

Letter Sounds

[z] as in zebu

Resource Information

"The zebu is a type of hump-backed cattle from southern Asia. The large muscular hump on the shoulders makes it an easy animal to identify. Can you name another kind of animal that has a hump on its back?" (a camel)

"Most zebus have short horns, big floppy ears, and dewlaps (loose floppy skin that hangs under the throat). Just like other cattle, a group of zebus is called a herd."

"In some countries Zebus are used as beasts of burden. Zebus are raised for milk and meat. Name some things that we make from milk?" (butter, cheese, cottage cheese, ice cream, etc.)

Work Page Directions

"Color your zebu a light tan or brown. Some Asian farmers put bells around their cows' necks to help them find the cows in large pastures. If you wish, draw a rope around the zebu's neck and put a bell on it."

Review

See Student Worktext pages 137-138

Lesson Focus
A review of capital letters

Y, W, V, K, X, Z

Lesson Description

This is the final capital letter review. Before students begin this page, Sky Write each of these letters (see pg. 9) reviewing letter formation. Praise students to help reinforce the correct counter-clockwise stroke of each letter.

Lesson Directions[1]

(page 137) "Draw a line from each capital letter to its lowercase letter."

(page 138) "Write a capital letter to match each lowercase letter. Be sure to use the start dots."

[1] No animal name *starts* with X, so this example uses a word that *ends* with the X sound.

To The Teacher

Page 138 in the Student Worktext completes the introduction and review of all capital and lowercase alphabet letters.

The rest of the book contains comprehensive review lessons which focus on specific letter groups. These not only serve as a final review, but also provide a tool to help you verify individual student mastery.

See Student Worktext pages 139-140

Lesson Focus
A review of circle letters
c, a, o, d, e, g

Lesson Description
This is a comprehensive review of lowercase circle letters. It is designed to test individual student mastery of letter formation.

Lesson Directions
"Trace each circle letter, then finish the line with that letter. Be sure to use the start dots."

Lesson Focus
A review of curve letters
r, m, n, h, u, s

Lesson Description
This is a comprehensive review of lowercase curve letters. It is designed to test individual student mastery of letter formation.

Lesson Directions
"Trace each curve letter, then finish the line with that letter. Be sure to use the start dots."

See Student Worktext pages 141-142

Lesson Focus
A review of slant letters
k, v, w, x, y, z

Lesson Description
This is a comprehensive review of lowercase slant letters. It is designed to test individual student mastery of letter formation.

Lesson Directions
"Trace each slant letter, then finish the line with that letter. Be sure to use the start dots."

Lesson Focus
A review of downstroke letters
i, t, l, b, h, f

Lesson Description
This is a comprehensive review of lowercase downstroke letters. It is designed to test individual student mastery of letter formation.

Lesson Directions
"Trace each downstroke letter, then finish the line with that letter. Be sure to use the start dots."

See Student Worktext pages 143-144

Lesson Focus
A review of tail letters
g, j, p, q, y

Lesson Description
This is a comprehensive review of lowercase tail letters. It is designed to test individual student mastery of letter formation.

Lesson Directions
"Trace each tail letter, then finish the line with that letter. Be sure to use the start dots."

Lesson Focus
A review of tall letters
b, d, f, h, k, l

Lesson Description
This is a comprehensive review of lowercase tall letters. It is designed to test individual student mastery of letter formation.

Lesson Directions
"Trace each tall letter, then finish the line with that letter. Be sure to use the start dots."

WORKTEXT GUIDELINES
Manuscript, Transition, & Cursive

General Guidelines for
Teaching Handwriting

Handwriting is an essential skill for children and adults alike. Even in today's high-tech world (computers use Manuscript!); it's a skill we need and use every day!

Legible handwriting is a critical skill in the classroom, too. Students (even in high school and college) increasingly feel the need for quality handwriting as they face the essays required on many of today's standardized tests.

Unfortunately, there are no shortcuts in learning to write legibly. It does not occur automatically with age maturity, but is a learned motor skill that requires constant practice! And yet, "perfect" handwriting should never be an end in itself. Ultimately, the focus should be on the *message and readability* rather than the process.

A Reason For Handwriting® provides the ideal message for your students to focus on — God's Word! In short, since success is achieved only by consistent, daily practice, why not focus that practice on the values found in Scripture verses?

Why Teach Manuscript?
It's much easier for students to imitate in writing what they see each day in reading. Manuscript is the style that dominates our world — from billboards, to street signs, to computer screens, to textbooks. Thus Manuscript writing is the logical starting point for beginning readers.

The Teacher's Role
Handwriting Worktexts don't teach handwriting—TEACHERS do! Simply put, the process of learning legible handwriting is greatly enhanced by continued monitoring and guidance from an informed teacher.

Because students tend to imitate the teacher in their handwriting, you should become thoroughly familiar with all the letter forms used in order to demonstrate the individual letter strokes correctly. Even though it's similar to many traditional methods, **A Reason For Handwriting®** is a unique handwriting style. Please take a few moments to review the Manuscript Letter Formation Chart. (See Appendix, page 231.)

The Weekly Schedule
Handwriting should be part of your daily schedule. Each section is designed to take 10 to 15 minutes to complete, since longer periods cause many students to tire and lose efficiency. Most students quickly grasp the simple weekly format, allowing them to focus their attention on the lesson tips, applications, and daily practice.

A great time to teach **A Reason For Handwriting®** is at the beginning of the day. The program's Scripture-based content makes it ideal for starting each day! And when you *begin* with handwriting, you can draw your student's attention to practice letters throughout other daily lessons.

Remember, it's counter-productive to let your students complete an entire week's lesson in one sitting! Only regular *daily* practice can bring effective results. The key is the *quality* of the practice, not just the quantity!

Scripture Translation

Since **A Reason For Handwriting**® was designed to teach elementary handwriting, using a Scripture translation with simple, easy-to-understand vocabulary was essential. Each Verse of the Week used in this series is taken from *The Living Bible* by Tyndale House Publishers.

Alternative Methods & Remediation

Many students are not visual learners, and need more than just a model to help them effectively improve their handwriting.

To maximize their learning experience, be sure to include some of the recommended alternatives (verbal description, board practice, Sky Writing, etc.) to demonstrate both letter size and formation. Chalkboard practice is especially helpful. It not only reinforces learning, but also makes it easier for you to spot letter formation problems.

If your students are having problems with specific letters, take time to review letter formation. (See "letter formation charts," Appendix, page 231.) It's really amazing how quickly a child's handwriting will improve when a specific problem area is remediated!

Evaluation & Motivation

Letting students know exactly what's expected is always helpful — especially when it comes to legible handwriting! As students are made aware of the evaluation system (see "Tips on Grading," page 57 and "How To Become a Five Star Student," Student Worktext, page 6), their work will improve remarkably. The evaluation system also provides a reference point to pinpoint specific areas: Alignment, Slant, Size, Shape, and Spacing, and facilitates parent/student interaction. Scripture Border Sheets are also a powerful component of **Handwriting**. When students know that their handwriting will be shared with others (see "Fun Ways to Share," p. 58), they're motivated to do their *very best* work. Assign specific Border Sheets each week, or let students select their own. (Note: Several Border Sheets feature holiday themes.

Have your students save these until the appropriate time.) Sharing Scripture Border Sheets will generate positive interaction, as children discover the joy of sharing God's Word!

Weekly
Lesson Format

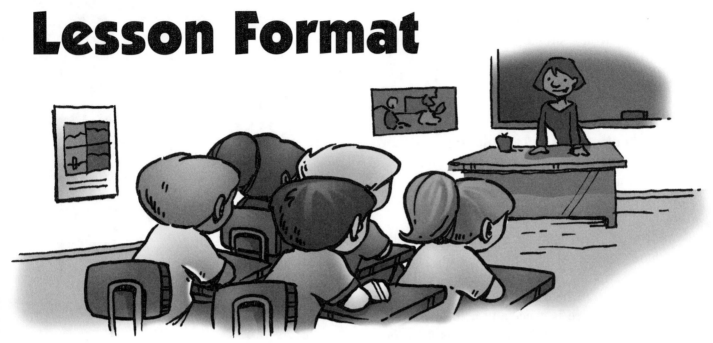

The pattern of daily lessons in **A Reason For Handwriting**® repeats from week to week. This format minimizes the time needed each day for verbal instruction, and maximizes student's time on task. Specific lesson tips, answers to discussion questions, and Extended Teaching suggestions for each lesson are found in the Daily Lesson Plans section, for each book.

Here is the suggested weekly lesson format:

Day 1

Read the Verse of the Week together. Discuss the daily lesson tip. Point out the focus letters or words for the day.

Day 2

Read the Verse of the Week together. Review the focus letters or words for the day. Use the Extended Teaching tips as time permits.

Day 3

Same as Day 2.

Day 4

Read the Verse of the Week together. Have students practice the entire verse once or twice on a sheet of paper. Ask the students to select a Scripture Border Sheet from the back of their Worktexts and begin decorating it.

Day 5

Challenge students to repeat the Verse of the Week from memory. Have students carefully write the Verse of the Week on their chosen Scripture Border Sheet, then finish decorating it. Discuss ways children can share their finished Scripture verses. (See page 58 for ideas.)

Tips on
Grading

Grading System

There are five basic areas the teacher should consider when evaluating handwriting. They are **Alignment, Slant, Size, Shape,** and **Spacing**. The "How To Become a Five Star Student" section in the Student Worktext (page 6) has detailed descriptions of each area, and is designed to help reinforce the evaluation process. (See Black Line Masters, pages 242 & 243.) Allowing two points for each item results in an easy-to-understand 10 point grading scale. (See Black Line Masters, page 246 & 247.) If this system is used regularly, it helps students identify areas for improvement.

General Guidelines

It is important to keep handwriting evaluation as positive as possible. Look for the student's *best* work! Also, emphasize consistent writing from day to day, and focus on the *quality* of the student's handwriting rather than just quantity.

Student Folders

It's a good idea to keep a folder for each student with samples of his/her work. This should include pages from the beginning and ending of each grading period (either the alphabet or Day 4 practice). Thus, when grading time arrives, evaluation can be based on the student's progress.

Evaluation Sentence

The practice sentence at the bottom of the page (See also Student Worktext, page 6.) contains all the letters of the alphabet. Ask students to write this sentence at the beginning of the grading period — then again at the end. Comparing the two will help pinpoint specific letter problems.

This sentence may also be used for one-minute timed writings. While speed is not the primary concern in handwriting, some students may benefit from this practice. Be sure to encourage readability as well as speed!

The following practice sentence contains all the letters of the alphabet:

God created zebras and foxes to walk, jump, and hide very quickly.

Fun Ways to Share the Scripture Border Sheets

Each week, students have fun sharing God's Word with others. From the back of their Worktext, students choose, write out, and decorate the Verse of the Week. (Kindergarten features Creation) But, the real excitement begins when they then **share** God's Word—in **their very own handwriting**—with others!

- Place the verse in a spot where members of the family will see it every day.

- Make a placemat! Center the sheet on construction paper or a plain paper placemat. Laminate or cover with clear contact paper.

- Find someone who is housebound. Deliver the verse in person, and stay to visit.

- Give the decorated verse to grandparents. Don't forget a personal note on the back.

- Share the verse with someone who works in your neighborhood: the postman, grocery store clerks, law enforcement, etc.

- Encourage other Christians. The church secretary can often provide names of those who'd appreciate a Scripture verse of encouragement.

- Take a trip to a nursing home. Have a pair of students visit each resident, then leave their verses to decorate the room.

- Give the verse to someone who is sick. Some hospitals will cooperate by placing the verses on patients' breakfast trays.

- Create an attractive bulletin board using the Scripture Border Sheets. Or select a special one each week, and display it in a special place in your home.

- If your church has a central display case, ask permission to periodically post a Scripture Border Sheet.

- Check to see if your church would like to enclose copies along with the church newsletter.

- Ask for a church mailing list. Send each family a Scripture Border Sheet and a personal note. Do a few each week. Students will be delighted with the positive response this will generate!

Suggested Cover Letter

People receiving the decorated Verses are even more responsive when a note, describing the sharing activity, is included. Here's a sample note you can use or adapt:

Dear Friend,

Each week I write a Scripture Verse as part of my Handwriting lesson. This week I want to share my Verse with you.

I hope you have a good week with God's blessings. I will be praying for you.

Sincerely,
(Child's name)

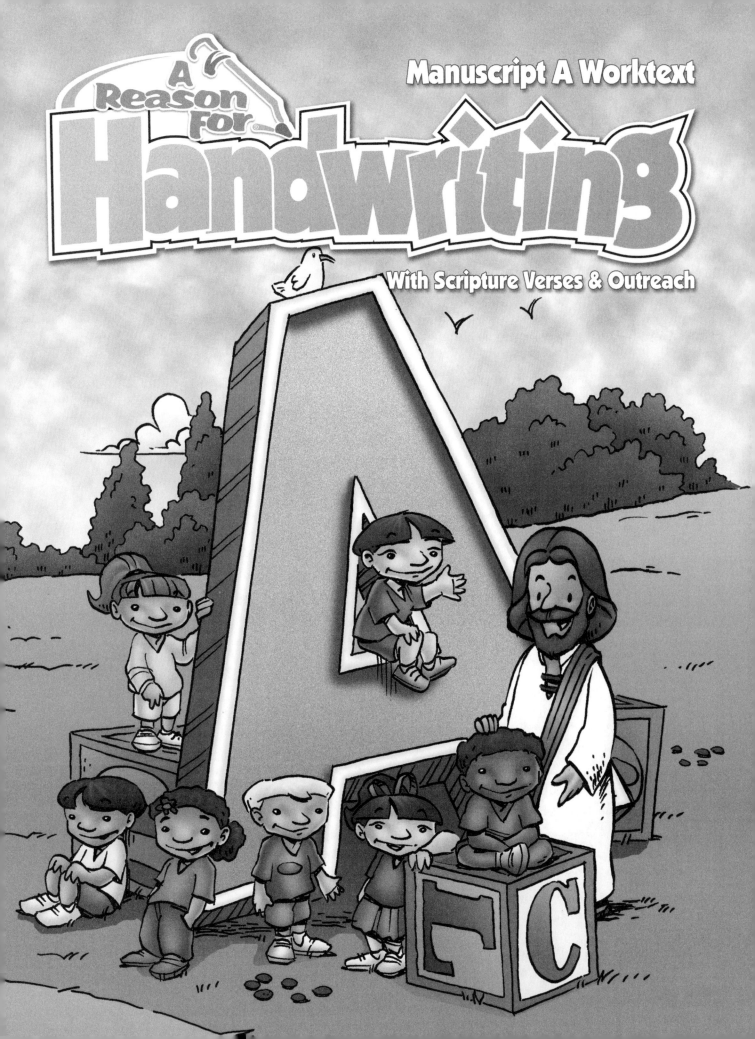

LESSONS

To The Teacher

After the summer break, students often benefit from a focused review. The following **Practice Lessons** provide a quick, efficient method for reviewing Manuscript letter formation.

These lessons are designed for one page each day, for a total of six weeks.

Another option is to begin immediately with Lesson 1, and use these review pages as concurrent extra practice.

Important Notice:

The basic strokes in Manuscript handwriting are the downstrokes (top to bottom), and circles (counter-clockwise and clockwise). Practicing the direction of these strokes may not seem important, but it's the *key* to ease and readability. Focusing on basic strokes *first* makes teaching letter formation much easier. And mastering these strokes now helps smooth the transition from Manuscript to Cursive later.

The concepts of "top to bottom" and "left to right" are also foundational. You'll find yourself returning to them again and again as students need remedial help.

As the year begins, proper attention to these fundamental lessons will pay big dividends in letter formation as the weeks progress. Letter formation descriptions are given in the Appendix (pages 226-230) to help as you introduce new letters.

(See Student Worktext, page 9)

Lesson Focus: Circles/Downstrokes

Directions: Have students complete page 9, carefully following the arrows and start dots.

Teaching Tip: Tell students that circles start at the two o'clock position, and go up and around counter-clockwise. Have students Sky Write letters (page 9) to show the direction and stroke. Verbalize the movement as you make circles in the air. Make large circles, then smaller circles — all going the same direction (counter-clockwise). Note: While two lowercase letters (b, p) have a clockwise stroke, most circle letters are written with a counter-clockwise stroke (a, c, d, e, g, o, q).

Sky Write a top-down stroke, verbalizing to help emphasize that downstrokes are "top to bottom." Encourage students to reach high and come down to waist level, using the pointer finger of their writing hand. Some students have learned to write letters bottom to top. This is a hard habit to break, but well worth the effort. Many experts believe it takes at least 12 repetitions to repattern the brain, so spend plenty of time Sky Writing downstrokes. Board or finger painting practice may also be helpful.

Extended Teaching: Blow bubbles with your students, pointing out the round shapes and

different sizes. Tell them that circle letters are like bubbles. Have them draw bubbles of different colors on unlined paper, using a counter-clockwise stroke. They may also enjoy drawing pictures using only downstrokes and circles. (Make sure their downstrokes are written "top to bottom.")

(See Student Worktext, page 10)

Lesson Focus: Downstrokes / Straight Lines / Slanted Lines

Directions: Have students complete page 10, carefully following the arrows and start dots.

Teaching Tip: Before moving to the practice page, Sky Write these downstroke lines. Students may benefit from saying "down, down, down" aloud as they write each line.

Using the start dots and arrows as direction cues, have students follow the pattern for each line. Correct posture and paper position will greatly improve consistency of slant as students write. Encourage students to hold their pencils correctly as well.

Extended Teaching: Using stick pretzels, have students make as many letters as possible, especially the straight line capitals (A, E, F, H, I, K, L, M, N, T, V, W, X, Y, Z). Students not only enjoy this unique form of letter practice, they enjoy *eating* their practice too!

(See Student Worktext, page 11)

Lesson Focus: Number Focus

Directions: Have students complete page 11, carefully following the arrows and start dots.

Teaching Tip: Remind students that most numbers are written with one stroke. (The exception is the number 4.) For practice using multiple learning styles, have students describe the numbers, Sky Write them, and practice them on the board.

Extended Teaching: Encourage students to write numbers in sand, salt, or finger paint. They will also enjoy making the numbers out of clay or dough. Provide number cards and counting activities (buttons, cubes, toothpicks, etc.) to reinforce number recognition.

(See Student Worktext, page 12)

Lesson Focus: Circle Letters (c, o)

Directions: Have students complete page 12, carefully following the arrows and start dots. Read aloud the practice words "cook" and "come" with your students.

Teaching Tip: Begin the lesson by Sky Writing each letter to help imprint its shape in students' minds. Students will also benefit from board practice.

Extended Teaching: Students enjoy blowing bubbles. Expand this activity by talking about the shape of bubbles, then transferring the concept to the shape of circle letters (see Extended Teaching, Lesson 1).

(See Student Worktext, page 13)

Lesson Focus: Circle Letters (a, d)

Directions: Have students complete page 13, carefully following the arrows and start dots. Remind students to completely fill the space with each letter. Read aloud the practice words "dad" and "do" with your students.

Teaching Tip: Have students Sky Write these one-stroke circle letters, beginning at the two o'clock position. Describe the letters as students move with them. It's important to write these letters with one stroke to minimize letter reversals. (When the d is begun as a circle letter, with the strokes around, up and down, then there's no question about which side gets the tall stroke.) Name the letters. Name the sounds. Name the letter formation.

Extended Teaching: Students may draw a picture of Dad, or of themselves doing something with Dad.

(See Student Worktext, page 14)

Lesson Focus: Circle Letters/Tail Letters (g, q)

Directions: Have students complete page 14, carefully following the arrows and start dots. Read aloud the practice words "dog" and "go" with your students.

Teaching Tip: Using the Treehouse (page 7), review the tail letters g and q. Focus on the direction of both the circle and tail. Sky Write each letter. Describe each letter.

Extended Teaching: Using pipe cleaners or clay, have students make the g — then turn it into a q!

Practice Lesson 7

(See Student Worktext, page 15)

Lesson Focus: Downstrokes/Tall Letter (b) /Circle Letter (e)

Directions: Have students complete page 15, carefully following the arrows and start dots. Read aloud the words "be" and "bed" with your students.

Teaching Tip: Using the Treehouse (page 7), review the letters b and e. Focus on the beginning point and direction of stroke. The letter b is one letter that is written with a clockwise stroke. Have students Sky Write this letter as you describe it. There will be fewer reversals if the b is completed without picking up the pencil.

Extended Teaching: Show students that the word "bee" is written by adding an additional "e." They may wish to draw a bee flying to a hive, a tree, or a flower.

Practice Lesson 8

(See Student Worktext, page 16)

Lesson Focus: Downstroke Letters (p, i)

Directions: Have students complete page 16, carefully following the arrows and start dots. Read aloud the practice words "pig" and "did" with your students.

Teaching Tip: Using the Treehouse (page 7), review the letters p and i. Both letters begin with a downstroke from the Ceiling. Point out that the p goes down the ladder, and is completed with a clockwise stroke. Also remind students that the i is dotted in the attic.

Extended Teaching: Practice other words containing the letters p and i: pit, dip, sip, rip, etc.

Practice Lesson 9

(See Student Worktext, page 17)

Lesson Focus: Downstroke/Tall letters (t, l)

Directions: Have students complete page 17, carefully following the arrows and start dots. Read aloud the practice words "tall" and "it" with your students.

Teaching Tip: Using the Treehouse, review the starting point for the tall letters t and l. Both letters begin at the Roofline and go down to the Floor. The letter t is crossed at the Ceiling. Have students Sky Write these letters. Describe the letters as students move.

Extended Teaching: Help the students understand the concepts of "tall, taller, tallest" by showing photos of three family members and saying, "(name) is tall, (name) is taller, (name) is tallest." Emphasize that like letters, each one of us is special — and just the right size!

Practice Lesson 10

(See Student Worktext, page 18)

Lesson Focus: Downstroke/Curve Letters (h, r)

Directions: Have students complete page 18, carefully following the arrows and start dots. Read aloud the practice words "hat" and "rat" with your students.

Teaching Tip: Using the Treehouse, review the starting point for the tall letter h. The h begins at the Roofline, and the r begins at Ceiling. Point out that the r is contained in the h. Sky Write and verbally describe each letter.

Extended Teaching: Have students draw "a rat wearing a hat," and write the words "hat" and "rat" below the picture.

Lesson 11

(See Student Worktext, page 19)

Lesson Focus: Downstroke/Curve Letters (n, m)

Directions: Have students complete page 19, carefully following the arrows and start dots. Read aloud the practice words "not" and "man" with your students.

Teaching Tip: Sky Write and describe the curve letters n and m. Encourage students to make an n with their left hand (thumb pointing up and facing them, fingers curved around and down). Add right hand with thumb tucked in fingers curved to make an m.

Extended Teaching: Find pictures or describe camels with one hump (dromedary) and two humps (bactrian). This may help some students form a mental picture of the m and n.

Lesson 12

(See Student Worktext, page 20)

Lesson Focus: Tall/Two-Stroke Letters (f, k)

Directions: Have students complete page 20, carefully following the arrows and start dots. Read aloud the practice words "fill" and "kind" with your students.

Teaching Tip: Using the Treehouse, review the tall/two-stroke letters f and k. Point out that the letter f begins just below the Roofline of the Treehouse and curves up and around, then down. Talk about the second stroke of the letters f and k. While most letters are written without picking up a pencil, these letters need a second stroke.

Extended Teaching: The first stroke of the letter f looks much like a shepherd's staff. In the story of the lost sheep (see Luke 15:4-6), the Shepherd probably used his staff to help rescue the little lost lamb. Share this story with the students. You can play a variation of hide and seek with students hiding and one being the shepherd. The shepherd calls out "Little lamb! Little lamb! Where are you?" The "sheep" must then respond with "Baa! Baa!" When found, the sheep must go to the "fold" (designated area). The last one found becomes the shepherd for the next game.

Lesson 13

(See Student Worktext, page 21)

Lesson Focus: Tail/Two-Stroke Letters (j, y)

Directions: Have students complete page 21, carefully following the arrows and start dots. Read aloud the practice words "jet" and "may" with your students.

Teaching Tip: Using the Treehouse, review the formation of the j and y. Point out that even though these are both tail letters, the tails are different! Ask students what else is different about these letters. (The j is a downstroke letter; the y is a slant letter).

Extended Teaching: Have each student write the word "joy," then draw a picture that illustrates the concept. (Note: This is an abstract concept, so they may need some examples: smiling child jumping rope; laughing child on swings; smiling child sharing toys; etc.)

Lesson 14

(See Student Worktext, page 22)

Lesson Focus: Slantstroke Letters (v, w)

Directions: Have students complete page 22, carefully following the arrows and start dots. Read aloud the practice words "vine" and "want" with your students.

Teaching Tip: Ask students how the lowercase v and w are alike. (They begin with the same strokes. There are two v's in the w.) Ask several students to describe how to write these letters. Then have one student lead out in the Sky Writing activity.

Extended Teaching: Using construction paper, have students make a crown by drawing the slanted down/up pattern of the v and w. To finish their crown, have them cut out the design, then staple or tape the ends of paper together.

Lesson 15

(See Student Worktext, page 23)

Lesson Focus: Curve Letters (u, s)

Directions: Have students complete page 23, carefully following the arrows and start dots. Read aloud the practice words "yes" and "us" with your students.

Teaching Tip: To help students recognize shapes, ask them what other letter they might see if they turned the u around and upside down (the letter n). Also ask them, "What number begins like the letter s?" (the number 8).

Extended Teaching: Have students draw a picture of themselves with their friends or family, then at the bottom of the picture, write the word "us."

Lesson 16

(See Student Worktext, page 24)

Lesson Focus: Slantstroke Letters (x, z)

Directions: Have students complete page 24, carefully following the arrows and start dots. Read aloud the practice words "ax" and "zoo" with your students.

Teaching Tip: Review the slantstroke letter formation for x and z.

Extended Teaching: Using half-inch or one-inch grid paper, suggest that students make a cross-stitch pattern for the letter x using different colored crayons.

Lesson 17

(See Student Worktext, page 25)

Lesson Focus: Capital/Circle Letters (O, Q)

Directions: Have students complete page 25, carefully following the arrows and start dots. Read aloud the practice words "Obed" and "Queen" with your students.

Teaching Tip: Sky Write with students the circle letters O and Q. Begin at the two o'clock position, and go up and around. Challenge students to describe how the Q is different from the O (the added line).

Extended Teaching: Students often enjoy talking about names. Who are some famous Queens in the Bible? (Queen Esther; the Queen of Sheba) Who was Obed? (Actually there were *several* men in the Old Testament named Obed. Check a concordance.) Challenge students to identify other people whose names are the same. Perhaps there are even some in your family.

Lesson 18

(See Student Worktext, page 26)

Lesson Focus: Capital/Circle Letters (C, G)

Directions: Have students complete page 26, carefully following the arrows and start dots. Read aloud the practice words "Christ" and "God" with your students.

Teaching Tip: Review the letter formation of the capital letters C and G. After Sky Writing these letters, ask students to point out how these letters are alike and how they are different. (They begin alike. They are both circle capitals. The capital G has an added ledge.) Remind students that all names are capitalized, as well as pronouns that refer to God.

Extended Teaching: Just for fun, have students write several C's and G's, then let them add hair, eyes, and noses to make "people."

Lesson 19

(See Student Worktext, page 27)

Lesson Focus: Forward Curve/Two-Stroke Capitals (P, B)

Directions: Have students complete page 27, carefully following the arrows and start dots. Read aloud the practice words "Paul" and "Bible" with your students.

Teaching Tip: Challenge students to see the P in the B. Review the P letter formation — downstroke, back to the top, and around. Also, review the B — downstroke, back to the top, then around and around.

Extended Teaching: Point out that Paul was an Apostle in the Bible. He was a man who was not kind to Christians — until he understood God's love for him. Then he wanted to tell everyone about God. He traveled many places and wrote many letters to people to share that good news. Ask students what lessons there might be for us in Paul's story.

Lesson 20

(See Student Worktext, page 28)

Lesson Focus: Forward/Curve Capitals (D, R)

Directions: Have students complete page 28, carefully following the arrows and start dots. Read aloud the practice words "David" and "Ruth" with your students.

Teaching Tip: Review the letter formation for the capital letters D and R. Point out that they are in the same letter group as P and B. Students will benefit from verbally describing how these letters are alike and different.

Extended Teaching: King David was once a shepherd boy. He was very brave, and even fought the giant Goliath for God's people. David wrote many songs, which we can find in Scripture as the Psalms (Psalm means song). Ask students to name some of their favorite songs about God.

(See Student Worktext, page 29)

Lesson Focus: Downstroke/Three-Stroke Capitals (F, E)

Directions: Have students complete page 29, carefully following the arrows and start dots. Read aloud the practice words "Father" and "Eve" with your students.

Teaching Tip: Review the downstroke letter formation for the capital letters E and F. Ask students to discover the F inside the E. Sky Write the letter E and describe it: down across, across, across. (Note: The first stroke is down and across the bottom to the right. Emphasize that this is one stroke.)

Extended Teaching: Count the strokes of the capital F with the students. Have them practice on the board (or their paper) counting "one, two, three, rest; one, two, three, rest." Place the students in groups of two, one can write the letter while the other counts and claps the strokes.

(See Student Worktext, page 30)

Lesson Focus: Downstroke Capitals (H, U)

Directions: Have students complete page 30, carefully following the arrows and start dots. Read aloud the practice words "Holy" and "Uz" with your students.

Teaching Tip: Review the letter formation of the capital H and U. Both begin with a downstroke. Encourage students to touch the Roofline with both ends of the U, as well as both downstrokes in the letter H.

Extended Teaching: Uz is the name of a person in Scripture, and also a place. In fact, at one time Job probably had many cattle and sheep grazing in the land of Uz. Have students draw a picture of Job's cattle and sheep on a grassy hillside, then label their picture "Uz."

(See Student Worktext, page 31)

Lesson Focus: Downstroke Capitals (I, T)

Directions: Have students complete page 31, carefully following the arrows and start dots. Read aloud the practice words "Isaac" and "Terah" with your students.

Teaching Tip: Review the letter formation for the downstroke capitals I and T. These two letters have similarities. Ask the students how they are the same and different. (Both begin with a downstroke. Both have a top stroke. One has two strokes; one has three. One has a shorter top stroke.)

Extended Teaching: Isaac was the son of Abraham and Sarah. Terah was Abraham's father. Scripture says Terah lived to be 205 years old. Ask students, "How long do most people live today?" Take this opportunity to discuss with students the concepts of age and aging.

(See Student Worktext, page 32)

Lesson Focus: Downstroke Capitals (K, L)

Directions: Have students complete page 32, carefully following the arrows and start dots. Read aloud the practice words "King" and "Luke" with your students.

Teaching Tip: Review the letter formation of the capital letters K and L. Both begin with a downstroke. The capital L is a one-stroke letter. The K is a two-stroke letter. Ask students, "What other capital letter begins like the capital L?" (the letter E)

Extended Teaching: Luke was one of Jesus' disciples. He also was a doctor and wrote the book of Scripture that bears his name. There are many Kings mentioned in Scripture. See if students can name a few. (Saul, David, Solomon, Ahab, Joash, etc. Check a concordance for many more… including the King of Kings, Jesus!)

Practice Lesson 25

(See Student Worktext, page 33)

Lesson Focus: Downstroke/Two-Stroke Capitals (M, N)

Directions: Have students complete page 33, carefully following the arrows and start dots. Read aloud the practice words "Mary" and "Naomi" with your students.

Teaching Tip: Review letter formation for the downstroke capital letters M and N. These are two-stroke letters. Remind students to write top to bottom, and to connect the second stroke at the top where they began.

Extended Teaching: Students may draw a picture of Mary with baby Jesus, or Jesus as a young boy helping Mary.

Practice Lesson 26

(See Student Worktext, page 34)

Lesson Focus: Slantstroke Capitals (A, X)

Directions: Have students complete page 34, carefully following the arrows and start dots. Read the practice words "Adam" and "Xerxes" [pronounced zurk'-seez] with your students.

Teaching Tip: As students Sky Write and describe the letters A and X, point out that they have two similar strokes that are simply arranged differently. Also, remind students that the A is a three-stroke letter; the X is a two-stroke letter.

Extended Teaching: Xerxes is not a common word, and has unusual pronunciation — but it's a great practice word for X's. Xerxes was a king of Persia.

Practice Lesson 27

(See Student Worktext, page 35)

Lesson Focus: Slantstroke Capitals (V, W)

Directions: Have students complete page 35, carefully following the arrows and start dots. Read aloud the practice words "Vashti" and "Word" with your students.

Teaching Tip: Review the slantstroke down/up strokes used in both the V and W. Point out that there are two V's found in the W.

Extended Teaching: Vashti was Xerxes' queen. Her name means "beautiful woman." Remind students that it's very important to be beautiful and handsome on the inside. Ask students how this happens (being kind and helpful to others, etc.). Also point out that when Word is capitalized, it refers to God's Word — the Scriptures — or to Jesus (see John 1:3, 14).

Practice Lesson 28

(See Student Worktext, page 36)

Lesson Focus: Curvestroke Capitals (J, S)

Directions: Have students complete page 36, carefully following the arrows and start dots. Read aloud the practice words "Jesus" and "Samuel" with your students.

Teaching Tip: As students practice the curvestroke capitals, encourage them to Sky Write the letters and describe them.

Extended Teaching: Samuel was known for being an obedient child. When he thought priest Eli was calling him, he replied quickly, "Here I am!" Actually it was God calling Samuel, and when he realized this, he said, "Speak, Lord for your servant is listening." Ask students what lessons we can learn from the experience of the boy Samuel (to obey, to be respectful, to listen, etc.).

Lesson 29

(See Student Worktext, page 37)

Lesson Focus: Slantstroke Capitals (Y, Z)

Directions: Have students complete page 37, carefully following the arrows and start dots. Read aloud the practice words "Yahweh" and "Zion" with your students.

Teaching Tip: Review the letter formation for the capital letters Y and Z. Point out that the capital Y is written with a small v at the top, and a stem connecting at the Ceiling.

Extended Teaching: Yahweh is a special name for God. Zion is another name for heaven. Students may wish to draw a picture of what they think heaven might look like.

Lesson 30

(See Student Worktext, page 38)

Lesson Focus: Alphabet/Number, Start Dot Practice

Directions: Have students complete page 38, carefully following the arrows and start dots, writing the entire alphabet and all the numbers.

Teaching Tip: This is a good page to use as a posttest.

Extended Teaching: This lesson provides a great opportunity to identify letters that may need further practice or instruction.

GENERAL
LESSONS

To The Teacher

Before beginning the daily lessons, have students review the following:

The mechanics of handwriting
(See **Proper Positioning**, page 10.)
The format of the class
(See **Weekly Lesson Format**, page 56.)
The evaluation process
(See **Tips on Grading**, page 57.)

It's also very important to have students write the alphabet (capital and lowercase letters) on a sheet of paper, then sign his or her name and date it. Use this sheet later to pinpoint areas of special need.

Most importantly, remember that as you acknowledge and reward progress, the learning process is greatly enhanced!

Scripture Verse

"Oh, give thanks to the Lord, for He is good." Psalm 136:1

Letter Focus

Oo

Tip of the Week

Just like you have your own place to sit, each letter has its own place on the lines and spaces. Take the extra effort to place your letters right where they belong.

Extended Teaching

As you begin the weekly lessons, review the **Five Star** evaluation goals with your students (See Student Worktext, page 6.)

Save a sample of each student's handwriting of the alphabet, capital and lowercase. Ask them to put their name and date on the page. This is a good reference point for future evaluation.

For Discussion

Encourage students to think of ways they "give thanks" to God. Then have each student tell you three things they plan to do this week to tell God "thank you!"

Scripture Verse

"All day long I'll praise and honor You, oh God, for all that You have done for me." Psalm 71:8

Letter Focus

Aa

Tip of the Week

The capital A looks like a teepee with a line in the middle. The lowercase a is easy to write since it begins just like the lowercase o.

Extended Teaching

Sky Write (page 9) the lowercase o and a with students so that they can see that the a contains the o. As they Sky Write, it is easy to spot areas where they may need additional help with formation.

Sky Write the capital letter A. It is important to get the "slant down, slant down, and across," movement in students' minds.

For Discussion

Discuss specific ways to praise God (through song, prayer, actions, etc.). Ask students, "How does the way we treat others show praise to God?" (See Matthew 25:40 — "When you did it to these my brothers, you were doing it to me!")

Scripture Verse
"We should make plans — counting on God to direct us." Proverbs 16:9

Letter Focus
Cc

Tip of the Week
The capital and lowercase c's look alike, but are different sizes. Try to make your c's very round. Make certain the capital C touches the top and bottom lines.

Extended Teaching
Show students that the word "count" in this verse has a special ending (ing). Ask if anyone can find another word with a special ending in this verse (the s on plans).

Remind students that Proverbs was written by Solomon, a very wise man. This book of Scripture gives us good advice for living happy lives.

For Discussion
Discuss some ways that God might direct us (through Scripture; through people in our lives — parents, friends; etc.).

Scripture Verse
"God delights in those who keep their promises." Proverbs 12:22

Letter Focus
Dd

Tip of the Week
It's easier to remember how to write the lowercase d if you begin it like the c: around, up, then back down.

Extended Teaching
Encourage students to sit up straight as they write. Remind them to keep their feet flat on the floor.

Have students check the direction of their paper as they write. Slanting the paper at the same angle as the writing arm makes it easier to write neatly (page 10).

For Discussion
Ask students what it means to "keep a promise." Have them share how they feel if someone lets them down. Ask them to suggest ways they can be better promise keepers.

Scripture Verse

"Compose new songs of praise to God."
Psalm 33:3

Letter Focus

Gg

Tip of the Week

The bottom part of the lowercase g is like a monkey's tail. It goes down the ladder all the way to the Ground! Be sure to write the g without picking up your pencil.

Extended Teaching

In addition to practicing the capital G this week, have students practice their numbers. With the exception of the number 4, the numbers 0 through 9 are written with one stroke.

Point out that the colon in the text separates the numbers into chapter and verse. This tells where the verse is located in Scripture, just as an address tells where someone lives.

For Discussion

Since many children make up tunes and sing to themselves, they often relate to this verse better than adults. Have students generate a list of words they might use in a song praising God.

Scripture Verse

"The earth belongs to God! Everything in all the world is His!" Psalm 24:1

Letter Focus

Ee

Tip of the Week

The capital E is written with three strokes. Start by making a capital L, then go across the top, then across the middle.

Extended Teaching

Point out the similarities between the circle lowercase c and e. Have students Sky Write these letters, describing them as they write.

Establish a rhythm as students practice the capital E. Count slowly with a "one-two-three" count, emphasizing the first count.

For Discussion

This verse makes a great starting point for a discussion of ecology. Ask students, "If the earth belongs to God, how should we treat it?" Discuss specific ways students can impact the local ecology (pick up trash, avoid disturbing wildlife, etc.).

Scripture Verse
"It is hard to stop a quarrel once it starts, so don't let it begin." Proverbs 17:14

Letter Focus
Qq

Tip of the Week
The lowercase q looks like the g, but the q's tail curves to the right. The capital letter Q looks a lot like an O, but the added line makes it unique. Write your q's carefully this week!

Extended Teaching
Remind students that all their letters need to "sit" on the line — not float in the air or sink below the line.

Caution students that circle letters are a big challenge to place exactly on the line.

For Discussion
Ask students, "What are some ways you can *stop* a quarrel before it even begins?" (learning to share, trying to see other points of view, being less quarrelsome, etc.)

Scripture Verse
"Be with wise men and become wise. Be with evil men and become evil." Proverbs 13:20

Letter Focus
Bb

Tip of the Week
Think of the lowercase b as a baseball bat standing on end with a ball connected to it. To write the b, go down, up, and around. Spend time this week "Sky Writing" the b.

Extended Teaching
Use a die-cut b (or one you cut out of paper) to show students how a b can become other letters, depending how it is turned (b, p, d, or even a q with no tail). Remind students the lowercase b is written with a downstroke first, then the circle to the right is added without picking up the pencil.

For Discussion
Remind students that we often become like the people we're with. Think about how they might affect their friends. Now make two lists: one of character traits they'd like to develop (kindness, generosity, cheerfulness, etc.); the other of character flaws they'd like to avoid (selfishness, meanness, grouchiness, etc.).

Scripture Verse

"Help me to do your will, for You are my God. Lead me in good paths." Psalm 143:10

Letter Focus

Pp

Tip of the Week

Remember, your name is the most important word you write! To make it as special as you are, make certain you take time to write it clearly and carefully.

Extended Teaching

Point out that there are two sentences in this week's verse, thus there are two periods. Remind students that periods sit right on the line.

Remind students of the "b" turned upside down for the p (Lesson 8). The description of the downstroke p and b are similar with the circle at a different point and the letter placed differently on the line.

For Discussion

Ask students, "What kind of 'good paths' is this verse talking about?" (living right, being kind, caring for others, etc.) Discuss why we all need God's help to act this way.

Scripture Verse

"God blesses those who obey Him; happy the man who puts his trust in the Lord." Proverbs 16:20

Letter Focus

Ee, Uu

Tip of the Week

Vowels are important letters. Every word has a vowel: a, e, i, o, u (and sometimes y). As you write your vowels this week, pay close attention to their shape and size.

Extended Teaching

As students Sky Write the u, describe it: "down curve, around, up and down."

Have students Sky Write the other letters from this week's lesson. Remember, students will benefit from a clear description of the starting point of each letter.

For Discussion

Ask students, "What makes someone trustworthy?" (they always keep promises, always keep our best interest in mind, etc.) Talk about the importance of trust-based relationships (especially with God), and what trust really means.

 **Lesson 11**

Scripture Verse

"I will sing to the Lord because He has blessed me so richly." Psalm 13:6

Letter Focus

I i

Tip of the Week

Sometimes the letter I is used as a word by itself. When I is a word, it is always capitalized. What other capitalized word do you write every day? (Hint: You sign your papers with it.)

Extended Teaching

When practicing the letter I, encourage each student to make a list of some things that he or she can do. Have them write simple sentences: I can read. I can run. I can play.

Discuss homophones (words that are pronounced alike, but are different in meaning) with your students. Examples from this lesson: I/eye; so/sew; to/two/too.

For Discussion

Ask students to name their favorite songs about God. Talk about what makes each of these songs special. If time allows, sing a favorite song or two.

 **Lesson 12**

Scripture Verse

"To help the poor is to honor God." Proverbs 14:31

Letter Focus

T t

Tip of the Week

The capital and lowercase t's look very different, but they are similar, too! Both t's are tall letters, and both have a second stroke.

Extended Teaching

Sing the song *Michael, Row the Boat Ashore* with your students. Using that tempo, have students practice first the lowercase t, then the capital T, to the beat of the music (Rhythm: down, across; down, across).

For Discussion

Discuss ways students can help the poor (share outgrown clothes, share food, etc.). After discussion, ask the students to talk about ways they could put these ideas into practice. Challenge them to discuss these ideas with their friends.

Scripture Verse

"The Lord's blessing is our greatest wealth." Proverbs 10:22

Letter Focus

Ll

Tip of the Week

The capital and lowercase l's are both tall letters. They look a lot alike, but the capital L needs a leg to stand on! Make your l's as straight as you can.

Extended Teaching

Ask students what capital letter might look like the lowercase l. Now, point out the differences between the capital I and the lowercase l.

Suggest that the l is a good letter to help check letter slant. Also, remind students that when the writing paper is placed the same direction as the writing arm, it's easier to maintain consistent letter slant.

For Discussion

Ask students, "Does wealth always refer to money?" Discuss the concept of "wealth" and have students make a list of other things that enrich our lives (good health, friends, beauty of nature, etc.).

Scripture Verse

"Help me to love Your every wish." Psalm 119:80

Letter Focus

Hh

Tip of the Week

The capital letter H is a three-stroke letter. Go down, down, and across. How is this similar to the capital A? How is it different?

Extended Teaching

Remind students that when a car is out of alignment the passengers can get a bumpy ride. Writing is like that too. It can be "bumpy" if the letters are not all on the line.

Challenge students to visualize as many letters as possible in the h. Tell them they can turn it around or even take parts away (examples: n, l, u, r).

For Discussion

Ask students what they think Jesus would wish for (peace on earth, kindness to others, etc.).

Lesson 15

Scripture Verse

"The Lord is my fort where I can enter and be safe."
Psalm 18:2

Letter Focus

Rr

Tip of the Week

As you write the lowercase r, don't pick up your pencil. Go down, up, and curve around — but not too far!

Extended Teaching

Help students identify the forward curve capital letters that are very similar to the capital R (the letters B, D, and P). As they get letter groups in their mind, formation will be much easier. Stress the beginning downstroke.

For Discussion

Ask students, "How can the Lord be a fort?" (He is our protection, our shelter, our safety, etc.) This is an abstract concept, but guided discussion can help students increase their understanding.

Lesson 16

Scripture Verse

"Never forget to be truthful and kind."
Proverbs 3:3

Letter Focus

Nn

Tip of the Week

Compare the lowercase n with the h, r, and m. Even though they are a lot alike, each one is a little different. God made each of us a little different, too — that's what makes us special!

Extended Teaching

Students will enjoy "tongue twister" sentences composed of all "n" words. (Example: Nine nice nurses name newborns. New nests never need nails. Nice neighbors never need notes.) Challenge students to think of others.

Ask students to name letters similar to the n (h, r, m, etc.). Also ask, "What letter do you get when you turn the n upside down?" (u)

For Discussion

Ask students, "How does it make you feel when someone is unkind to you? How should this affect the way we treat others?" Have students make a list of kind things they might do for others.

Scripture Verse

"Just tell me what to do and I will do it, Lord. Make me walk along the right paths." Psalm 119:33, 35

Letter Focus

M m

Tip of the Week

Remember, you only pick your pencil up once as you write the capital M. The same is true for the capital N. Practice these letters, describing the strokes as you write them.

Extended Teaching

Challenge students to write three letter words that begin with m (mom, mop, mob, mad, met, mud, map, etc.).

Students may wish to practice the capital letter M by writing names that begin with M (Mary, Martha, Mike, Matthew, Melissa, etc.).

For Discussion

Continue and expand on the discussion of "right paths" from Lesson 9.

Scripture Verse

"A true friend is always loyal and a brother is born to help in time of need." Proverbs 17:17

Letter Focus

A a, O o

Tip of the Week

Our focus letters for this week are the capital and lowercase a and o. See how many words you can find during the week that contain the circle letters a or o.

Extended Teaching

Students will benefit from practice of two-letter words with either an a or an o in them (as, at, am, or, on, do, go, no).

Sky Write (page 9) this week's focus letters. As students Sky Write, it's easy to spot individuals that need additional formation help. Be sure to describe the letters as you Sky Write them.

For Discussion

Ask students the meaning of "friend" and "brother" as used in this week's Scripture. This is another abstract concept, but students can expand their understanding through guided discussion.

Lesson 19

Scripture Verse

"Fill all who love You with Your happiness."
Psalm 5:11

Letter Focus

F f

Tip of the Week

The capital letter F is a three-stroke letter. The capital letter E is also a three-stroke letter. Which stroke makes the E different from the capital F? (the L-shaped downstroke).

Extended Teaching

Ask students to find all the tall letters in this week's Scripture Verse (f, h, l, t). Remind them that tall letters need to touch the lines.

Challenge students to put all the words from this week's Scripture in alphabetical order (all, fill, happiness, love, who, with, you, your).

For Discussion

Sometimes we look for happiness in the wrong places. We may think a new toy would really make us happy, then when we get it, we still want something more. Can *things* make us happy? (maybe for a short time) How does God fill us with the kind of happiness this verse talks about? (helps us think of others first; teaches us to love others; etc.)

Lesson 20

Scripture Verse

"I delight to do Your will, my God, for Your law is written upon my heart!" Psalm 40:8

Letter Focus

U u

Tip of the Week

Make certain your paper is slanted the same direction as your writing arm. This will make it much easier to keep your letters straight as you write.

Extended Teaching

Remind students to watch spacing between words as they write. To get the point across, write this week's verse on the board without spaces, then have them try to read it.

A good rule for spacing is to use a letter space between words. If eye spacing is difficult for students, have them "finger space" between words.

For Discussion

Ask students, "What does it mean to have God's law 'written' upon our hearts?" Another abstract concept — but students' understanding will expand through guided discussion.

Scripture Verse

"Joy rises in my heart until I burst out in songs of praise to God." Psalm 28:7

Letter Focus

 J j

Tip of the Week

Here's a trick to help you remember how to form the capital and lowercase j's. Think about the shape of the staff that David (the shepherd boy) used to reach down and rescue a fallen lamb!

Extended Teaching

Review tail letters: g, j, p, q, and y. Remind students that the tail should touch the bottom line. Challenge students to think of short words that begin with each tail letter (go, get, joy, pay, put, quit, yes, you, etc.).

For Discussion

This is a good week to continue and expand on the discussion from Lesson 11. Focus on the part "joy" plays in singing and spontaneous praise.

Scripture Verse

"You made my body, Lord; now give me sense to heed Your laws." Psalm 119:73

Letter Focus

 Y y

Tip of the Week

The capital and lowercase Y are two-stroke letters. Practice these letters describing the strokes as you write.

Extended Teaching

Teach students what a synonym is. Give students a synonym for the word "heed" in this verse (follow, notice). Have students talk about other words and possible synonyms.

Ask students to name and practice the other slantstroke letters (w, x, z).

For Discussion

Discuss what "laws" this verse might be talking about. This verse provides a good opportunity to discuss substance abuse, exercise, drinking water, proper diet, etc. Remind students that God wants us to be sensible in all things that affect our bodies and minds.

Scripture Verse

"In everything you do, put God first, and He will direct you." Proverbs 3:6

Letter Focus

V v

Tip of the Week

It's a lot easier to make the sharp point on the lowercase v if your pencil is sharp. Slant down, slant up — and don't pick up your pencil.

Extended Teaching

Point out the commas in this week's Scripture verse. Read it aloud to demonstrate the pauses for commas. Remind students that the comma sits on the line, with the tail dropping slightly below the base line.

Challenge students to find the v in a capital letter (Y). Remind them that this v is written before the downstroke in the capital Y.

For Discussion

Encourage students to ask the question, "What would Jesus do?" in every aspect of their lives. Discuss this concept and how to put it into practice.

Scripture Verse

"What a wonderful thing it is for a nation to know and keep God's laws!" Proverbs 29:18

Letter Focus

W w

Tip of the Week

Both the capital and lowercase w's look like two v's that are stuck together. For extra practice, Sky Write the w's while saying the strokes aloud: slant down, up, down, up.

Extended Teaching

Remind students that there are other capital and lowercase letters that are look-alikes. See how many they can name (Cc, Jj, Oo, Ss, Uu, Vv, Ww, Xx, and Zz).

Remind students that when capital and lowercase letters are alike, size is very important! Capitals should fill the whole space; lowercase letters should fill half the space.

For Discussion

See if students can name some of God's laws that are also U.S. laws (do not kill, do not steal, etc.). Tell students about other forms of government that exist in the world (Examples: Great Britain, China, India, etc.).

Scripture Verse

"Kind words are like honey — enjoyable and healthful." Proverbs 16:24

Letter Focus

Kk

Tip of the Week

Here's another trick to help you remember a letter shape. There's a ∨ hidden in both the capital and lowercase k's. Can you see it? (Hint: Turn your head sideways.)

Extended Teaching

Have students spend some extra time practicing the slant letters Vv, Ww, Xx, and Kk.

Share some honeycomb with your students. (It's available at many grocery stores.) Point out the beautiful geometric shapes in the comb. Let them taste the honeycomb and remind them that their words should be as sweet as honey!

For Discussion

Ask students, "How can your words be like honey?" (always sweet and kind) Once again, we're dealing with an abstract concept — but students' understanding will expand through guided discussion.

Scripture Verse

"Sing a new song to the Lord! Each day tell someone that He saves." Psalm 96:1, 2

Letter Focus

Ss

Tip of the Week

When you think of the letter s, think of a snake and the sound it makes — hiss! Both the capital and lowercase s look a little like a snake, and they make the "hiss" sound, too.

Extended Teaching

Ask students what number is similar to the capital S (the number 8). Sky Write the letter s and describe the moves: up and around, slide down, curve to the left.

Have students practice their numbers this week. Remind them that except for the number 4, the numbers 0 through 9 are made with a single stroke.

For Discussion

This verse provides a good opportunity to expand on the discussion from Lessons 11 and 21. If time allows, sing some favorite songs about God together.

Scripture Verse

"The godly man's life is exciting." Proverbs 14:14

Letter Focus

X x

Tip of the Week

You can make a giant letter X by crossing your arms in front of you. When you write the X, be sure you use two slanting downstrokes.

Extended Teaching

Tell students that if a person doesn't know how to write their name, they are asked to make an X.

Remind students that their name is the most important word they write. Encourage them to write it using the correct size letters.

For Discussion

Remind students that their name really is the most important word they write. Challenge students to write their names in their very best writing.

Scripture Verse

"Lazy men are soon poor; hard workers get rich." Proverbs 10:4

Letter Focus

Z z

Tip of the Week

Compare your writing now with your writing at the beginning of this Worktext. Doesn't it look much better? Remember, writing clearly and correctly is always worth the extra effort!

Extended Teaching

Encourage students to continue to be **Five Star** writers. Remind them to watch spacing, slant, shape, size, and alignment when writing.

Have students write the alphabet, capital and lowercase letters. Compare this with an earlier writing sample. Commend progress and give encouraging suggestions as you review each student's work with them.

For Discussion

Ask students, "Does 'rich' always refer to money?" Discuss ways that hard work can enrich our lives. You may wish to relate this concept to students' summer plans.

Scope & Sequence - Level A

Skills/letters emphasized in Student Worktext A are found in the following lessons.

Practice Letters

A
Capital: 26*, 2, 18
Lowercase: 5*, 2, 18

B
Capital: 19*, 8, 15
Lowercase: 7*, 8

C
Capital: 18*, 3
Lowercase: 4*, 3

D
Capital: 20*, 4, 15
Lowercase: 5*, 4

E
Capital: 21*, 6, 10, 19
Lowercase: 7*, 6, 10

F
Capital: 21*, 19
Lowercase: 12*, 19

G
Capital: 18*, 5
Lowercase: 6*, 5, 7, 21

H
Capital: 22*, 14
Lowercase: 10*, 14, 16

I
Capital: 23*, 11
Lowercase: 8*, 11

J
Capital: 28*, 21
Lowercase: 13*, 21

K
Capital: 24*, 25
Lowercase: 12*, 25

L
Capital: 24*, 13
Lowercase: 9*, 13

M
Capital: 25*, 17
Lowercase: 11*, 16, 17

N
Capital: 25*, 16
Lowercase: 11*, 16

O
Capital: 17*, 1, 7, 18
Lowercase: 4*, 1, 2, 18

P
Capital: 19*, 9, 15
Lowercase: 8*, 9, 21

Q
Capital: 17*, 7
Lowercase: 6*, 7, 21

R
Capital: 20*, 15
Lowercase: 10*, 15, 16

S
Capital: 28*, 26
Lowercase: 15*, 26

T
Capital: 23*, 12
Lowercase: 9*, 12

U
Capital: 22*, 20
Lowercase: 15*, 16, 20

V
Capital: 27*, 23
Lowercase: 14*, 23

W
Capital: 27*, 24
Lowercase: 14*, 22, 24

X
Capital: 26*, 27
Lowercase: 16*, 22, 27

Y
Capital: 29*, 22
Lowercase: 13*, 21, 22

Z
Capital: 29*, 28
Lowercase: 16*, 22, 28

Manuscript Terms

CAPITAL GROUPS
Circle (C, G, O, Q)
Curve (J, S, U)
Downstroke (B, D, E, F, H, I, J, K, L, M, N, P, R T, U)
Forward curve (B, D, P, R)
Slantstroke (A, K, M, N, V, W, X, Y, Z)
Two-stroke (B, D, K, M, N, P, Q, R, T, X)
Three-stroke (A, E, F, H, I)

LOWERCASE GROUPS
Circle (a, b, c, d, e, g, o, p, q)
Curve (h, m, n, r, s, u)
Downstroke (b, f, h, i, j, k, l, m, n, p, r, t)
Slantstroke (k, v, w, x, y, z)
Tail (g, j, p, q, y)
Tall (b, d, f, h, k, l, t)
Two-stroke (f, i, j, k, t, x, y)

General Skills

IN EVERY VERSE
Letter formation
Connecting strokes
Number formation
Sentence structure
Punctuation
Capitalization

LETTER PRACTICE
Capital Letters
Circle: 16*, 17*, 5, 7
Curve: 27*, 26
Downstroke: 20*, 21*, 22*, 23*, 24*, 6, 11, 12, 13, 15, 17, 27
Forward curve: 18*, 15
Slantstroke: 25*, 28*, 17, 23, 24, 25, 27, 28
Two-stroke: 12, 17, 22
Three-stroke: 6, 11, 14, 19

Lowercase Letters
Circle: 3*, 4*, 5*, 6, 18
Curve: 8*, 9*, 13*, 16
Downstroke: 6*, 7*, 8, 9, 12, 27
Slantstroke: 12*, 14*, 22, 24, 25, 27
Tail: 11*, 9, 21, 25
Tall: 10*, 12, 13, 19
Two-stroke: 10*, 13, 22

FIVE STAR SKILLS
Alignment: 1, 7, 14
Letter shape: 2, 3, 7, 10, 13, 21
Letter size: 5, 7, 10, 19, 24, 27
Letter slant: 8, 13, 20
Letter spacing: 20

MECHANICS
Paper position: 4, 20
Pencil position: 23
Posture: 4

OTHER PRACTICE
Evaluation: 1, 28
Name focus: 9, 11, 27
Number review: 5, 26
Punctuation: 5, 9, 11, 23
Similar cap/lowercase: 3, 12, 24, 26
Verbal Description: 2, 5, 6, 8, 10, 14, 15, 18, 26
Visualize letter formation: 2, 6, 18, 21, 25
Vowels: 2, 6, 18, 21, 25

* Practice Lessons (See page 7, Student Worktext)

Vocabulary List

This list is composed of all the practice words from Lessons 1-28 in Student Worktext A.

Aa
after
all
along
always
and
are

Bb
be
because
become
begin
belongs
blesses
blessings
body
born
brother
burst

Cc
can
compose
count
counting

Dd
day
delight
delights
direct
do
does
done

Ee
each
earth
enjoyable
enter
every

everything
evil
except
exciting
exit

Ff
face
fill
first
for
forget
fort
from

Gg
get
give
God
godly
good
greatest

Hh
hard
happiness
happy
has
have
he
heed
healthful
heart
help
his
honey
honor

Ii
I
is
it

Jj
joy
just

Kk
keep
kind
know

Ll
law
laws
lazy
lead
life
like
long
Lord
Lord's
love
loyal

Mm
make
man
man's
me
men
my

Nn
nation
never
new

Oo
obey
of
oh
once
our

Pp
paths
plans
poor
praise
promises
Proverbs
Psalms
put
puts

Qq
quarrel

Rr
rich
richly
right
rises

Ss
safe
saves
should
sing
so
someone
song
songs
soon
stop

Tt
tell
that
the
thing
those
time
to
trust
truthful

Uu
until
up
upon
us

Vv
very

Ww
walk
wealth
what
where
who
will
wish
wise
with
wonderful
words
workers
world
written

Yy
you
your

Zz
zip

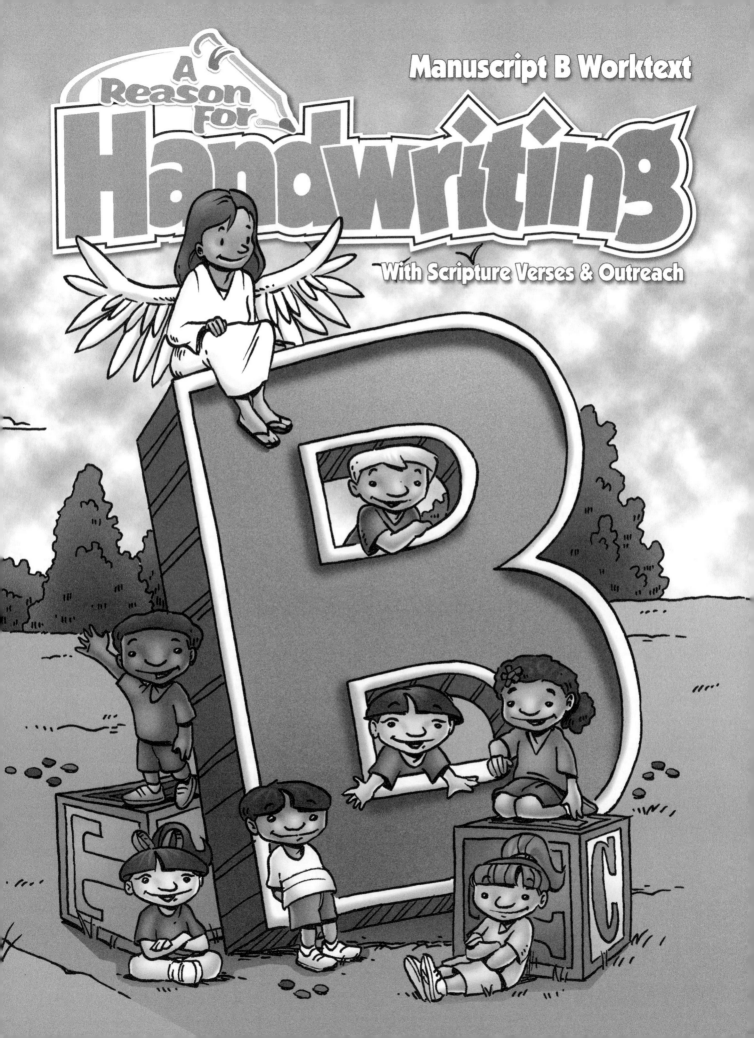

Please
Read This First!

Before beginning this section, please review **How & When to Use the Transition Worktext** on page 232 of this Guidebook.

Since the **Transition** Student Worktext is designed to replace either the **Level B** Student Worktext (earlier transition) or the **Level C** Student Worktext (later transition), careful review of the various options is essential. This will help determine the "correct curriculum sequencing" best suited to meet student needs.

PRACTICE
LESSONS

To The Teacher

After the summer break, students often benefit from a focused review. The following **Practice Lessons** provide a quick, efficient method for reviewing Manuscript letter formation.

These lessons are designed for one page each day, for a total of 10 days.

Another option is to begin immediately with Lesson 1 (page 21 in the Student Worktext), and use these review pages as concurrent extra practice.

(See Student Worktext, page 9)

Lesson Focus: Alphabet practice

Directions: Have students write the entire alphabet — capital and lowercase. Start dots are provided to make this self-directed activity easier.

Teaching Tip: Be sure to review the proper way to hold the pencil, as well as the correct posture and paper position, before students start this first page. (See page 10.) While it's difficult to change the way a student holds a pencil, it's not impossible. Correcting problems now can impact a student's writing for the rest of his/her life. Positive praise can help make these changes permanent.

(See Student Worktext, page 10)

Lesson Focus: Circle Letter practice
(c, o, a, d, e)

Directions: Have students fill each line with the appropriate circle letter. Again, start dots are provided to make this self-directed activity easier.

Teaching Tip: All circle letters begin at the two o'clock position and go up and around to the left. The exception is the letter e. The e begins in the middle of the space and then goes up and around to the left. Have students look for the c as part of the e.

(See Student Worktext, page 11)

Lesson Focus: Tall Letter practice
(l, h, b, t, k)

Directions: Have students fill each line with the appropriate tall letter.

Teaching Tip: Most tall letters begin with a downstroke. The first stroke begins at the Roofline and goes straight down to the Floor. Other tall letters include the d and f. However, the d begins like the circle letters; the f begins just below the line and curves up and around before the downstroke.

(See Student Worktext, page 12)

Lesson Focus: Two-Stroke Letters
(t, f, k, j, i)

Directions: Have students fill each line with the appropriate two-stroke letter.

Teaching Tip: Although the majority of Manuscript letters may be written without picking up the pencil, the letters in this lesson require a second stroke. Sky Write and verbally describe these letters to imprint them in students' minds. These letters can also be written in rhythm to a one-two count. For example: The t is down/across, or one/two. Several students can write these letters on the board in rhythm as other students clap in time and chant: "one, two, one, two…"

Lesson 5

(See Student Worktext, Page 13)

Lesson Focus: Slantstroke Letters

(v, w, x, y, z)

Directions: Have students fill each line with the appropriate slant stroke letter.

Teaching Tip: Challenge students to see the v in other letters. The obvious ones are w and y — however, the v is also in the x and k if you look sideways! Point out that two of this lesson's letters (x and y) are made with two strokes. The other slant line letters are made without picking up the pencil (v, w, z). Challenge students to identify another letter that contains slant lines (k).

Lesson 6

(See Student Worktext, page 14)

Lesson Focus: Curve Letters

(r, n, m, s, u)

Directions: Have students fill each line with the appropriate curve letter.

Teaching Tip: While some curve letters begin with a downstroke, they also curve around. Challenge students to find other letters that begin like the letter r (n and m). Help them visualize the r as a part of an h. Use a cut-out letter n to help students discover a u when you turn it around and upside down. Identifying such similarities and differences will help strengthen the students' mental picture of these letters.

Lesson 7

(See Student Worktext, page 15)

Lesson Focus: Tail Letters

(p, q, y, g, j)

Directions: Have students fill each line with the appropriate tail letter.

Teaching Tip: Ask students to imagine sitting in a chair that's too tall. Remind them how tired their legs get when they can't reach the ground. Now, point out that tail letters want to touch the Ground, too! (See "Using the Treehouse," page 7.) Challenge them to make all their tail letters carefully so the tails touch the Ground.

Lesson 8

(See Student Worktext, page 16)

Lesson Focus: Capital Letters
(C, O, G, Q, P, R, B, D)

Directions: Have students fill each line with the appropriate capital letter.

Teaching Tip: Remind students to use start dots and arrow direction to have the best letter practice. Also, read aloud the two sentences that students can write after they have practiced the capital letters. Point out the exclamation point at the end of each sentence. Remind students that both sentences are something to be excited about!

Lesson 9

(See Student Worktext, page 17)

Lesson Focus: Capital Letters
(A, X, M, N, K, V, W, Y, Z)

Directions: Have students fill each line with the appropriate capital letter.

Teaching Tip: For the most effective practice, these slant line capitals are grouped in similar stroke letter groups. Remind students to follow the arrows, and use the start dots to begin each letter.

Lesson 10

(See Student Worktext, page 18)

Lesson Focus: Capital Letters
(I, L, T, F, E, H, J, U, S)

Directions: Have students fill each line with the appropriate capital letter.

Teaching Tip: For the most effective practice, these downstroke and curve capitals are grouped in similar stroke letter groups. Remind students to follow the arrows, and use the start dots to begin each letter.

GENERAL LESSONS

To The Teacher

Before beginning the daily lessons, have students review the following:

    The mechanics of handwriting
    (See **Proper Positioning**, page 10.)
    The format of the class
    (See **Weekly Lesson Format**, page 56.)
    The evaluation process
    (See **Tips on Grading**, page 57.)

It's also very important to have students write the alphabet (capital and lowercase letters) on a sheet of paper, then sign his or her name and date it. Use this sheet later to pinpoint areas of special need.

Most importantly, remember that as you acknowledge and reward progress, the learning process is greatly enhanced!

Scripture Verse
"Love the Lord your God with all your heart, soul, and mind." Matthew 22:37

Letter Focus
A a, D d

Tip of the Week
Manuscript handwriting is a skill you will use the rest of your life. This year, we'll be sharing ways to make your handwriting even better!

Extended Teaching
As you begin the weekly lessons, review the **Five Star** evaluation goals with your students (Student Worktext, page 6).

Remind students that the books written by Matthew, Mark, Luke, and John are often referred to as the "Gospels."

For Discussion
Encourage students to think of ways they can show God they love Him. Ask them how this affects the way they treat others.

Scripture Verse
"Your care for others is the measure of your greatness." Luke 9:48

Letter Focus
G g, O o

Tip of the Week
The letter o forms one part of the letter g — can you see it? Write both of these letters in one stroke, without picking up your pencil.

Extended Teaching
Remind students that both the g and the o begin just below the center line and are written with a counter-clockwise circle without picking up the pencil.

When a student is having difficulty with a letter, it's helpful to practice the similar letter group. (See page 230.) Similar circle letters are o, a, d, g, and q.

For Discussion
Discuss the concept of "random acts of kindness." Encourage students to watch for such opportunities this week. Remind them: "Your kind act is a secret! Don't let anyone know!"

Lesson 3

Scripture Verse
"Come to terms quickly before it is too late." Matthew 5:25

Letter Focus
Qq, Uu

Tip of the Week
Your name is important — just like you! Write your letters carefully. Make certain they are the correct size and sit firmly on the line.

Extended Teaching
Students will benefit from extra practice of the g and q. Remind them to watch the direction of the tail!

Visual and tactile learners will benefit from making these letters from pipe cleaners or clay.

For Discussion
Talk about the phrase "come to terms" with students. Challenge them to come up with helpful ways to settle an argument. Discuss these and look for specific applications.

Lesson 4

Scripture Verse
"Live in peace with each other." Mark 9:50

Letter Focus
Cc, Ee

Tip of the Week
How are the lowercase c and e alike? How are they different? As you write these letters, make sure they fill the entire space.

Extended Teaching
Explore letter relationship by pointing out that the c is part of the e. Remind students that the beginning stroke of the e starts in the middle of the meeting room.

Ask the students how this Scripture Verse relates to the last week's verse. (One deals with the problem, the other one suggests the goal or solution.)

For Discussion
Ask students, "Is it always easy to live in peace?" Explore ways to make your home or neighborhood more peaceful and less argumentative.

Lesson 5

Scripture Verse
"Be prepared, for you don't know what day your Lord is coming." Matthew 24:42

Letter Focus
Bb, Pp

Tip of the Week
How are the lowercase b and p different? How are they alike? Be sure the tail of the p goes all the way to the Ground.

Extended Teaching
As the students practice the b and p, it's important that they make the letters with one stroke, beginning with the downstroke. Have students describe these letters aloud as they Sky Write. This will help them picture the letters in their minds.

Remind students the letter b should touch the Roofline, and the p should touch the Ground.

For Discussion
Discuss the importance of being prepared. Ask students, "What are some other areas of our lives where being prepared is very important?" (taking tests, receiving visitors, home fire drills, etc.)

Lesson 6

Scripture Verse
"Your strong love for each other will prove to the world that you are my disciples." John 13:35

Letter Focus
Ll, Vv

Tip of the Week
Are your letters and words sitting firmly on the line? Think of your letters as birds sitting on a wire. Don't let them fall off!

Extended Teaching
Help students to focus on making sure their letters touch the line. Also, have them check spacing. Positive encouragement will help students do their best.

As they practice the focus letter v, remind students of other slantstroke letters (k, w, x, y, and z). (pages 226-230).

For Discussion
Ask students, "What are some ways that we can show we care for each other?" Have them make a list of nice things they could do for a friend. Now, challenge them to apply this attitude to everyone they know.

Lesson 7

Scripture Verse
"Go home to your friends, and tell them what wonderful things God has done for you." Mark 5:19

Letter Focus
Mm, Nn

Tip of the Week
Who was Mark and why will you be writing his name this week? Other names this year are Matthew, Luke and John. Who were they? (They were disciples of Jesus, and the writers of the Gospels.)

Extended Teaching
Ask students to practice the overcurve letters h, n, m, and r. Have them Sky Write these letters, describing them aloud as they write them.

Have your students verbally describe the lowercase h while you write it on the board following their directions. Take turns and do again with the n, m, and r.

For Discussion
Now have them make a list of good things God has blessed them with.

Lesson 8

Scripture Verse
"If you are filled with light within, then your face will be radiant too." Luke 11:36

Letter Focus
F f, Hh

Tip of the Week
Think how you have to stretch to reach the top shelf. This week, help your tall letters (d, f, h, l, and t) stretch all the way to the top line.

Extended Teaching
Point out the two-stroke tall letters in this Scripture Verse (f, k, and t). The downstroke is written first. Ask students to find the k in this verse. (See "Luke" in the text reference.)

Even though d is a tall letter, the circle part is written first.

For Discussion
Ask students to come up with ways they can be "filled with light." Talk about the relationship between our "inside" and our "outside."

Lesson 9

Scripture Verse
"Oh, how I praise the Lord. How I rejoice in God my Savior!" Luke 1:46, 47

Letter Focus
Ii, Jj

Tip of the Week
Two lowercase letters that are almost look-alikes are i and j. Remember the j has a tail just like a monkey. Don't forget to dot both letters.

Extended Teaching
Remind students that the i and j are written with a downstroke, and that the dot is added after the letter is written. Make sure students use a dot — not a small circle or dash.

Point out the size difference between the i and j. Verbally describe the letters as students practice them (page 227).

For Discussion
Have students make a list of things that make them joyful — things for which they "praise the Lord."

Lesson 10

Scripture Verse
"Love your neighbor as much as you love yourself." Matthew 22:39

Letter Focus
Uu, Y y

Tip of the Week
The lowercase y is one of the two-stroke letters. How many other two-stroke letters can you find in this week's verse?

Extended Teaching
Point out the two-stroke letters found in this verse (i, f, and t).

Remind students that the capital letter Y is written like a v with a stem, and that both the capital and lowercase y's are two-stroke letters.

Make a point to commend students who are using correct posture and paper position.

For Discussion
In this verse, Jesus gives a fundamental guideline about how we should treat others. Discuss with your students the meaning of this verse, then have them share their thoughts with you.

Lesson 11

Scripture Verse
"Though all heaven and earth shall pass away, yet My words remain forever true." Luke 21:33

Letter Focus
Rr, Ww

Tip of the Week
The capital R begins with a straight downstroke. The capital W is written with all slanting lines. Sit straight like the R as you write your words this week.

Extended Teaching
Encourage students to practice slantstroke letters k, w, v, x, y, and z. Show students that two letters (k and z) are a combination of slant and straight.

Describe differences in making the w and v versus the x and y. (The w and v are written without picking up the pencil; the x and y are two-stroke letters.)

For Discussion
In view of this week's Scripture Verse, discuss what things are always the same, and what things change in life. (Same: basic principles found in Scripture, Jesus, God, etc. Change: seasons, food preferences, where we live, etc.)

Lesson 12

Scripture Verse
"He created everything there is — nothing exists that He didn't make." John 1:3

Letter Focus
Kk, Xx

Tip of the Week
How are you holding your pencil? Is it sharp? It is much easier to write well when you hold your pencil correctly, and it is sharp!

Extended Teaching
When students have to rest their writing hand — or shake it because of too much tension — remind them of the correct method to hold the pencil (page 10).

Suggest students relax the wrist by rotating it in a circle — then reversing the circle. Also have them rotate the shoulders forward and backward.

For Discussion
Have students list three things God created that they especially enjoy. Next, have them share their lists with you. Ask students, "What do all these wonderful things tell us about how much God loves us?"

Lesson 13

Scripture Verse
"If anyone wants to be a follower of mine, let him take up his cross and follow Me." Matthew 16:24

Letter Focus
Ss, Tt

Tip of the Week
The capital T and lowercase t both have a cross, but in different places. Watch where you cross the lowercase t.

Extended Teaching
Use the letter t as an opportunity to talk of the cross. Suggest that as students write it, they think of how the cross shows God's great love for each of us.

The capital S and lowercase s are look-alikes. Help students remember formation by showing them the s "begins just below the line and slithers and slinks around the curves."

For Discussion
Ask what "taking up a cross" means to students. Remind them that following Jesus includes doing our very best at whatever task or job God gives us.

Lesson 14

Scripture Verse
"Never criticize or condemn — or it will all come back on you." Luke 6:37

Letter Focus
Cc, Zz

Tip of the Week
Make sure your letters are all the correct size and that they fill the space completely! This makes your writing easier to read.

Extended Teaching
Ask students, "What number begins like the letter z?" (the number 7) Remind them that except for the 4, numbers 0 through 9 are written without picking up the pencil.

Since few words contain the letter z, give the students these extra z words for practice this week: zip, zap, quiz, and zone.

For Discussion
Talk about ways that "criticizing others can end up hurting you, too."

Lesson 15

Scripture Verse

"I came to bring truth to the world. All who love the truth are My followers." John 18:37

Letter Focus

Bb, Oo

Tip of the Week

As you write the lowercase b, be sure to start at the top! Tell a friend exactly how to make this letter.

Extended Teaching

Use a tall letter with a downstroke to check letter slant. Some tall downstroke letters to help reinforce proper slant are f, h, k, l, and t.

Have your students verbally describe the lowercase f while you attempt to write it on the board following their directions. Do again with the h, k, l, and t.

For Discussion

Ask students "What does it mean to 'love the truth?'" Discuss why honesty is always the best policy.

Lesson 16

Scripture Verse

"We must worship God, and Him alone. So it is written in the Scriptures." Luke 4:8

Letter Focus

Ss, Ww

Tip of the Week

Two of this week's focus letters are capital and lowercase look-alikes: the S and s; and the W and w. See how the S slithers around?

Extended Teaching

Start planning early this week on ways to share the Scripture Border Sheet (page 58). Sending the suggested letter helps create positive feedback for students.

Encourage students to share experiences from sending Scripture Border Sheets in the past.

For Discussion

Remind students that "worship" includes spending special time with God. Ask them for suggestions on how to do this (prayer, church, reading Scripture stories, etc.).

Scripture Verse
"Praise the Lord, for He has come to visit His people and has redeemed them." Luke 1:68

Letter Focus
Ee, Pp

Tip of the Week
Make good, straight lines for the downstrokes on the capital E, H, L, and P. All these letters are found in this week's lesson.

Extended Teaching
Point out the similarities and differences in the focus capital letters. (E, H, and L are made with all straight lines. All begin with a downstroke. The L is hidden in the E.)

Encourage students to watch letter spacing as they write. A letter space is needed between words or practice letters. Remind them that even spacing makes handwriting more readable.

For Discussion
Challenge students to make a list of ways to praise God. Encourage them to use these ideas to thank God for His love.

Scripture Verse
"I am with you always, even to the end of the world." Matthew 28:20

Letter Focus
Vv, Xx

Tip of the Week
Look around your classroom for a sign that contains the letter X. (Here's a clue: It should be by the door where you go out.)

Extended Teaching
Encourage students to describe the V and X as they practice them. The V is slant down, slant up, while the X is slant right, slant left.

Students will enjoy seeing how many body parts they can cross to look like the letter X (fingers, arms, legs — but not eyes, please!).

For Discussion
Ask students what they think God means when He says, "I am with you always." Discuss how God's presence impacts our lives (protection, comfort, security, etc.).

Lesson 19

Scripture Verse

"God will take care of your tomorrow. Live one day at a time." Matthew 6:34

Letter Focus

A a, L l

Tip of the Week

The capital letter A is a three-stroke letter. So are the letters E, F, H, and I. Count the strokes as you write these letters this week.

Extended Teaching

Have students discuss the similarities and differences between the capital A and X. (Each has two slant downstrokes. The A is slant left, slant right; the X is slant right, slant left.)

Encourage students to always write their names carefully. Praise them for any paper that has their name written neatly with the correct size letters.

For Discussion

Have students make a list of things that worry them. Now ask them how this text relates to worrying.

Lesson 20

Scripture Verse

"There is joy in the presence of the angels of God when one sinner repents." Luke 15:10

Letter Focus

T t, G g

Tip of the Week

If your hand gets tired while you are writing, you may be holding your pencil too tightly. Try to loosen up a bit!

Extended Teaching

The t and g are good letters to practice in rhythm. Sing, "When the Saints Go Marching In," making the strokes on the first and third beat. (Start the downstroke or circle on the word "Saints.")

Challenge students to discover other letters and songs that can be practiced together.

For Discussion

This verse says there is joy in heaven when we repent. Ask students, "What other things can we do that might make God happy?"

Scripture Verse
"If you have ears, listen! Be sure to put into practice what you hear." Mark 4:23, 24

Letter Focus
Ii, Zz

Tip of the Week
Some letters are tall, some have tails, and some sit in the middle. But even though your letters are different, they should all be the correct size.

Extended Teaching
Remember to save samples of student writing throughout the year to show progress and note areas for improvement.

Encourage students to review letters by similar letter practice: tall, tail, circle, two-stroke, etc. (See "Letter Groups," page 230.) Note that letters are often included in more than one group.

For Discussion
Read the verse aloud to the students. Ask them what they think Mark is trying to tell us.

Scripture Verse
"Your heavenly Father will give the Holy Spirit to those who ask for Him." Luke 11:13

Letter Focus
Hh, Yy

Tip of the Week
Using your index finger, outline a letter on a friend's back. See if they can tell what you wrote. Now trade places and try it again.

Extended Teaching
Ask students to practice curve letters h, m, n, and r. As a letter family there are certain similarities. Encourage students to verbalize these similarities.

Suggest that students watch for homophones in the practice words this week. (Homophones are words pronounced alike, but different in meaning — like "four" and "for.")

For Discussion
See how many pairs of homophones students can recall (tail, tale; bear, bare; red, read; to, two, too; etc.).

Lesson 23

Scripture Verse
"Blessed are all who hear the Word of God and put it into practice." Luke 11:28

Letter Focus
Bb, Rr

Tip of the Week
How are the capital B and R alike? How are they different? Name some people whose name begins with a B or an R.

Extended Teaching
Have students describe the ways that the capital B and R are alike. Ask them what other capital letter might fit into this group? (The capital P)

Ask students to write the tall letter pair b and h, then describe the similarities and differences (page 92).

For Discussion
Have students name some things God asks us to do in Scripture (be kind, love our enemies, help the poor, etc.). Ask them what this verse says will happen if we do what God asks.

Lesson 24

Scripture Verse
"Do for others what you want them to do for you." Matthew 7:12

Letter Focus
A a, D d

Tip of the Week
Writing is easier if your paper is slanted the same way as your writing arm. This is true not only in handwriting, but in your other subjects as well.

Extended Teaching
For the left-handed student, note that the paper must slant the same direction as the writing arm. This is very important to prevent an awkward writing hand position.

Positive comments will help students focus on good posture as they write.

For Discussion
Remind students that this verse is often called the "Golden Rule." Ask them how the world might be different if everyone followed this rule.

Lesson 25

Scripture Verse
"God is ready to give blessings to all who come to Him." Luke 4:19

Letter Focus
Gg, Qq

Tip of the Week
If you make a lowercase g with a pipe cleaner or clay, can you turn it into a q? Write these letters without picking up your pencil.

Extended Teaching
Writing Manuscript letters with one stroke (when possible) is vital to helping students make an easier transition to Cursive writing. It also diminishes the letter reversal problem.

Point out that when the students begin Cursive writing, the tails of the g and q will extend into the connecting stroke.

For Discussion
Have students make a list of blessings. Read some of the blessings aloud. Remind students that blessings surround us, but sometimes we miss them because we're not looking.

Lesson 26

Scripture Verse
"You will know the truth, and the truth will set you free." John 8:32

Letter Focus
Ee, Tt

Tip of the Week
When you sit up straight, it is easier to write and your handwriting improves. When your letters "sit up straight" on the line, they are easier to read.

Extended Teaching
Remind students that a slight slant in Manuscript writing is acceptable as long as the letter slant is consistent.

Have students draw a line through some of the tall letters in the practice pages using a different color pencil or crayon. This will help them see if their letters are consistent.

For Discussion
Challenge students to think about someone to share this verse with. Perhaps there's a person in their neighborhood who might be lonely. Suggest that they can make a difference by planning to help just one person this week.

Lesson 27

Scripture Verse

"If you are friendly only to your friends, how are you different from anyone else?" Matthew 5:47

Letter Focus
F f, M m

Tip of the Week

Two letters in this verse are crossed at the mid-line after the downstroke. Can you find them? (Here's a clue: Both are tall letters.)

Extended Teaching

The two-stroke letters in this verse are f and t. There are more two-stroke letters in Manuscript than in Cursive. See how many your students can name (f, i, j, k, t, x, and y).

The capital M is easier to write when it is written with a downstroke. Pick up the pencil, connect to the downstroke, and slant down right, slant up and down.

For Discussion

Who does this verse imply we should be friendly and kind towards? (our enemies, not just our friends) Discuss some ways we can do this.

Lesson 28

Scripture Verse

"Turn from sin, and turn to God, for the Kingdom of heaven is near." Matthew 4:17

Letter Focus
K k, N n

Tip of the Week

You probably don't like it when people crowd you. Your letters don't look right when they are crowded too closely either!

Extended Teaching

When grading this week, pay special attention to spacing. Some students are challenged with too much spacing instead of not enough. Either extreme is a problem.

While the K and N look like three-stroke letters, they are actually two-stroke letters. Both begin with the downstroke.

For Discussion

Ask students to describe how someone might "turn from sin" (ask God for help; avoid certain places, people, things; pray about it, etc.).

Lesson 29

Scripture Verse

"There will be great joy for those who are ready and waiting for His return." Luke 12:37

Letter Focus

J j, R r

Tip of the Week

Watch for tail letters this week. You will be writing quite a few (g, j, and y). Make sure their tails touch the bottom line!

Extended Teaching

Remind students that their letters must always fill the appropriate space. Capital letters should fill the entire space, and some lowercase letters should fill half the space.

Continue to have students describe the letters aloud as they Sky Write, using words like up, down, around, etc. This will help them picture the letters in their minds.

For Discussion

Ask students, "What are some things you think God would want us to do to get ready for His return?" Also ask them, "Why would being ready make a person joyful?"

Lesson 30

Scripture Verse

"Unless you are honest in small matters, you won't be in large ones." Luke 16:10

Letter Focus

L l, U u

Tip of the Week

You will use your Manuscript writing many ways throughout your life. It will be very helpful and is something you will use often. A kind written word will brighten someone's day!

Extended Teaching

Have students write the Manuscript alphabet letters (capital and lowercase) and compare this page with what they wrote at the start of the year.

Review the blessings that have come from students sharing their Scripture Border Sheets this year. Perhaps you have received some letters or calls. Count your blessings together.

For Discussion

What are some "small matters" we can be honest about? Challenge students to be as strictly honest as the verse implies. Ask them how they think this might affect their lives.

Scope & Sequence - Level B

Skills/letters emphasized in Student Worktext B are found in the following lessons.

Practice Letters

A
Capital: 9*, 1, 19, 24
Lowercase: 2*, 1, 19, 24

B
Capital: 8*, 5, 15, 23
Lowercase: 3*, 5, 15, 23

C
Capital: 8*, 4, 14
Lowercase: 2*, 4, 14

D
Capital: 8*, 1, 24
Lowercase: 2*, 1, 8, 24

E
Capital: 10*, 4, 17, 19, 26
Lowercase: 2*, 4, 17, 26

F
Capital: 10*, 8, 19, 27
Lowercase: 4*, 8, 27

G
Capital: 8*, 2, 20, 25
Lowercase: 7*, 2, 20, 25, 29

H
Capital: 10*, 8, 17, 19, 22
Lowercase: 3*, 8, 22

I
Capital: 10*, 9, 19, 21
Lowercase: 4*, 9, 21

J
Capital: 10*, 9, 29
Lowercase: 4*, 7*, 9, 29

K
Capital: 9*, 12, 28
Lowercase: 3*, 4*, 12, 28

L
Capital: 10*, 6, 17, 19, 30
Lowercase: 3*, 6, 8, 19, 30

M
Capital: 9*, 7, 27
Lowercase: 6*, 7, 27

N
Capital: 9*, 7, 28
Lowercase: 6*, 7, 28

O
Capital: 8*, 2, 15
Lowercase: 2*, 2, 15

P
Capital: 8*, 5, 17
Lowercase: 7*, 5, 17

Q
Capital: 8*, 3, 25
Lowercase: 7*, 3, 25

R
Capital: 8*, 11, 23, 29
Lowercase: 6*, 11, 23, 29

S
Capital: 10*, 13, 16
Lowercase: 6*, 13, 16

T
Capital: 10*, 13, 20, 26
Lowercase: 3*, 4*, 8, 13, 20, 26

U
Capital: 10*, 3, 10, 30
Lowercase: 6*, 3, 10, 30

V
Capital: 9*, 6, 18
Lowercase: 5*, 6, 18

W
Capital: 9*, 11, 16
Lowercase: 5*, 11, 16

X
Capital: 9*, 12, 18
Lowercase: 5*, 12, 18

Y
Capital: 9*, 10, 22
Lowercase: 5*, 7*, 10, 22, 29

Z
Capital: 9*, 14, 21
Lowercase: 5*, 14, 21

Manuscript Terms

CAPITAL GROUPS
Circle (C, G, O, Q)
Curve (J, S, U)
Downstroke (B, D, E, F, H, I, J, K, L, M, N, P, R T, U)
Forward curve (B, D, P, R)
Slantstroke (A, K, M, N, V, W, X, Y, Z)
Two-stroke (B, D, K, M, N, P, Q, R, T, X)
Three stroke (A, E, F, H, I)

LOWERCASE GROUPS
Circle (a, b, c, d, e, g, o, p, q)
Curve (h, m, n, r, s, u)
Downstroke (b, f, h, i, j, k, l, m, n, p, r, t)
Slantstroke (k, v, w, x, y, z)
Tail (g, j, p, q, y)
Tall (b, d, f, h, k, l, t)
Two stroke (f, i, j, k, t, x, y)

General Skills

IN EVERY VERSE
Letter formation
Connecting strokes
Number formation
Sentence structure
Punctuation
Capitalization

LETTER PRACTICE
Capital Letters
Circle: 8*
Curve: 10*
Downstroke: 10*, 17, 23, 27
Forward curve: 8*, 23
Slantstroke: 9*, 10, 11, 18, 19, 27
Two stroke: 8*, 10, 13, 23, 28
Three stroke: 19

Lowercase Letters
Circle: 2*, 2
Curve: 6*, 7, 22
Downstroke: 5*, 5, 9, 11, 15, 18
Slantstroke: 5*, 6, 11, 18
Tail: 7*, 25, 29
Tall: 3*, 5, 6, 8, 15, 23
Two stroke: 4*, 8, 9, 10, 11, 18, 27

FIVE STAR SKILLS
Alignment: 3, 6, 26
Letter shape: 2, 5, 10, 14, 25
Letter size: 4, 8, 14, 21, 29
Letter slant: 6, 15, 26
Letter spacing: 1, 17, 28

MECHANICS
Paper position: 10, 24
Pencil position: 12, 20
Posture: 10, 11, 24, 26

OTHER PRACTICE
Evaluation: 1, 21, 30
Cap/lowercase review: 1*
Name focus: 3, 19
Number review: 14
Similar cap/lowercase: 13, 16
Verbal Description: 4*, 5, 7, 15, 19, 22, 29
Visualize letter formation: 6*, 10*, 5, 17, 18, 22

* Practice Lessons (See page 7, Student Worktext)

Vocabulary List

This list is composed of all the practice words from Lessons 1-30 in Student Worktext B.

Aa
all
always
and
angels
anyone
are
as
ask
at
away

Bb
back
be
before
bless
blessed
blessings
bring

Cc
came
care
come
condemn
coming
criticize
created
cross

Dd
day
didn't
different
disciples
do
done
don't

Ee
each
ears
earth
else
end
even
everything
exist
exists
exit

Ff
face
Father
filled
followers
for
forever
free
friends
friendly
from

Gg
get
give
go
God
great
greatness

Hh
he
hear
heart
heaven
heavenly
Him

holy
home
honest
how

Ii
in
into

Jj
joy

Kk
kingdom
know

Ll
large
late
let
light
listen
live
Lord
love
Luke

Mm
make
matters
Matthew
Mark
measure
mind
mine
much
must
my

Nn
near
never
neighbor
nothing

Oo
of
oh
on
one
other
others

Pp
peace
people
practice
praise
prepare
prepared
prove
presence

Qq
quickly
quit

Rr
radiant
ready
redeemed
rejoice
remain
repents
return

Ss
Savior
Scriptures
set

sin
size
small
so
strong
sure

Tt
take
terms
the
them
then
there
things
those
time
to
tomorrow
too
true
truth
turn

Uu
unless

Vv
visit

Ww
waiting
want
wants
we
what
when
who
will
with
within

wonderful
word
words
world
worship
written

Yy
you
your
yourself

Please
Read This First!

Before beginning this section, please review **How & When to Use the Transition Worktext** on page 232 of this Guidebook.

Since the **Transition** Student Worktext is designed to replace either the **Level B** Student Worktext (earlier transition) or the **Level C** Student Worktext (later transition), careful review of the various options is essential. This will help determine the "correct curriculum sequencing" best suited to meet student needs.

TRANSITION LESSONS

To The Teacher

The following 45 lessons are designed to be presented one per day for a total of nine weeks. Before beginning this section, please review the **How & When to Use the Transition Worktext** on page 232 of this Guidebook.

Please note that Transition lessons (especially Student Worktext pages 77-122) should never be used as homework! To maximize each practice session, first introduce each new letter to the class, then monitor and encourage the students as they work.

As each new letter is presented, encourage students to use a variety of practice techniques. Sky Writing, back writing, board practice, verbal descriptions, etc., can all help imprint letter formation in the brain. Also, remind students that handwriting is a learned motor skill, and requires consistent daily practice for mastery.

And don't forget to encourage and *praise* correct letter formation! Creating positive writing experiences now can greatly impact students' future writing success.

To The Teacher

As students begin these Transition lessons, it's important to help them discover the similarities and differences between the Manuscript and Cursive versions of each letter. This activity helps students form clear mental models of letters and strokes, leading to more accurate letter formation and better handwriting.

Also, many letters in Cursive writing use similar patterns in their formation. Be sure to emphasize these similarities by using the information found in the Cursive Letter Chart (page 234). This will greatly enhance student understanding as you introduce new letters.

Note: Lessons 1 through 5 introduce the vowels. Since vowels are the most commonly used letters, it's important to master them thoroughly at the start. Lessons 6 through 26 cover the remaining letters in alphabetical order. (After completing Lessons 1 through 26, students have practiced the entire alphabet.) Lessons 27 through 34 are group letter review lessons. Finally, Lessons 35 through 45 are a review of capital and lowercase letters.

(See Student Worktext, page 77)

Letter Focus A a $\mathcal{A}$ a

Directions: Sky Write each letter, verbally describing its formation and pointing out similarities to other Cursive letters. (See Cursive Letter Chart, page 234.) Show students how to use the start dots and arrows as they practice the letters $\mathcal{A}$ a. Also, have students practice the lowercase a in sets of three to help them master the letter as well as the connecting stroke. Space is given on the first two lines for students to practice their name.

Extended Teaching: While students practice the a in sets of three, point out that the lowercase a is also a word that can stand alone.

(See Student Worktext, page 78)

Letter Focus E e $\mathcal{E}$ e

Directions: Sky Write each letter, verbally describing its formation and pointing out similarities to other Cursive letters. (See Cursive Letter Chart, page 234.) Encourage students to use the start dots and arrows as they practice the letters $\mathcal{E}$ e. Also, have students practice the lowercase e in sets of three to help them master the letter as well as the connecting stroke. Space is given on the first two lines for students to practice their name.

Extended Teaching: The vowel e is a loop letter. Remind students to leave the loop open — similar to the loop on their shoelace.

(See Student Worktext, page 79)

Letter Focus Ii *ℐ i*

Directions: Sky Write each letter, verbally describing its formation and pointing out similarities to other Cursive letters. (See Cursive Letter Chart, page 234.) Encourage students to use the start dots and arrows as they practice the letters *ℐ i*. Also, have students practice the lowercase *i* in sets of three to help them master the letter as well as the connecting stroke. Space is given on the first two lines for students to practice their name.

Extended Teaching: Point out that the capital *ℐ* is also a word that stands alone. Remind students that when the *ℐ* is used as a word, it's always capitalized.

(See Student Worktext, page 80)

Letter Focus Oo *𝒪 o*

Directions: Sky Write each letter, verbally describing its formation and pointing out similarities to other Cursive letters. (See Cursive Letter Chart, page 234.) Encourage students to use the start dots and arrows as they practice the letters *𝒪 o*. Also, have students practice the lowercase *o* in sets of three to help them master the letter as well as the connecting stroke. Space is given on the first two lines for students to practice their name.

Extended Teaching: Several verses in Psalms begin with the letter *𝒪*. (Example: "O Lord our God, the majesty and glory of your name fills all the earth and overflows the heavens." Psalm 8:1). The modern spelling for that same word is "Oh."

(See Student Worktext, page 81)

Letter Focus Uu *𝒰 u*

Directions: Sky Write each letter, verbally describing its formation and pointing out similarities to other Cursive letters. (See Cursive Letter Chart, page 234.) Encourage students to use the start dots and arrows as they practice the letters *𝒰 u*. Also, have students practice the lowercase *u* in sets of three to help them master the letter as well as the connecting stroke. Space is given on the first two lines for students to practice their name.

Extended Teaching: As students write the *u* in groups of three, remind them to avoid loops and to use clean upstrokes. This takes some practice as the stroke goes up and comes down on the same line.

(See Student Worktext, page 82)

Letter Focus Bb *ℬ b*

Directions: Sky Write each letter, verbally describing its formation and pointing out similarities to other Cursive letters. (See Cursive Letter Chart, page 234.) Encourage students to use the start dots and arrows as they practice the letters *ℬ b*. Also, have students practice the lowercase *b* in sets of three to help them master the letter as well as the connecting stroke. Space is given on the first two lines for students to practice their name.

Extended Teaching: The lowercase *b* is found in several letter group families. It is a tall letter, a loop letter, an upstroke letter, and a bridgestroke letter. Pointing out letter groups can help students form an accurate mental picture of each letter.

Transition Lesson 7

(See Student Worktext, page 83)

Letter Focus C c *C c*

Directions: Sky Write each letter, verbally describing its formation and pointing out similarities to other Cursive letters. (See Cursive Letter Chart, page 234.) Encourage students to use the start dots and arrows as they practice the letters *C c*. Also, have students practice the lowercase *c* in sets of three to help them master the letter as well as the connecting stroke. Space is given on the first two lines for students to practice their name.

Extended Teaching: Have students write the word *cab* several times for practice. This will give them practice connecting three letters they have already learned.

Transition Lesson 8

(See Student Worktext, page 84)

Letter Focus D d *D d*

Directions: Sky Write each letter, verbally describing its formation and pointing out similarities to other Cursive letters. (See Cursive Letter Chart, page 234.) Encourage students to use the start dots and arrows as they practice the letters *D d*. Also, have students practice the lowercase *d* in sets of three to help them master the letter as well as the connecting stroke. Space is given on the first two lines for students to practice their name.

Extended Teaching: Have students write the words *dad* and *did* several times for practice. This will give them practice connecting three letters they have already learned.

Transition Lesson 9

(See Student Worktext, page 85)

Letter Focus F f *F f*

Directions: Sky Write each letter, verbally describing its formation and pointing out similarities to other Cursive letters. (See Cursive Letter Chart, page 234.) Encourage students to use the start dots and arrows as they practice the letters *F f*. Also, have students practice the lowercase *f* in sets of three to help them master the letter as well as the connecting stroke. Space is given on the first two lines for students to practice their name.

Extended Teaching: Show students that the lowercase *f* is a tall letter, a loop letter, and a tail letter, and that the capital *F* is a three-stroke letter. Remind students that the downstroke for the capital *F* is written first, then the top line, then the middle cross.

Transition Lesson 10

(See Student Worktext, page 86)

Letter Focus G g *G g*

Directions: Sky Write each letter, verbally describing its formation and pointing out similarities to other Cursive letters. (See Cursive Letter Chart, page 234.) Encourage students to use the start dots and arrows as they practice the letters *G g*. Also, have students practice the lowercase *g* in sets of three to help them master the letter as well as the connecting stroke. Space is given on the first two lines for students to practice their name.

Extended Teaching: Show students that the capital *G* is a boatstroke letter that does not connect to the rest of the word. Practice words: *God*, *bag*, *gab*

Lesson 11

(See Student Worktext, page 87)

Letter Focus H h ℋ ℎ

Directions: Sky Write each letter, verbally describing its formation and pointing out similarities to other Cursive letters. (See Cursive Letter Chart, page 234.) Encourage students to use the start dots and arrows as they practice the letters ℋ ℎ. Also, have students practice the lowercase ℎ in sets of three to help them master the letter as well as the connecting stroke. Space is given on the first two lines for students to practice their name.

Extended Teaching: Remind students that the lowercase ℎ is a tall, loop letter. Point out that the capital ℋ is a two-stroke capital that starts with a canestroke, then goes down, up and across to connect to the rest of the word. Practice words: *had*, *hid*

Lesson 12

(See Student Worktext, page 88)

Letter Focus J j ℐ 𝒿

Directions: Sky Write each letter, verbally describing its formation and pointing out similarities to other Cursive letters. (See Cursive Letter Chart, page 234.) Encourage students to use the start dots and arrows as they practice the letters ℐ 𝒿. Also, have students practice the lowercase 𝒿 in sets of three to help them master the letter as well as the connecting stroke. Space is given on the first two lines for students to practice their name.

Extended Teaching: Remind students that the lowercase 𝒿 is a two-stroke letter. The dot is added after the word is written. Practice word: *jade*

Lesson 13

(See Student Worktext, page 89)

Letter Focus K k 𝒦 𝓀

Directions: Sky Write each letter, verbally describing its formation and pointing out similarities to other Cursive letters. (See Cursive Letter Chart, page 234.) Encourage students to use the start dots and arrows as they practice the letters 𝒦 𝓀. Also, have students practice the lowercase 𝓀 in sets of three to help them master the letter as well as the connecting stroke. Space is given on the first two lines for students to practice their name.

Extended Teaching: Point out that the capital 𝒦 is a two-stroke capital. The lowercase 𝓀 is a tall, loop letter. Challenge students to discover the similarities between the lowercase ℎ and 𝓀 (both are tall, loop letters).

Lesson 14

(See Student Worktext, page 90)

Letter Focus L l ℒ 𝓁

Directions: Sky Write each letter, verbally describing its formation and pointing out similarities to other Cursive letters. (See Cursive Letter Chart, page 234.) Encourage students to use the start dots and arrows as they practice the letters ℒ 𝓁. Also, have students practice the lowercase 𝓁 in sets of three to help them master the letter as well as the connecting stroke. Space is given on the first two lines for students to practice their name.

Extended Teaching: The lowercase 𝓁 is another tall, loop letter. Practice words: *fill*, *hill*, *jello*, *lab*, *leg*

(See Student Worktext, page 91)

Letter Focus M m 𝓜 𝓶

Directions: Sky Write each letter, verbally describing its formation and pointing out similarities to other Cursive letters. (See Cursive Letter Chart, page 234.) Encourage students to use the start dots and arrows as they practice the letters 𝓜 𝓶. Also, have students practice the lowercase 𝓶 in sets of three to help them master the letter as well as the connecting stroke. Space is given on the first two lines for students to practice their name.

Extended Teaching: The capital 𝓜 is a canestroke capital. The word *mom* provides good 𝓶 practice. Remind students that the words mom and dad are capitalized when used as a name ("I thanked Mom."), but not when used as a simple noun ("I thanked my mom.").

(See Student Worktext, page 92)

Letter Focus N n 𝓝 𝓷

Directions: Sky Write each letter, verbally describing its formation and pointing out similarities to other Cursive letters. (See Cursive Letter Chart, page 234.) Encourage students to use the start dots and arrows as they practice the letters 𝓝 𝓷. Also, have students practice the lowercase 𝓷 in sets of three to help them master the letter as well as the connecting stroke. Space is given on the first two lines for students to practice their name.

Extended Teaching: Practice words: *man*, *mine*, *name*

(See Student Worktext, page 93)

Letter Focus P p 𝓟 𝓹

Directions: Sky Write each letter, verbally describing its formation and pointing out similarities to other Cursive letters. (See Cursive Letter Chart, page 234.) Encourage students to use the start dots and arrows as they practice the letters 𝓟 𝓹. Also, have students practice the lowercase 𝓹 in sets of three to help them master the letter as well as the connecting stroke. Space is given on the first two lines for students to practice their name.

Extended Teaching: The capital 𝓟 is a forward oval capital that begins with a slight upstroke. The lowercase 𝓹 is a tail letter, as well as an oval letter. Show students that this oval letter does not begin like the lowercase c and a. Practice words: *help*, *peg*, *Pam*

(See Student Worktext, page 94)

Letter Focus Q q 𝓠 𝓺

Directions: Sky Write each letter, verbally describing its formation and pointing out similarities to other Cursive letters. (See Cursive Letter Chart, page 234.) Encourage students to use the start dots and arrows as they practice the letters 𝓠 𝓺. Also, have students practice the lowercase 𝓺 in sets of three to help them master the letter as well as the connecting stroke. Space is given on the first two lines for students to practice their name.

Extended Teaching: Since the 𝓾 always tags along with the 𝓺, encourage students to practice the 𝓺𝓾 combination. Practice words: *equip*, *quack*

Lesson 19

(See Student Worktext, page 95)

Letter Focus R r *R r*

Directions: Sky Write each letter, verbally describing its formation and pointing out similarities to other Cursive letters. (See Cursive Letter Chart, page 234.) Encourage students to use the start dots and arrows as they practice the letters *R r*. Also, have students practice the lowercase *r* in sets of three to help them master the letter as well as the connecting stroke. Space is given on the first two lines for students to practice their name.

Extended Teaching: Ask students to look for the similarities between the capital *R*, *P*, and *B*. These three capitals begin alike and have the same first three strokes. *R* is the only one of these capitals that connects to the rest of the word. Practice words: *ran*, *run*

Lesson 20

(See Student Worktext, page 96)

Letter Focus S s *S s*

Directions: Sky Write each letter, verbally describing its formation and pointing out similarities to other Cursive letters. (See Cursive Letter Chart, page 234.) Encourage students to use the start dots and arrows as they practice the letters *S s*. Also, have students practice the lowercase *s* in sets of three to help them master the letter as well as the connecting stroke. Space is given on the first two lines for students to practice their name.

Extended Teaching: Practice the words: *same*, *sees*, *sea*

Lesson 21

(See Student Worktext, page 97)

Letter Focus T t *T t*

Directions: Sky Write each letter, verbally describing its formation and pointing out similarities to other Cursive letters. (See Cursive Letter Chart, page 234.) Encourage students to use the start dots and arrows as they practice the letters *T t*. Also, have students practice the lowercase *t* in sets of three to help them master the letter as well as the connecting stroke. Space is given on the first two lines for students to practice their name.

Extended Teaching: Point out the boatstroke in the capital *T*. Ask students to identify other boatstroke capitals (*B*, *F*, *G*, *I*, *S*).

Lesson 22

(See Student Worktext, page 98)

Letter Focus V v *V v*

Directions: Sky Write each letter, verbally describing its formation and pointing out similarities to other Cursive letters. (See Cursive Letter Chart, page 234.) Encourage students to use the start dots and arrows as they practice the letters *V v*. Also, have students practice the lowercase *v* in sets of three to help them master the letter as well as the connecting stroke. Space is given on the first two lines for students to practice their name.

Extended Teaching: Practice the words: *vase*, *vine*, *vet*

Transition Lesson 23

(See Student Worktext, page 99)

Letter Focus W w $\mathcal{W}$ w

Directions: Sky Write each letter, verbally describing its formation and pointing out similarities to other Cursive letters. (See Cursive Letter Chart, page 234.) Encourage students to use the start dots and arrows as they practice the letters $\mathcal{W}$ w. Also, have students practice the lowercase w in sets of three to help them master the letter as well as the connecting stroke. Space is given on the first two lines for students to practice their name.

Extended Teaching: Point out the boatstroke in the lowercase w. Ask students to identify other lowercase letters with boatstrokes (b, o, v). Practice words: bow, $book$, vow

Transition Lesson 24

(See Student Worktext, page 100)

Letter Focus X x $\mathcal{X}$ x

Directions: Sky Write each letter, verbally describing its formation and pointing out similarities to other Cursive letters. (See Cursive Letter Chart, page 234.) Encourage students to use the start dots and arrows as they practice the letters $\mathcal{X}$ x. Also, have students practice the lowercase x in sets of three to help them master the letter as well as the connecting stroke. Space is given on the first two lines for students to practice their name.

Extended Teaching: Remind students that the capital and lowercase x are both two-stroke letters. Practice words: $exit$, $exam$

Transition Lesson 25

(See Student Worktext, page 101)

Letter Focus Y y $\mathcal{Y}$ y

Directions: Sky Write each letter, verbally describing its formation and pointing out similarities to other Cursive letters. (See Cursive Letter Chart, page 234.) Encourage students to use the start dots and arrows as they practice the letters $\mathcal{Y}$ y. Also, have students practice the lowercase y in sets of three to help them master the letter as well as the connecting stroke. Space is given on the first two lines for students to practice their name.

Extended Teaching: Point out that the capital and lowercase $\mathcal{Y}$ y are both tail letters. Practice words: yet, $yellow$, yam

Transition Lesson 26

(See Student Worktext, page 102)

Letter Focus Z z $\mathcal{Z}$ z

Directions: Sky Write each letter, verbally describing its formation and pointing out similarities to other Cursive letters. (See Cursive Letter Chart, page 234.) Encourage students to use the start dots and arrows as they practice the letters $\mathcal{Z}$ z. Also, have students practice the lowercase z in sets of three to help them master the letter as well as the connecting stroke. Space is given on the first two lincs for students to practice their name.

Extended Teaching: The capital $\mathcal{Z}$ is a tail capital. Ask students to identify other tail capitals ($\mathcal{J}$ and $\mathcal{Y}$). The capital $\mathcal{Z}$ also has a beginning stroke that is very similar to a number. Ask students to identify that number (the 2). Practice words: zoo, zip

(See Student Worktext, page 103)

Letter Focus: Upstroke Letters *e, l, h, k*.

Directions: Have students practice the upstroke, loop letters *e, l, h, k*. Remind them to follow the start dots and arrows. Practice word: *help*

Extended Teaching: Remind students to write the *e* with a clear loop. Incorrectly written, the *e* and *i* cause many spelling errors.

(See Student Worktext, page 105)

Letter Focus: Oval, Tail Letters *g, q, p*

Directions: Have students practice the oval tail letters *g, q,* and *p*. Remind them to follow the start dots and arrows. Practice words: *good, equip, gold*

Extended Teaching: Show students the different starting point for the tail letter *p*. Also, point out the differences between the tails of the *g, q,* and *p*.

(See Student Worktext, page 104)

Letter Focus: oval letters *o, a, c, d*

Directions: Have students practice the oval letters *o, a, c, d*. Remind them to follow the start dots and arrows. Practice word: *coal*

Extended Teaching: Point out that carefully closing oval letters will prevent misreading. If the oval is not closed, the *a* can easily be misread as a *u*.

(See Student Worktext, page 106)

Letter Focus: upstroke letters *i, u, w*

Directions: Have students practice the upstroke letters *i, u,* and *w*. Remind them to follow the start dots and arrows. Practice words: *with, quick, will*

Extended Teaching: Ask students to find similarities and differences in the three focus letters. (Alike: all begin alike, all are non-loop letters. Different: the *i* is a two-stroke letter, the *w* is a bridgestroke letter, etc.)

 **Lesson 31**

(See Student Worktext, page 107)

Letter Focus: Upstroke Letters *j, f, t*

Directions: Have students practice the upstroke, two-stroke letters *j, f, t*. Remind them to follow the start dots and arrows. Practice words: *jump, fit, jet*

Extended Teaching: Help students see similarities and differences between the tall letter *t*; the tall, tail letter *f*; and the tail letter *j*. Note that some are loop, and some are non-loop strokes.

 **Lesson 32**

(See Student Worktext, page 108)

Letter Focus: Upstroke Letters *r, s, b*

Directions: Have students practice the upstroke letters *r, s, b*. Remind them to follow the start dots and arrows. Practice words: *right, sure, boat*

Extended Teaching: Remind students to write the *r* and *s* with distinctive points. Also note the bridgestroke of the *b*. Additional practice words: *bass, rabbits, raspberry*

 **Lesson 33**

(See Student Worktext, page 109)

Letter Focus: Overstroke Letters *m, n, v*

Directions: Have students practice the overstroke letters *m, n, v*. Remind them to follow the start dots and arrows. Practice words: *men, jam, verse*

Extended Teaching: Ask students to verbalize how the Manuscript m and n are similar to the Cursive overstroke *m* and *n*. Additional practice words: *van, many, noon, vat*

 **Lesson 34**

(See Student Worktext, page 110)

Letter Focus: Overstroke Letters *x, y, z*

Directions: Have students practice overstroke letters *x, y, z*. Remind them to follow the start dots and arrows. Practice words: *year, zebra, exit*

Extended Teaching: Remind students that the *x* is a two-stroke letter with the second stroke added after the word is written. Additional practice words: *extra, exam, eye, you, yes, zap, zero*

Lesson 35

(See Student Worktext, page 111)

Letter Focus Aa, Oo

Directions: Have students practice Aa and Oo as well as the three-letter group practice. Remind them that the capital A is connected to the rest of the word, but the capital O is not. Monitor students' use of start dots and arrows. Practice words: *Abba*, *Adam*, *Obadiah*, *Omega*

Extended Teaching: Some of these words or names may not be familiar to the students. Abba is another name for Father God. Adam was the first man. Obadiah was a prophet from Old Testament times. Omega is the name of the last letter of the Greek alphabet and is also a word that means the last or the end.

Lesson 36

(See Student Worktext, page 112)

Letter Focus Cc, Ee

Directions: Have students practice Cc and Ee as well as the three-letter group practice. Monitor students' use of start dots and arrows. Practice words: *Caleb*, *Canaan*, *Esther*, *Eve*

Extended Teaching: Help students discover more about these people and places. Caleb and Joshua worked with Moses and were encouragers. Esther was a famous, beautiful queen. Eve was the first woman.

Lesson 37

(See Student Worktext, page 113)

Letter Focus: Boatstroke Capitals Gg, Ss, Tt

Directions: Have students practice Gg, Ss, Tt as well as the three-letter group practice. Monitor students' use of start dots and arrows. As they practice these boatstroke capitals, remind them that boatstroke capitals do not connect to the rest of the word. Practice words: *God*, *Son*, *Timothy*

Extended Teaching: Timothy was a young man who traveled with Paul. An interesting view of his life is found in Philippians 2:19-22. Son is capitalized when it refers to God's Son, Jesus.

Lesson 38

(See Student Worktext, page 114)

Letter Focus Upstroke Capitals Ii, Jj, Qq

Directions: Have students practice Ii, Jj, and Qq as well as the three-letter group practice. Monitor students' use of start dots and arrows. Practice words: *Isaac*, *Jesus*, *Queen*

Extended Teaching: Isaac was Abraham's promised son. Remind students that queen is not capitalized, except when used as part of a title. (Example: Queen Esther)

Lesson 39

(See Student Worktext, page 115)

Letter Focus *Hh, Kk, Xx*

Directions: Have students practice *Hh, Kk,* and *X x* as well as the three-letter group practice. Monitor students' use of start dots and arrows. Practice words: *Hebrews, Kingdom, Xerxes* [pronounced zurk[1]-seez]

Extended Teaching: Xerxes does not have an *x* pronunciation, however it does give good *x* practice! Xerxes was a Persian king named in the Old Testament. You'll find his story in the book of Esther. (Note: "Xerxes" is a Greek word. The Hebrew word is "Ahasuerus." Both refer to the same person. Usage in Scripture varies depending on the translation.)

Lesson 40

(See Student Worktext, page 116)

Letter Focus *Mm, Nn, Uu*

Directions: Have students practice *Mm, Nn,* and *Uu* as well as the three-letter group practice. Monitor students' use of start dots and arrows. Practice words: *Messiah, Numbers, Ur*

Extended Teaching: Numbers is capitalized in this lesson as it refers to a book in the Old Testament. Ur is the early home of Abraham as mentioned in Genesis.

Lesson 41

(See Student Worktext, page 117)

Letter Focus *Ff, Vv, Ww*

Directions: Have students practice *Ff, Vv,* and *Ww* as well as the three-letter group practice. Monitor students' use of start dots and arrows. Practice words: *Father, Victory, Worship*

Extended Teaching: Why would we capitalize the words victory and worship, other than for practice? Challenge students to think of when it's appropriate to capitalize these words. (They're capitalized when they begin a sentence! Examples: Victory is ours in Jesus! Worship the Lord!)

Lesson 42

(See Student Worktext, page 118)

Letter Focus *Dd, Ll*

Directions: Have students practice *Dd* and *Ll* as well as the three-letter group practice. Monitor students' use of start dots and arrows. Practice words: *Daniel, David, Lazarus, Lord*

Extended Teaching: Daniel and David are men mentioned in the Old Testament. The Psalms were written mostly by David. The book Daniel wrote bears his name. Lazarus is the man Jesus raised from the dead. His story is found in John 11:1-12, 19.

Lesson 43

(See Student Worktext, page 119)

Letter Focus *Pp, Rr, Bb*

Directions: Have students practice *Pp, Bb,* and *Rr* as well as the three-letter group practice. Monitor students' use of start dots and arrows. Practice words: *Bible, Paul, Ruth*

Extended Teaching: What are some other words we use for the Bible? (Holy Scriptures, Holy Bible, etc.) Paul is the man who changed his name when God changed his life. Challenge students to discover what his name was before it was Paul. (Saul) Ruth is a woman whose story is told in the Old Testament book of that name. She was a very kind, helpful woman.

Lesson 45

(See Student Worktext, page 121)

Letter Focus: Alphabet & Number Review

Directions: (Read to the student.) "Write your name on the top line." (pause) "Now write the entire alphabet, both capital and lowercase letters, then write all the numbers. Remember your letters should be the correct size and fill the space."

Extended Teaching: Students have now had a thorough introduction and practice of the alphabet, so this makes an excellent posttest. You may want to date and file this page to help evaluate future progress. Remember to praise improvement and to encourage students as they write.

Lesson 44

(See Student Worktext, page 120)

Letter Focus *Yy, Zz*

Directions: Have students practice *Yy* and *Zz* as well as the three-letter group practice. Monitor students' use of start dots and arrows. Practice words: *Yoke, You, Zacchaeus, Zion*

Extended Teaching: Not many people are famous because they climbed a tree! Students can read the story of Zacchaeus in Luke 19:1-6.

CURSIVE LESSONS

To The Teacher

Before beginning the daily lessons, have students review the following:

>The mechanics of handwriting
>(See **Proper Positioning**, page 10.)
>The format of the class
>(See **Weekly Lesson Format**, page 56.)
>The evaluation process
>(See **Tips on Grading**, page 57.)

It's also very important to have students write the alphabet (capital and lowercase letters) on a sheet of paper, then sign his or her name and date it. Use this sheet later to pinpoint areas of special need.

Most importantly, remember that as you acknowledge and reward progress, the learning process is greatly enhanced!

Lesson 1

Scripture Verse
"God who began the good work within you will keep right on helping you grow in His grace." Philippians 1:6

Letter Focus
Dd, Oo, Yy

Tip of the Week
As you get taller and smarter this year, make sure your handwriting grows too! Strive to be a **Five Star** student (Student Worktext, page 6). Good handwriting helps others read what you have to say.

Extended Teaching
Review the **Five Star** evaluation with your students (Student Worktext, page 6). Encourage students to stay aware of these five areas as they write.

File a dated sample of each student's writing to help you evaluate future progress. Note: It's important to evaluate each student based on his/her own improvement, not just comparison with the model.

For Discussion
How much have you grown since last year? Is physical growth the only way we can grow? What do you think it means to "grow in God's grace?"

Lesson 2

Scripture Verse
"May God our Father and the Lord Jesus Christ give you all of His blessings, and great peace of heart and mind." I Corinthians 1:3

Letter Focus
Aa, Ee, Jj

Tip of the Week
Close your eyes and picture the strokes for the capital and lowercase *Aa, Ee,* and *Jj.* With your eyes still closed, write these six letters with your index finger on the palm of your other hand.

Extended Teaching
Remind students to be careful as they write the loop in the lowercase *e.* It can easily be mistaken for the non-loop lowercase *i.* Poorly written, these two letters account for many spelling errors.

Practice the capital letters in this week's lesson: *M, G, F, L, J, C, H.* Remind students that the capital *M, J, H,* and *C* connect to the rest of the word.

For Discussion
Make a list of some "blessings" that make you happy. Now compare your list with a friend's. How are they similar? How are they different?

Scripture Verse

"Don't worry about anything; instead, pray about everything; tell God your needs and don't forget to thank Him for His answers." Philippians 4:6

Letter Focus

Rr, Tt, Uu

Tip of the Week

Letters are different heights, just like people! Some lowercase letters fill only half the space, while tall letters (*b*, *d*, *f*, *h*, *k*, *l*, and *t*) fill the whole space, and touch the top lines.

Extended Teaching

Have students practice the *r* combinations from this lesson (*er*, *or*, *ur*, *pr*, and *ry*). Remind them to write the *r* with definite points.

All the tall letters (*b*, *d*, *f*, *h*, *k*, *l*, *t*) are used in this week's lesson. Remind students that tall letters must touch the top line.

For Discussion

Ask students, "Does God always answer prayers with 'yes?'" "What other answers might God give?" "Why?" Encourage students to share some answers to prayers.

Scripture Verse

"Dwell on the fine, good things in others. Think about all you can praise God for and be glad about." Philippians 4:8

Letter Focus

Bb, Ll, Pp

Tip of the Week

When you tie your shoes you make loops for the bows. When you write some letters, you use loops, too. Make certain that the loops in *b*, *e*, *f*, *h*, *k*, and *l* are open — but don't put loops in *t* or *d*.

Extended Teaching

Students will benefit from Sky Writing the focus letters (see page 9). Sky Writing allows the teacher to see at a glance when students are unsure of letter formation.

Have students practice the capital *B* and *P* on practice paper. Point out similarities. Ask students, "What other letter begins like these two letters?" (the *R*)

For Discussion

What are some of the "fine, good things" that you can see in your classmates? Which of these traits would you like to have, too?

 **Lesson 5**

Scripture Verse
"Anyone who believes and says that Jesus is the Son of God has God living in him, and he is living with God." I John 4:15

Letter Focus
Gg, Ss, Vv

Tip of the Week
The capital *G* and *S* are boatstroke capitals. The other boatstroke capitals are *B, F, I,* and *T*. Remember, boatstroke capitals are not joined to the rest of the word.

Extended Teaching
As they write this week, remind students to check their letters to make sure they fill the whole space.

Challenge students to think of someone who needs encouragement this week (neighbor, family member, someone in church). Suggest that they share their Scripture Border Sheet with that person.

For Discussion
When God is living in our hearts, how does this affect our behavior? Name some traits that might show we are "living with God."

 **Lesson 6**

Scripture Verse
"I can do everything God asks me to with the help of Christ who gives me the strength and power." Philippians 4:13

Letter Focus
Cc, Hh, Ww

Tip of the Week
Is your hand getting tired as you write? You may be holding your pencil incorrectly, or too tightly. Have your teacher check your pencil position. Relax your wrist by rotating it in a circle.

Extended Teaching
It's hard to write smoothly and neatly when you're not relaxed. Encourage your students to breathe deeply and use good posture.

Remind students that the capital *C* and *H* are connected to the rest of the word. Good practice names include: *Carol, Charles, Harold, Hans, Hannah*. Ask students to check their name to see if the capital letter is connected to the rest of the letters.

For Discussion
What sort of things might God ask you to do? How does this verse say we should get the "strength and power" to do them?

Scripture Verse

"Be kind to each other, tenderhearted, forgiving one another, just as God has forgiven you."
Ephesians 4:32

Letter Focus

Ii, Kk, Tt

Tip of the Week

There are four lowercase letters (*i*, *j*, *t*, and *x*) that require an extra stroke after the word is written. Pay close attention to these letters as you practice.

Extended Teaching

Remind students that the focus letters *K* and *T* are two-stroke capital letters. The other two-stroke capitals are *H* and *X*.

Ask students to find the words in this week's Scripture Verse that contain suffixes (tenderhearted, forgiving, forgiven).

For Discussion

List some ways you can show kindness to your classmates . . . your family . . . your neighbors. Try to put at least one of these ideas into action this week.

Scripture Verse

"Follow God's example in everything you do just as a much loved child imitates his father."
Ephesians 5:1

Letter Focus

Ff, Mm, Xx

Tip of the Week

The bridgestroke family includes the lowercase *b*, *o*, *v*, and *w*. As you write the connecting stroke, don't let your bridge sag!

Extended Teaching

Show students that the capital *F* is the only three-stroke capital. Encourage students to practice this letter on the board while counting one-two-three.

Since there are very few words that contain an *x*, here are some extra words to practice: *extreme, exact, exit, except*

For Discussion

What are some good ways we might imitate God? Watch for opportunities to put these into practice!

Lesson 9

Scripture Verse
"Let everyone be sure that he is doing his very best, for then he will have the personal satisfaction of work well done." Galatians 6:4

Letter Focus
Aa, Ll, Rr

Tip of the Week
A train won't work unless it's on the track. Keep your handwriting on track by making sure your letters rest firmly on the line.

Extended Teaching
Review the **Five Star** evaluation with the students. Encourage them to demonstrate each "star" on the board, showing what is good practice and what isn't. (See Student Worktext, page 6.) Ask them to identify at least one area of the five that they could improve in.

The capital *L* is a downstroke capital. Have students look for the similar stroke in the capital *D*.

For Discussion
Why is it important to always do your very best? Make a list of some areas you'd like to improve in. Don't forget to ask God to help you!

Lesson 10 through Lesson 27

The remaining 18 lessons from the Transition Student Worktext are identical to Lessons 10-27 from the Cursive C Student Worktext. See pages 144-153 in this Guidebook for directions.

Scope & Sequence - Transition

Skills/letter emphasized in the Transition Worktext are found in the following lessons.

Practice Letters

A
Capital: 9*, *1, 19, 24*, **2, 9, 16, 21, 27**
Lowercase: 2*, *1, 19, 24*, **2, 9, 16, 21**

B
Capital: 8*, *5, 15, 23*, **4, 5, 11, 13, 19**
Lowercase: 3*, *5, 15, 23*, **3, 4, 6, 8, 13, 19**

C
Capital: 8*, *4, 14*, **6, 11, 21, 24**
Lowercase: 2*, *4, 14*, **6, 16, 21, 24**

D
Capital: 8*, *1, 24*, **1, 16, 20, 27**
Lowercase: 2*, *1, 8, 24*, **1, 3, 4, 16, 20, 27**

E
Capital: 10*, *4, 17, 19, 26*, **2, 11, 20**
Lowercase: 2*, *4, 17, 26*, **2, 4, 11, 20**

F
Capital: 10*, *8, 19, 27*, **5, 8, 12, 15, 20**
Lowercase: 4*, *8, 27*, **3, 4, 8, 15, 20**

G
Capital: 8*, *2, 20, 25*, **5, 13, 19, 26**
Lowercase: 7*, *2, 20, 25*, **5, 13, 16, 19, 26**

H
Capital: 10*, *8, 17, 19, 22*, **6, 12, 17**
Lowercase: 3*, *8, 22*, **3, 4, 6, 12, 17, 19**

I
Capital: 10*, *9, 19, 21*, **5, 7, 15, 22**
Lowercase: 4*, *9, 21*, **7, 15, 22, 26**

J
Capital: 10*, *9*, **2, 15, 22**
Lowercase: 4*, *7*, *9*, **2, 7, 9, 15, 22**

K
Capital: 9*, *12*, **7, 12, 19, 23**
Lowercase: 3*, *4*, *12*, **3, 4, 7, 19, 23**

L
Capital: 10*, *6, 17, 19*, **4, 9, 12, 21**
Lowercase: 3*, *6, 8, 19*, **3, 4, 12, 21**

M
Capital: 9*, *7, 27*, **8, 10, 21, 25**
Lowercase: 6*, *7, 27*, **10, 18, 21, 25**

N
Capital: 9*, *7*, **10, 18**
Lowercase: 6*, *7*, **10, 18**

O
Capital: 8*, *2, 15*, **1, 10, 14, 25**
Lowercase: 2*, *2, 15*, **1, 8, 10, 14, 25**

P
Capital: 8*, *5, 17*, **4, 11, 18**
Lowercase: 7*, *5, 17*, **4, 11, 18**

Q
Capital: 8*, *25*, **13, 22**
Lowercase: 7*, *3, 25*, **13, 16, 22**

R
Capital: 8*, *11, 23*, **3, 9, 11, 16, 26**
Lowercase: 6*, *11, 23*, **3, 9, 16, 26**

S
Capital: 10*, *13, 16*, **5, 11, 17**
Lowercase: 6*, *13, 16*, **5, 11, 17**

T
Capital: 10*, *13, 20, 26*, **3, 5, 7, 12, 26**
Lowercase: 3*, *4*, *8, 13, 20, 26*, **3, 4, 7, 12, 26**

U
Capital: 10*, *3, 10*, **3, 14, 23**
Lowercase: 6*, *3, 10*, **3, 13, 14, 18, 23**

V
Capital: 9*, *6, 18*, **5, 8, 17**
Lowercase: 5*, *6, 18*, **5, 8, 10, 17**

W
Capital: 9*, *11, 16*, **6, 18, 25**
Lowercase: 5*, *11, 16*, **6, 8, 18, 25**

X
Capital: 9*, *12, 18*, **8, 21, 23**
Lowercase: 5*, *12, 18*, **7, 8, 10, 21, 23, 12**

Y
Capital: 9*, *10, 22*, **1, 14, 21, 24**
Lowercase: 5*, *7*, *10, 22*, **1, 10, 14, 21, 24**

Z
Capital: 9*, *14, 21*, **21, 24, 27**
Lowercase: 5*, *14, 21*, **10, 21, 24, 27**

General Skills

IN EVERY VERSE
Letter formation
Number formation
Sentence structure
Punctuation
Capitalization

LETTER PRACTICE

Capital Letters
Boatstroke: **5**
Canestroke: **4, 14, 17, 19**
Circle: 8*, *25*
Curve: 10*
Downstroke: 10*, *7, 8, 9, 17, 23, 27*, **9, 21**
Forward curve: 8*, *23*
Forward oval: **11**
Oval: *2*, **11**
Slantstroke: 9*, *7, 10, 11, 18, 19, 27*
Tail: *1, 2, 14, 15*
Two stroke: 8*, *10, 13, 23, 28*, **7, 12, 19**
Three stroke: *8, 19*
Upswing: **22**

Lowercase Letters
Bridgestroke: **8, 18**
Circle: 2*, *2, 4, 5, 15, 24*
Curve: 6*, *7, 11, 22, 23*
Downstroke: 5*, *5, 8, 9, 11, 15*
Loop: **4, 19**
Oval: **16, 21**
Overstroke: **10**
Slantstroke: 5*, *6, 11, 18*
Tail: 7*, *25, 29*, **8, 13, 22**
Tall: 3*, *5, 6, 8, 15, 23*, **3, 6, 19**

Two stroke: 4*, *8, 9, 10, 11, 12, 13, 18, 27*, **7, 15, 26,**
Upstroke: **9**

FIVE STAR SKILLS
Alignment: *3, 6, 26*, **9, 27**
Letter shape: *2, 5, 10, 14, 25*, **8, 16, 22**
Letter size: *4, 8, 14, 21, 29*, **3, 16, 22, 25, 30**
Letter slant: *6, 15, 26*, **11, 22, 28**
Letter spacing: *1, 17, 28*, **10, 17, 27**

MECHANICS
Paper position: *10, 24*, **23**
Pencil position: *12, 20*, **6, 12**
Posture: *10, 11, 24, 26*, **23**

OTHER PRACTICE
Evaluation: *1, 21, 30*, **1, 20, 27, 32**
Cap/lowercase review: 1*
Connected capitals: **2, 7, 17, 19, 29**
Connecting stroke: **13, 28**
Loop/Non-loop: **2, 4, 5, 17**
Manuscript review: **14**
Name focus: *3, 19*, **14, 30**
Number review: *14*
Similar cap/lowercase: *13, 16*, **14, 18, 21**
Verbal Description: 4*, *5, 7, 15, 19, 22, 29*
Visualize letter formation: 6*, 10*, *5, 17, 18, 22*

Vocabulary List

This lesson is composed of all the practice words from the Transition Student Worktext.

Key
italics = Manuscript Lessons 1-27
bold = Cursive Lessons 1-27
* = Manuscript and Cursive Lessons

Aa
abilities
about
against
all*
allowance
always
and*
angels
another
anyone*
anything
answers
are*
as*
ask
asks
at*
away

Bb
back*
be*
beautiful
because
began
before
believes
belong
best
bless
blessed
blessings*
bring*
brothers

Cc
came
can
care
charm
child
children
Christ
Christian
church
citizens
Colossians
come
comes
coming
condemn
continue
country
created

criticize*
cross

Dd
day
dear
deep
deeper
didn't
different
disciples
do*
doing
done
don't*
down
dwell

Ee
each*
ears
earth
else
end
even
ever
everything*
evil
example
exception
exists
exit

Ff
face
family
Father*
faults
fellowship
filled
fine
first
follow
followers
for
forever
forgave
forgive
forgiven
forgiving
free
friendly
friends
from*

Gg
Galatians
gentle
gentleness
get
give*
given
glad
glory
go
God*
God's
good
grace
great
greatness
grow
grudges

Hh
harmony
has
have
he
hear
heart*
hearts
heaven
heavenly
help
helping
high
Him*
his
hold
holy*
home*
household
how*
humble

Ii
if
imitates
important
in
inside
instead
into*
is

Jj
James
Jesus
John
joy
just

Kk
kind
know

Ll
lasting
late
law
let*
life
light*
listen
listening
live
living
Lord*
love
loved
loving

Mm
make*
makes
making
many
Mark
marvelous
Matthew
may
measure
members
mind*
minds
mine
more
most
much*
must*
my

Nn
neighbor
never*
nothing

Oo
obey
of
oh
on
one*
other*
others*

Pp
patience
patient
peace*
people
perfect
personal
Peter
Philippians
power
practice

praise*
pray
prayers
precious
prepare
prepared
presence*
prove
pure

Qq
quickly
quiet
quit

Rr
radiant
ready*
redeemed
rejoice
remain
remember
repay
repents
roots

Ss
satisfaction
Savior
says
Scriptures
set
should
show
size
snap
so
soil
some
Son
speak
special
spirit
strength
strong
sure*
sympathy

Tt
take
tell
tender
tenderhearted
terms
thank
that
the*
their
them
then*
there

Thessalonians
things
think
those*
time
to*
tomorrow
too
toward
true
trust
truth

Uu
understand
understanding
unkind
unless
use

Vv
visit

Ww
want*
wants*
watching
we*
well
what*
when
which
who*
whole
wide
will*
with*
within*
wonderful*
word
words
work
world
worry
worship
written

Yy
you*
your*
yourself

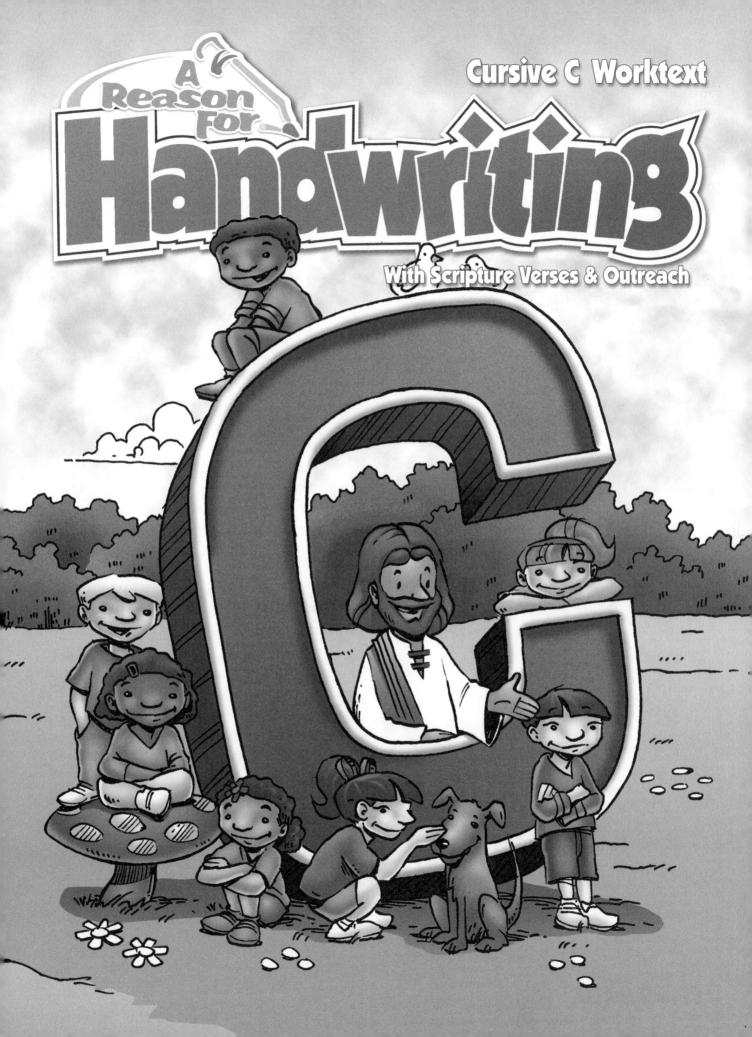

A Reason For Handwriting

Cursive C Worktext

With Scripture Verses & Outreach

Please
Read This First!

Before beginning this section, please review **How & When to Use the Transition Worktext** on page 232 of this Guidebook.

Since the **Transition** Student Worktext is designed to replace either the **Level B** Student Worktext (earlier transition) or the **Level C** Student Worktext (later transition), careful review of the various options is essential. This will help determine the "correct curriculum sequencing" best suited to meet student needs.

GENERAL LESSONS

To The Teacher

Before beginning the daily lessons, have students review the following:

    The mechanics of handwriting
    (See **Proper Positioning**, page 10.)
    The format of the class
    (See **Weekly Lesson Format**, page 56.)
    The evaluation process
    (See **Tips on Grading**, page 57.)

It's also very important to have students write the alphabet (capital and lowercase letters) on a sheet of paper, then sign his or her name and date it. Use this sheet later to pinpoint areas of special need.

Most importantly, remember that as you acknowledge and reward progress, the learning process is greatly enhanced!

Lesson 1

Scripture Verse
"Make the most of every opportunity you have for doing good." Ephesians 5:16

Letter Focus
Dd, Oo, Yy

Tip of the Week
As you get taller and smarter this year, make sure your handwriting grows too! Strive to be a **Five Star** student (see Student Worktext, page 6). Good handwriting helps others read what you have to say.

Extended Teaching
Review the **Five Star** evaluation with your students. Explain the grading procedure, and encourage students to set personal goals within these five areas.

Have each student write the alphabet (capital and lowercase) on a sheet of paper, adding their name and date at the top. File these papers as a starting point for future evaluation.

For Discussion
What are some "opportunities for doing good" you might find? (pick up trash, help parents, help younger siblings, etc.) Try to make the most of at least one opportunity this week.

Lesson 2

Scripture Verse
"Always give thanks for everything to our God and Father in the name of our Lord Jesus Christ." Ephesians 5:20

Letter Focus
Aa, Ee, Jj

Tip of the Week
Close your eyes and picture the strokes for the capital and lowercase *Aa, Ee,* and *Jj.* With your eyes still closed, write these six letters with your index finger on the palm of your other hand.

Extended Teaching
Remind students to form the loop in the lowercase *e* carefully. Otherwise it might be mistaken for the non-loop lowercase *i.*

Note that this week's lesson contains the capital letters: *A, C, E, F, G, J* and *L.* Oval capital letters that connect to the rest of the word are *A, C,* and *E.*

For Discussion
Make a list of things you are thankful for. Now compare your list with a friend's. How are they similar? How are they different?

Scripture Verse
"The earnest prayer of a righteous man has great power and wonderful results." James 5:16

Letter Focus
Rr, Tt, Uu

Tip of the Week
Letters are different heights, just like people! Some lowercase letters fill only half the space, while tall letters (*b*, *d*, *f*, *h*, *k*, *l*, and *t*) fill the whole space, and touch the top lines.

Extended Teaching
Have students practice the *r* combinations from this lesson (*ar*, *pr*, *ri*, *gr*, *er*, *ra*, and *re*). Remind them to form the *r* with definite points.

To enhance understanding of this week's verse, ask students to define "earnest" and "righteous." (Earnest: serious in intention, purpose, or effort. Righteous: acting in a moral, upright way.)

For Discussion
Does God always answer prayers with a "yes?" What other answers might God give? Why?

Scripture Verse
"Whatever happens, dear friends, be glad in the Lord." Philippians 3:1

Letter Focus
Ll, Pp, Ww

Tip of the Week
When you tie your shoes you make loops for the bows. When you write some letters, you use loops, too. Make certain that the loops in *b*, *e*, *f*, *h*, *k*, and *l* are open — but don't put loops in *t* or *d*.

Extended Teaching
Have students practice the canestroke *W* on practice paper. Point out that the formation of the *W* and *V* are very similar.

Students will benefit from Sky Writing the focus letters occasionally. Sky Writing also allows the teacher to see at a glance if a student is unsure of a letter's formation.

For Discussion
Is it possible to be "glad in the Lord" even when you're having a bad day? Explain.

Scripture Verse
"Long ago, even before He made the world, God chose us to be His very own." Ephesians 1:4

Letter Focus
Gg, Ss, Vv

Tip of the Week
The capital G and S are boatstroke capitals. The other boatstroke capitals are B, F, I and T. Remember, boatstroke capitals are not joined to the rest of the word.

Extended Teaching
Have students put the boatstroke capitals in similar stroke groups (G and S; F and T). The B and I are part of other letter groups ($B, P,$ and R), ($I, J,$ and Q).

Challenge students to think of someone who needs encouragement this week, and to plan how they can share their Scripture Border Sheet with them.

For Discussion
How does it make you feel that God has chosen you? How should this relationship affect your behavior? Be specific.

Scripture Verse
"Because of what Christ has done we have become gifts to God that He delights in." Ephesians 1:11

Letter Focus
Bb, Cc, Hh

Tip of the Week
Is your hand getting tired as you write? You may be holding your pencil incorrectly, or too tightly. Have your teacher check your pencil position. Relax your wrist by rotating it in a circle.

Extended Teaching
It's difficult for students to write smoothly and neatly if they're not relaxed. Encourage them to breathe deeply and use good posture. Relaxing exercises are also helpful. Have students rotate their shoulders, their head, and their elbows to reduce stress.

The lowercase letters b and h are both tall letters. Combinations to practice include Ch, be, wh, He, ght, and Eph.

For Discussion
Is a gift always an object, or can our actions be a gift, too? Name some gifts that you might share with God.

Scripture Verse

"If you want a happy, good life, keep control of your tongue, and guard your lips from telling lies." I Peter 3:10

Letter Focus

Ii, Kk, Tt

Tip of the Week

There are four lowercase letters (*i*, *j*, *t*, and *x*) that require an extra stroke after the word is written. Pay close attention to these letters as you practice.

Extended Teaching

Remind students that the focus letters *K* and *T* are two-stroke capital letters. The other two-stroke capitals are *H* and *X*.

Encourage students to refer to the alphabet chart when they need to be reminded which capitals connect to the rest of the word.

For Discussion

Everyone knows that lying is wrong. But are there other ways that things we say might cause problems? Explain.

Scripture Verse

"Be full of love for others, following the example of Christ Who loved you." Ephesians 5:2

Letter Focus

Ff, Vv, Xx

Tip of the Week

The bridgestroke family includes the lowercase *b*, *o*, *v*, and *w*. As you write the connecting stroke, don't let your bridge sag!

Extended Teaching

Note that the capital *F* is the only three-stroke capital. Encourage students to practice this letter on the board.

Remind students the *f* is the only lowercase tall letter that's also a tail letter and loop letter.

Show students the differences in formation of the *u* and the *v* — both in beginning strokes and in the connecting strokes.

For Discussion

List some ways you can show your love for your family . . . your friends . . . your neighbors.

Lesson 9

Scripture Verse
"Always be full of joy in the Lord; I say it again, rejoice! . . . Remember that the Lord is coming soon." Philippians 4:4, 5

Letter Focus
Aa, Jj, Rr

Tip of the Week
A train won't work unless it's on the track. Keep your handwriting on track by making sure your letters rest firmly on the line.

Extended Teaching
There are three capital letters that have tails — the *J*, the *Y*, and the *Z*. Have students practice these letters, making sure they touch both the top line and the lower line.

Point out that the lowercase *j* begins with an upstroke — like the *e, i, p, r, s, t, u,* and *w*.

For Discussion
Look up Psalm 118:24. ("This is the day the Lord has made. We will rejoice and be glad in it.") How is it similar to this week's verse? How is it different?

Lesson 10

Scripture Verse
"Most important of all, continue to show deep love for each other, for love makes up for many of your faults." I Peter 4:8

Letter Focus
Mm, Nn, Oo

Tip of the Week
This verse contains most of the overstroke letters (*m, n, v, y*). Think of some words that contain the other overstroke letters (*x* and *z*) and practice them, too!

Extended Teaching
Remind students to leave a letter space between their words as they write.

Practice words that contain overstroke letters are *man, yes, excuse, extra, zip,* and *zone.* Ask students to check these words carefully for correct letter formation.

For Discussion
Why is it so important for Christians to love one another? (Have students read John 13:34, 35. "Love each other just as much as I love you. Your strong love for each other will prove to the world that you are my disciples.")

Scripture Verse
"God has given each of you some special abilities; be sure to use them to help each other."
I Peter 4:10

Letter Focus
Ee, Pp, Ss

Tip of the Week
Just like the capital *C*, the oval capital *E* begins just below the top line. Also, remember that the forward oval capitals *B*, *P*, and *R* begin with a "flagstroke." (Notice the flagpole is leaning a bit!)

Extended Teaching
Encourage students to write numbers with one stroke (except for the number *4*).

Special letter combinations to practice this week are *ch*, *sp*, *ab*, *th*, *lp*, and *al*. Remind students that the connecting stroke in all these combinations needs to touch the baseline.

For Discussion
What special ability, knowledge, or talent has God given you? List some things that all of us can do to be helpful.

Scripture Verse
"The Lord is watching His children, listening to their prayers." I Peter 3:12

Letter Focus
Hh, Ll, Tt

Tip of the Week
The *H*, *T*, and *K* are two-stroke capital letters. There is also one three-stroke capital letter. Can you guess what it is? Here's a hint: It's just like a *T*, but with one stroke more (the letter *F*).

Extended Teaching
Challenge students to write the Evaluation Sentence (page 57) as many times as possible in one minute. Students should work on speed, but without sacrificing legibility.

Suggest that students relax their wrists by doing circle wrist exercises before writing. This will help them write more smoothly.

For Discussion
Having someone watch us can make us feel very good. But sometimes it makes us feel bad. What are some possible reasons for this? (sometimes it depends on why people are watching us — to see how good we are doing, or to criticize our actions)

Scripture Verse
"Be beautiful inside, in your hearts, with the lasting charm of a gentle and quiet spirit which is so precious to God." I Peter 3:4

Letter Focus
Bb, Gg, Qq

Tip of the Week
The lowercase *g* and *q* are very similar. Be sure you know which way the tail goes for each. The *q* is usually found beside its best friend, the *u*. Practice the *qu* combination.

Extended Teaching
Have students practice the tail letters from this week's verse (*f*, *g*, *p*, *q*, and *y*). Remind them that practicing *any* letter in a set of three improves both the letter *and* the connecting stroke.

Remind students that what we're really like on the inside isn't visible in a mirror — but is visible to God. Ask, "What's something you can do today to develop inner beauty?"

For Discussion
Can someone be pretty on the outside, but ugly on the inside? How about the opposite? Explain. (The way we act often shows what we are really like inside.)

Scripture Verse
"You should be like one big happy family, full of sympathy toward each other, loving one another with tender hearts and humble minds." I Peter 3:8

Letter Focus
Oo, Uu, Yy

Tip of the Week
Everyone's name is special. You may be named after a relative, a family friend, or something totally unique! Be proud of your name and write it so anyone can read it.

Extended Teaching
Point out that the capital letters *Y* and *U* both begin with a canestroke. Ask students to identify other canestroke capitals (*K, M, N, V, W,* and *X*).

This would be a good verse to practice in Manuscript. Your students will use printing all their lives, so Manuscript writing is an important skill to maintain.

For Discussion
When someone you care about feels bad, do you feel bad, too? How does this relate to our Scripture Verse this week?

Scripture Verse

"If we are living in the light of God's presence . . . we have wonderful fellowship and joy with each other." I John 1:7

Letter Focus

Ff, Ii, Jj

Tip of the Week

There are two dotted letters this week — the *i* and *j*. Add a small dot (not a circle) after you finish the word. Also, check your lowercase *e*'s to make sure they don't look like *i*'s.

Extended Teaching

Remind students that incorrectly written *e*'s and *i*'s account for many spelling errors.

Point out the ellipsis (. . .) in this verse, and explain that it means some words were left out.

This lesson has a number of tricky bridgestroke *w* connections. Pay close attention to *we*, *wo*, *ous*, and *wi*.

For Discussion

According to this verse, how does our relationship with God affect the way we relate to each other? Explain.

Scripture Verse

"Don't repay evil for evil. Don't snap back at those who say unkind things about you . . . We are to be kind to others, and God will bless us for it." I Peter 3:9

Letter Focus

Aa, Dd, Rr

Tip of the Week

Your lowercase oval letters (*a*, *c*, *d*, *g*, *o*, and *q*) should be round and smooth, not squashed like someone sat on them! To look its best the oval part of each letter should fill the middle space.

Extended Teaching

A few extra *q* words to practice this week are *quick*, *quart*, and *quiz*.

Have students categorize the lowercase letters into loop and non-loop letters. To sharpen their writing skills, have them practice any difficult letters in sets of three.

For Discussion

How should you act when someone is being unkind? What should be our attitude toward those who are mean to us? Hint: see Luke 23:34. ("Father, forgive these people," Jesus said, "for they don't know what they are doing.")

Scripture Verse

"I pray that Christ will be more and more at home in your hearts, living within you as you trust in Him." Ephesians 3:17

Letter Focus

Hh, Ss, Vv

Tip of the Week

Just as you need space between a classmate's desk and your desk, so words need a letter space between them for easier reading. Wordsthataretooclosetogether are much too hard to read!

Extended Teaching

Have students practice the canestroke capitals *H* and *V*.

Point out that the capital *H* is connected to the rest of the letters in the word. Some words to practice are *He*, *Him*, and *His*.

Many New Testament books were written by Paul. Have students check first verses of the Epistles (Romans to Philemon) for clues.

For Discussion

What does it mean to make someone "feel at home?" Describe the kind of heart where Jesus could feel at home.

Scripture Verse

"God is at work within you, helping you want to obey Him, and then helping you do what He wants." Philippians 2:13

Letter Focus

Nn, Pp, Ww

Tip of the Week

Look for the similarities and differences between the lowercase *u - w*; and the *m - n*. Make sure you write these letters clearly and carefully so they can't be mistaken for each other.

Extended Teaching

This week's verse contains several *n*'s and *w*'s. They're almost the reverse of each other. Remind students that the *w* connecting stroke is a bridgestroke.

Helpful letter combinations to practice this week are *wo*, *wi*, *wa*, and *wh*.

Remind students that a sharp pencil makes writing much easier to read.

For Discussion

Where does this verse say the desire to obey comes from? List some ways that we can become closer to God.

Scripture Verse
"May you always be doing those good, kind things which show that you are a child of God, for this will bring much praise and glory to the Lord." Philippians 1:11

Letter Focus
Bb, Gg, Kk

Tip of the Week
Look for similarities and differences between the lowercase *h* and *k*. Like the lowercase *u* - *w* and *m* - *n*, these letters must be written clearly to avoid mistakes in reading.

Extended Teaching
Remind students that tall letters should touch the top line. The letters *b*, *h*, *k*, and *l* contain a similar loop. Good words to practice are *hike*, *bill*, and *bike*.

Remind students that the canestroke capital *K* is made with two strokes. It's a letter that is connected to the rest of the word. A good practice word is *King*.

For Discussion
List some ways we can help our neighbors. How does our kind behavior affect what people think about Christians?

Scripture Verse
"Be gentle and ready to forgive; never hold grudges. Remember, the Lord forgave you, so you must forgive others." Colossians 3:13

Letter Focus
Dd, Ee, Ff

Tip of the Week
Have you looked at the "stars" lately? The **Five Star** evaluation can help you determine areas in your handwriting that need work. Watch your **Alignment, Shape, Size, Slant, and Spacing.**

Extended Teaching
Review the **Five Star** evaluation. Using the board, let students show an exaggerated example of what *not* to do for each of the five areas. This helps students focus on the *true* goals.

This week's verse is similar to the "Golden Rule" (Matthew 7:12). Read Matthew 6:12 aloud, then encourage students to think of someone they need to forgive. Remind them God forgives us as we forgive others.

For Discussion
How can holding a grudge be harmful? Why do you think forgiving each other is important?

Scripture Verse
"Most of all, let love guide your life, for then the whole church will stay together in perfect harmony."
Colossians 3:14

Letter Focus
Cc, L l, Mm

Tip of the Week
Some of us look a lot like our parents. Some capital and lowercase pairs look alike too! The *Cc* is one such pair. Also look at the *Aa*, *Xx*, *Yy*, and *Zz*.

Extended Teaching
Have students identify and practice the similar down stroke in the capital *L* and *D*.

As your students practice the *c*, add the oval letter *o* (same letter family). Remind them that the *o* connecting bridgestroke doesn't touch the baseline. Challenging letter combinations in this verse to practice are *os*, *of*, *ov*, *ou*, *or*, *ol*, and *og*.

For Discussion
If you really love everyone, how might it affect your behavior? List some ways you can let love guide your life.

Scripture Verse
"But the wisdom that comes from heaven is first of all pure and full of quiet gentleness. Then it is peace-loving and courteous." James 3:17

Letter Focus
Ii, Jj, Qq

Tip of the Week
To help you remember the correct strokes, Sky Write the capital letters from this lesson (*I*, *J*, and *Q*), and see if a classmate can tell which one you're writing!

Extended Teaching
Allow students to practice writing the three upswing capitals (*I*, *J*, *Q*) on the board. Large strokes will help imprint the formation of these letters firmly in the brain. It's a challenge to keep the slant consistent.

Suggest that students practice the tail letters (*f*, *g*, *j*, *p*, *q*, *y*, and *z*), remembering that they touch the baseline.

For Discussion
Think of someone who seems "full of quiet gentleness." How do you think they became that kind of person?

Scripture Verse

"Be patient with each other, making allowance for each other's faults because of your love."
Ephesians 4:2

Letter Focus

Kk, Uu, Xx

Tip of the Week

Check your posture. It's amazing how much difference correct posture can make in your handwriting. Also, make sure your paper is going the same direction as your writing arm.

Extended Teaching

Remind students that whether they write with the right or left hand, it's easier to keep a consistent slant when the paper is going the same direction as their writing arm.

Expand students' vocabulary by discussing the several meanings of the word "allowance." 1) To make allowance for, to forgive 2) A sum of money "allowed" or granted for a particular purpose 3) A reduction in price.

For Discussion

Have you ever been impatient with someone, or critical? How can we learn to make allowances for another's weaknesses?

Scripture Verse

"You are members of God's very own family, citizens of God's country, and you belong in God's household with every other Christian."
Ephesians 2:19

Letter Focus

Cc, Yy, Zz

Tip of the Week

The apostrophe *s* on *God's* means we belong to God — we're part of God's family! To care for the rest of the family, share your Scripture Border Sheet with someone new this week.

Extended Teaching

Point out the punctuation in this week's verse (apostrophes, comma, period, and colon). Remind students that a colon is always used between the numbers in a Scripture text to show chapter and verse.

Explore the concept of being a member of "God's family." What does this mean? How should it affect our relationship with others?

For Discussion

Isn't it great to be part of God's family? List some ways you can share God's love with others.

Scripture Verse

"May your roots go down deep into the soil of God's marvelous love; and may you be able to feel and understand . . . how long, how wide, how deep, and how high His love really is."
Ephesians 3:17-19

Letter Focus
Mm, Oo, Ww

Tip of the Week

Make sure your letters are "planted" in the right space. Your tail letters need to touch the bottom line, and your tall letters need to reach the top line.

Extended Teaching

Encourage students to classify all the lowercase alphabet into groups. (See page 234 for letter group names.) Remind students that letters may be in more than one group.

Buy a live plant and show students the root structure. Remind them that as roots expand, they draw in more nourishment. In the same way, as our understanding of God's love expands it helps us grow spiritually.

For Discussion

What do you think this verse means when it says our "roots" should "go down deep" into God's love? Explain.

Scripture Verse

"May the Lord bring you into an ever deeper understanding of the love of God and of the patience that comes from Christ." II Thessalonians 3:5

Letter Focus
Gg, Rr, Tt

Tip of the Week

Remember, to help you write more rapidly and smoothly, dot your *i*'s and cross your *t*'s *after* you finish the entire word. The same is true for *j*'s and *x*'s, too.

Extended Teaching

Have students identify words with special word endings (*ing*, *s*, *ed*, *er*) in this week's verse.

Encourage students to talk about ways to demonstrate patience. Remind them that patience is not just sitting and waiting — it's cheerfully doing what God has given you to do *today*, while waiting for circumstances to change.

For Discussion

What have you learned about the love of God this year? Why not share your new insights with a friend?

Scripture Verse

"Don't criticize and speak evil about each other, dear brothers. If you do, you will be fighting against God's law of loving one another." James 4:11

Letter Focus

Aa, Dd, Zz

Tip of the Week

Always look for the good in each other. Trade papers with a classmate, then point out each other's best letters and words.

Extended Teaching

Coach students on specific things to look for as they exchange papers this week. Focus on spacing and alignment, or use all five goals of the **Five Star** evaluation.

The contraction don't is found in this verse. Encourage students to practice writing two word combinations and their contractions (do not = don't; can not = can't; would not = wouldn't; etc.)

For Discussion

Compare this verse with Ephesians 4:2. (See Lesson 23.) How are they different? How are they similar?

Scripture Verse

"May God who gives patience, steadiness, and encouragement help you to live in complete harmony with each other — each with the attitude of Christ toward the other." Romans 15:5

Letter Focus

Ee, Ii, Nn

Tip of the Week

This would be a good week to check your writing slant. Draw a line from top to bottom through each letter on Day Two. Are your lines parallel? (One challenging letter is the capital *I*.)

Extended Teaching

Students will benefit from practicing difficult letters in groups of three. (See page 244.)

Review the difference between a dash and a hyphen. (The dash is a horizontal line indicating a pause in speech. A hyphen is used to divide a word into syllables when it doesn't fit on a line.)

For Discussion

What are some ways you can promote harmony with your friends? Your family? Your neighbors? Explain.

Lesson 29

Scripture Verse

"Pray much for others; plead for God's mercy upon them; give thanks for all He is going to do for them." I Timothy 2:1

Letter Focus

Hh, Mm, Pp

Tip of the Week

Many canestroke capitals are connected to the rest of the word. They include the *H* and *M* from this lesson — plus *K*, *N*, *U*, *X*, and *Y*.

Extended Teaching

The *P* is a forward oval letter, as are the letters *B* and *R*. Have students find the letter *P* in both the *B* and *R*.

The verse that follows this week's Scripture (I Timothy 2:2) mentions others we can pray for. Suggest students pray for leaders in your city, your state, and your church.

For Discussion

Make of list of people who might need your prayers. Use it as a reminder as you pray this week.

Lesson 30

Scripture Verse

"If you want to know what God wants you to do, ask Him, and He will gladly tell you, for He is always ready to give a bountiful supply of wisdom to all who ask Him." James 1:5

Letter Focus

Bb, Kk, Ww

Tip of the Week

Your name is the most important word you write. As you write it on your papers in every class, take extra time to write it carefully and clearly.

Extended Teaching

Remind students that tall letters (*b*, *d*, *f*, *h*, *k*, *l*, and *t*) should touch the top line.

Ask students to describe ways we can listen to God (study God's word; listen to others' experiences; feel God's presence in nature; etc.).

For Discussion

List some situations where you might need a bountiful supply of wisdom. How does God help us in times like these?

Scripture Verse
"May God bless you richly and grant you increasing freedom from all anxiety and fear." I Peter 1:2

Letter Focus
Cc, Ff, Xx

Tip of the Week
For something "extra" this week, write the word *extra* several times. This provides good practice making the *x*. Don't forget to cross the *x* after you write the word.

Extended Teaching
Remind students of the four letters (*i*, *j*, *t*, and *x*) that require a second stroke after the word is finished. Some good words to practice containing these letters are *tie*, *ax*, *jet*, and *anxiety*.

Two synonyms (anxiety and fear) are found in this verse. Encourage students to find them. Remind them that God can take negatives and turn them into something wonderful in our life!

For Discussion
How does knowing God help us deal with our fears? What is your greatest fear? Why not ask God to help you with it right now?

Scripture Verse
"See that you go on growing in the Lord, and become strong and vigorous in the truth you were taught. Let your lives overflow with joy and thanksgiving for all He has done." Colossians 2:7

Letter Focus
Ll, Ss, Vv

Tip of the Week
As you write this last verse, remember the **Five Star** challenge (alignment, shape, size, slant and spacing). You've grown in handwriting skills this year. God wants you to keep growing more like Him, too!

Extended Teaching
Have students write the complete Cursive alphabet (capital and lowercase), then sign and date the paper. Compare this sheet with the one from the beginning of the year to help you evaluate individual progress.

Hold a mini-conference with each student to review their handwriting. Focus on positive areas of improvement, and review experiences they've had sharing Scripture Border Sheets.

For Discussion
Choose two character traits we've discussed this year that you'd like to improve this summer. Don't forget to ask God to help you!

Scope & Sequence - Level C

Skills/letters emphasized in Student Worktext C are found in the following lessons.

Practice Letters

A
Capital: 2, 9, 16, 27
Lowercase: 2, 9, 16, 27

B
Capital: 5, 6, 11, 13, 19, 30
Lowercase: 3, 4, 6, 8, 13, 19, 30

C
Capital: 6, 11, 21, 24, 31
Lowercase: 6, 16, 21, 24, 31

D
Capital: 1, 16, 20, 27
Lower case: 1, 3, 4, 16, 20, 27

E
Capital: 2, 11, 20, 28
Lowercase: 2, 4, 11, 20, 28

F
Capital: 5, 8, 12, 15, 20, 31
Lowercase: 3, 8, 15, 20, 31

G
Capital: 5, 13, 19, 26
Lowercase: 5, 13, 16, 19, 26

H
Capital: 6, 12, 17, 29,
Lowercase: 3, 6, 12, 17, 19, 29

I
Capital: 5, 7, 15, 22, 28
Lowercase: 7, 15, 22, 26, 28

J
Capital: 2, 9, 15, 22
Lowercase: 2, 7, 9, 15, 22

K
Capital: 7, 12, 19, 23, 29, 30
Lowercase: 3, 4, 7, 19, 23, 30

L
Capital: 4, 12, 21, 32
Lowercase: 3, 4, 12, 21, 32

M
Capital: 10, 21, 25, 29
Lowercase: 10, 18, 21, 25, 29

N
Capital: 10, 18, 28, 29
Lowercase: 10, 18, 28

O
Capital: 1, 10, 14, 25
Lowercase: 1, 8, 10, 14, 25

P
Capital: 4, 11, 18, 29,
Lowercase: 4, 11, 18, 29

Q
Capital: 13, 22
Lowercase: 13, 16, 22

R
Capital: 3, 9, 11, 16, 26
Lowercase: 3, 9, 16, 26

S
Capital: 5, 11, 17, 32
Lowercase: 5, 11, 17, 32

T
Capital: 3, 5, 7, 12, 26
Lowercase: 3, 4, 7, 12, 26

U
Capital: 3, 14, 23, 29
Lowercase: 3, 14, 18, 23

V
Capital: 5, 8, 17, 32
Lowercase: 5, 8, 10, 17, 32

W
Capital: 4, 18, 25, 30
Lowercase: 4, 8, 18, 25, 30

X
Capital: 8, 21, 23, 29, 31
Lowercase: 7, 8, 10, 23, 31

Y
Capital: 1, 14, 21, 24, 29
Lowercase: 1, 10, 14, 21, 24

Z
Capital: 21, 24, 27
Lowercase: 10, 21, 24, 27

Cursive Terms

CAPITAL GROUPS
Boatstroke (B, F, G, I, S, T)
Canestroke (H, K, M, N, U, V, W, X, Y, Z)
Downstroke (D, L)
Forward oval (B, P, R)
Oval (A, C, E, O)
Tail (J, Y, Z)
Two/Three stroke (F, H, K, T, X)
Upswing (I, J, K)

LOWERCASE GROUPS
Bridgestroke (b, o, v, w)
Loop (b, e, f, h, k, l)
Oval (a, c, d, g, o, p, q)
Overstroke (m, n, v, x, y, z)
Tail (f, g, j, p, q, y, z)
Tall (b, d, f, h, k, l, t)
Two-stroke (i, j, t, x)
Upstroke (i, j, p, r, s, t, u, w)

General Skills

IN EVERY VERSE
Letter formation
Connecting strokes
Number formation
Sentence structure
Punctuation
Capitalization

LETTER PRACTICE
Capital Letters
Boatstroke: 5
Canestroke: 4, 14, 17, 19
Downstroke: 21
Forward oval: 11, 29
Oval: 2, 11
Tail: 9
Two-stroke: 7, 12, 19
Upswing: 22

Lowercase Letters
Bridgestroke: 8, 18, 21
Loop: 4, 19
Oval: 16, 21
Overstroke: 10
Tail: 8, 13, 22
Tall: 3, 6, 19, 30
Two-stroke: 7, 15, 26, 31
Upstroke: 9

FIVE STAR SKILLS
Letter alignment: 9, 27
Letter shape: 8, 22
Letter size: 3, 16, 22, 25, 30
Letter slant: 11, 22, 28
Letter spacing: 10, 17, 27

MECHANICS
Paper position: 23
Pencil position: 6, 12
Posture: 23

OTHER PRACTICE
Connected capitals: 2, 7, 17, 19, 29
Connecting stroke: 13, 28
Loop/Non-loop: 2, 4, 15, 17
Manuscript review: 14
Name focus: 14, 30
Peer evaluation: 1, 20, 32
Similar cap/lowercase: 21

Vocabulary List

This list is composed of all the practice words from Lessons 1-32 in student Worktext C.

Aa
abilities
about
again
against
ago
all
allowance
always
and
another
anxiety
are
as
ask
at
attitude

Bb
back
be
beautiful
because
become
belong
bountiful
bring
brothers

Cc
charm
child
children
chose
Christ
Christian
church
citizens
Colossians
comes
coming
complete
continue
control
country
criticize

Dd
dear
deep

deeper
delights
do
doing
done
don't
down

Ee
each
earnest
encouragement
Ephesians
even
ever
everything
evil
example
exception
exciting
extra

Ff
family
Father
faults
fear
fellowship
first
following
for
forgave
forgive
freedom
friends
from
full

Gg
gentle
gentleness
gifts
gives
given
glad
gladly
glory
God
God's

good
grant
great
growing
grudges
guard

Hh
happens
happy
harmony
have
he
hearts
heaven
help
helping
high
his
hold
home
household
how
humble

Ii
if
important
in
increasing
inside
into

Jj
James
Jesus
John
joy

Kk
keep
kind
know

Ll
lasting
law
let
lies
life

light
lips
listening
live
lives
living
long
Lord
love
loved
loving

Mm
make
makes
making
many
marvelous
may
members
mercy
minds
more
most
much
must

Nn
name
never

Oo
obey
of
one
opportunity
other
others
overflow
own

Pp
patience
patient
peace
perfect
Peter
Philippians
plead
power

praise
pray
prayer
prayers
precious
presence
pure

Qq
quiet

Rr
ready
rejoice
remember
repay
results
richly
righteous
Romans
roots

Ss
say
see
should
show
snap
soil
some
soon
speak
special
spirit
steadiness
strong
supply
sure
sympathy

Tt
tell
telling
tender
thanks
thanksgiving
that
the
their
them

then
Thessalonians
those
to
tongue
toward
trust

Uu
understand
understanding
unkind
upon
us
use

Vv
very
vigorous

Ww
want
wants
watching
we
what
whatever
which
who
whole
wide
wisdom
with
within
wonderful
work
world

Yy
you

GENERAL
LESSONS

To The Teacher

Before beginning the daily lessons, have students review the following:

The mechanics of handwriting
(See **Proper Positioning**, page 10.)
The format of the class
(See **Weekly Lesson Format**, page 56.)
The evaluation process
(See **Tips on Grading**, page 57.)

It's also very important to have students write the alphabet (capital and lowercase letters) on a sheet of paper, then sign his or her name and date it. Use this sheet later to pinpoint areas of special need.

Most importantly, remember that as you acknowledge and reward progress, the learning process is greatly enhanced!

Scripture Verse

"And you must love God with all your heart and soul and mind and strength . . . You must love others as much as yourself." Mark 12:30, 31

Letter Focus

A a, G g, U u

Tip of the Week

A good goal for this year is to improve your handwriting as you share God's Word with others. Check the **Five Star** evaluation (Student Worktext, page 6) to see what areas need improvement.

Extended Teaching

Review the **Five Star** evaluation with your students. Explain the grading procedure, and encourage students to set personal goals within these five areas.

Have your students write the alphabet (capital and lowercase) on a sheet of paper, adding their name and date at the top. File these papers as a starting point for future evaluation.

For Discussion

List some ways you can show your love for others. How does our relationship with God affect how we treat those around us?

Scripture Verse

"I will send you the Comforter — the Holy Spirit, the source of all truth. He will come to you from the Father and will tell you all about Me." John 15:26

Letter Focus

C c, S s, F f

Tip of the Week

Although the lowercase "oval" letters (a, c, d, g, o, and q) are different in many ways, they share a common part. To practice connecting strokes, write these letters in sets of three.

Extended Teaching

Have students practice oval letters in sets of three — either on the board or on practice paper. This exercise will improve their connecting strokes and letter formation.

Remind students that the capital C begins at the one o'clock position and goes counter-clockwise. If you Sky Write these letters, it will help imprint letter formation in the brain.

For Discussion

Jesus shared several things about the role of the Holy Spirit in this verse (comforter, source of all truth, tell about Jesus). See how many you can discover!

Lesson 3

Scripture Verse
"Eternal life is in Him, and this life gives light to all mankind. His life is the light that shines through the darkness — and the darkness can never extinguish it." John 1:4, 5

Letter Focus
Ee, Hh, Kk

Tip of the Week
This year's verses are from books in Scripture that were written by different men. Notice their names as you write each verse. Remember that names, titles, and sentences always begin with capital letters.

Extended Teaching
Discuss the Gospel writers: Matthew, Mark, Luke, and John. All were disciples of Jesus, and each gave a slightly different perspective to some of the same events — just as different reporters would do today.

Point out that the oval capital *E* begins in the same spot as the capital *C*. Students may benefit from verbally describing how to write each of the focus capitals this week.

For Discussion
Darkness is caused by the absence of light. What kind of darkness is this verse talking about? (evil) List some things you can do to "spread the light." (share Scripture, be kind to others, etc.)

Lesson 4

Scripture Verse
"I am the Light of the world. So if you follow me, you won't be stumbling through the darkness, for living light will flood your path." John 8:12

Letter Focus
Ii, Ll, Dd

Tip of the Week
All the lowercase tall letters (*b, d, f, h, k, l,* and *t*) are found in this week's verse. You may wish to practice your connecting strokes by writing these letters in sets of three. Be sure the letters touch the top line!

Extended Teaching
Remind students that although the capital letters *L* and *D* have a similar downstroke, they begin at different positions.

Give students additional opportunities to practice the capital *L*. It's one of the more challenging letters to write with a consistent slant.

Challenge students to write all tall letters precisely so loops are only placed on loop letters.

For Discussion
Continue your discussion of light and darkness from last week. How are these verses similar? (both refer to Jesus as "the light") How are they different? (light gives life vs. light gives direction, etc.)

Lesson 5

Scripture Verse
Jesus told him, "I am the Way — yes, and the Truth and the Life. No one can get to the Father except by means of Me." John 14:6

Letter Focus
Jj, Tt, Xx

Tip of the Week
Since pronouns that refer to Jesus or God are often capitalized in Scripture, there are lots of capitals this week! Make certain the capital letters you write are the correct size.

Extended Teaching
Point out the quotation marks in this week's verse. Remind students that quotation marks are placed around a person's exact words.

Ask students to practice the lowercase overstroke letters *m*, *n*, *v*, *x*, *y*, and *z*. Words for practicing overstroke letters include *my*, *vine*, *zenith*, *man*, *excellent*, and *excavate*.

For Discussion
What are some characteristics of a good father? (kind, loving, protective, etc.) List some ways that God shows his fatherly love for us (not only earthly things, but eternal things as well).

Lesson 6

Scripture Verse
"You believe because you have seen Me. But blessed are those who haven't seen Me and believe anyway." John 20:29

Letter Focus
Yy, Mm, Bb

Tip of the Week
The capital *Y* and *M* are always connected to the rest of the word. The boatstroke capital *B* is not. Can you name all the boatstroke capitals?

Extended Teaching
Have students name as many boatstroke capitals as they can (*B, F, G, I, S,* and *T*). For added practice, challenge them to think of names of people that begin with these letters.

Suggest that students watch for "*b*" bridgestroke combinations this week, such as *ba*, *be*, *bi*, *bl*, *bo*, and *bu*.

For Discussion
Who was Jesus talking to that had seen Him? Who might He be talking about that can't see Him today?

Scripture Verse
"Remember, your Father knows exactly what you need even before you ask Him!" Matthew 6:8

Letter Focus
Rr, Xx, Aa

Tip of the Week
The letter *x* often follows the letter *e*. The word *exact* (and its forms) provides good practice for this combination. Remember to cross the *x* and *t* after you finish writing the word.

Extended Teaching
Draw attention to the connecting strokes in the word "*your*." This is a good word to practice.

As students contemplate the meaning of this verse, remind them that we can present our requests to God in prayer, trusting Him to answer according to our need.

For Discussion
List three things that you really want. Now, list three things that you really need. What is the difference between wants and needs?

Scripture Verse
"Take care to live in Me, and let Me live in you. For a branch can't produce fruit when severed from the vine. Nor can you be fruitful apart from Me." John 15:4

Letter Focus
Ff, Oo, Nn

Tip of the Week
Carefully watch the shape of your *o*'s and *a*'s this week. Also the *e*'s and *i*'s. When they are poorly written, these letters account for many spelling errors.

Extended Teaching
Suggest that students practice the letter combinations *ar* and *or*, making certain the *a* and *o* are closed.

Encourage students to practice the oval capital *O*. Have them start at the one o'clock position and go counter-clockwise, making the letter as oval as possible.

For Discussion
What kind of "fruit" is this verse talking about? (see Galatians 5:22 — love, joy, peace, etc.) How do we stay connected to God? (read scripture, pray, etc.)

Lesson 9

Scripture Verse
"When you obey Me you are living in My love, just as I obey My Father and live in His love." John 15:10

Letter Focus
Vv, Jj, Ww

Tip of the Week
Posture and paper position make a big difference! Keep your feet flat on the floor and your back straight. Lean forward slightly with your paper slanted in the direction of your writing arm.

Extended Teaching
To keep left-handed students from developing the "hooked wrist" habit, encourage them to keep the wrist in line with the elbow fairly close to the body. Also, their writing paper should be going the same direction as the writing arm.

Have students practice the canestroke capitals *V* and *W*, and the bridgestroke letter combinations *ve*, *vi*, *we*, and *wi*.

For Discussion
Why is it important for you to obey your parents? List some things that God asks us to do (love enemies, help poor, obey parents, etc.), then describe how you might obey each one.

Lesson 10

Scripture Verse
"Unless you are honest in small matters, you won't be in large ones. If you cheat even a little, you won't be honest with greater responsibilities." Luke 16:10

Letter Focus
Uu, Ee, Mm

Tip of the Week
This week's lesson contains the lowercase tail letters *f*, *g*, *p*, and *y*. As you write these letters, make sure they touch the bottom line. Which of these tail letters is also a tall letter? (the *f*)

Extended Teaching
All three of this week's capital letters are connected to the rest of the word as it is written. Have students identify which capital letters in the alphabet connect to the rest of the word, and which do not. (See Letter Group Charts, page 234.)

Ask students how they would describe an honest person.

For Discussion
Why is honesty important, even in little things? How does cheating harm the cheater most of all?

Scripture Verse

"Remember, I don't even own a place to lay My head. Foxes have dens to live in, and birds have nests, but I, the Messiah, have no earthly home at all." Luke 9:58

Letter Focus

Rr, Xx, Pp

Tip of the Week

If your hand gets tired from writing, you may be holding your pencil too tightly. Also, to keep your slant consistent, make sure your paper is at the same angle as your writing arm.

Extended Teaching

As a student is writing, you should be able to gently pull the pencil from between his/her fingers. This is a good way to remind students to lighten their grip.

Suggest students practice the capital *R*, *P*, and *B*. All these capitals begin with a forward oval stroke. Also, remind students that the lowercase *r* and *s* need to have sharp points, not rounded ones.

For Discussion

Jesus owned almost nothing, yet He was always sharing. Think about the things you own. What could you share with someone less fortunate?

Scripture Verse

"Don't criticize, and then you won't be criticized. For others will treat you as you treat them." Matthew 7:1, 2

Letter Focus

Zz, Tt, Dd

Tip of the Week

There are two contractions to practice this week. (*Don't* forget the apostrophe or we *won't* be able to read the word!) Also, pay close attention to the formation of the capital and lowercase *z*.

Extended Teaching

Remind students that the capital *Z* fills the total line space and is also a tail letter. Point out that capital letters *Y* and *J* are also capital tail letters.

Have students read Luke 1:5 to discover that Zacharias (practice word on "Day One") was the father of John the Baptist.

For Discussion

Read Luke 6:31 ("Treat others as you want them to treat you."). How is it similar to this week's verse? Describe how you like to be treated. Is this the way you treat others?

Lesson 13

Scripture Verse

"Love your enemies. Do good to those who hate you. Pray for the happiness of those who curse you; implore God's blessing on those who hurt you." Luke 6:27, 28

Letter Focus

L l, P p, G g

Tip of the Week

Do your letters bump around, some above and some below the line? Proper alignment is important for easy reading. As you write, make sure all your letters sit firmly on the line.

Extended Teaching

Why not give your weekly grade based only on alignment this week. Let the students know what you'll be looking for. Letters should be written to "sit" right on the baseline.

Remind students that it's easy to pray for your friends — but this verse tells us to even pray for those who seem to be our enemies, and do nice things for them. Challenge students to try this. They may have more friends than they realize!

For Discussion

Compare this week's verse with the verses we discussed last week. How are they different? How are they similar?

Lesson 14

Scripture Verse

"I am the Good Shepherd and know My own sheep, and they know Me, just as My Father knows Me and I know the Father; and I lay down My life for the sheep." John 10:14, 15

Letter Focus

S s, Y y, O o

Tip of the Week

A shepherd keeps his sheep within certain boundaries. Your letters need to stay within a certain space too! This week make sure all of your letters touch the lines and fill the space.

Extended Teaching

Have students practice writing numbers on the board this week. Efficient writing calls for numbers to start at the top and be written with one stroke. (The number *4* is the exception).

Point out that the capital *Y* is a tail capital, as is the *J* and the *Z*.

Students will benefit from occasionally practicing their verse in Manuscript.

For Discussion

Why will sheep follow their shepherd, but not someone else? (they know him) List some ways we can learn to know God better (read Scripture, associate with other Christians, etc.).

Lesson 15

Scripture Verse
"So it is with prayer — keep on asking and you will keep on getting; keep on looking and you will keep on finding; knock and the door will be opened." Luke 11:9

Letter Focus
Nn, Kk, Ii

Tip of the Week
How are you writing your name? Is it larger or smaller than the rest of your writing? This week, focus on making it the same size as the rest of your handwriting practice.

Extended Teaching
Point out the difference between the capital and lowercase *k*. The capital *K* begins with a canestroke and is a two-stroke letter. The lower case *k* is written with an upstroke loop before the "half-a-bow knot" stroke.

For Discussion
The more time you spend talking to God, the more "treasures" you discover! List at least three benefits of regular prayer.

Lesson 16

Scripture Verse
"Anyone who welcomes a little child like this in My name is welcoming Me, and anyone who welcomes Me is welcoming My Father who sent Me!" Mark 9:37

Letter Focus
Aa, Cc, Qq

Tip of the Week
The capital *Q* uses the same upstroke as the *L* and *J*. Practice all three to make the slant the same. Also, you'll write the name *Quirinius* this week. See Luke 2:2 to find out who he was. (Quirinius was governor of Syria, and was in charge of taking the census.)

Extended Teaching
Encourage students to practice the capital *Q*, making the slant consistent with the capital *L* and *J*. These letters share a common upswing stroke.

Point out that the lowercase *q* is similar to the *g*, but the tail goes in the opposite direction. The *q* is almost always followed by a *u*. Ask students to write a list of *q* words, using the dictionary if necessary.

For Discussion
How should we treat those younger and smaller than us? List some things you can do to make a young child's life happier (be a friend, play a game, read them a story, etc.).

 Lesson 17

 Lesson 18

Scripture Verse

"For God loved the world so much that He gave His only Son so that anyone who believes in Him shall not perish but have eternal life." John 3:16

Letter Focus

Ff, Oo, Ee

Tip of the Week

This week, pay close attention to your letter spacing. If you write your letters too close together, thentheywillbehardtoread. See what we mean?

Extended Teaching

Remind students to completely close the lowercase *o* to prevent misreading.

Point out that the oval focus letters *Oo* are capital/lowercase look-alikes. Ask students to identify others (*Aa, Cc, Yy, Zz*).

Since this is the most well-known verse in Scripture, encourage students to commit it to memory.

For Discussion

This is the most recognized verse in Scripture . . . but do you really know what it means? Copy it, and insert your name in place of "anyone."

Scripture Verse

"The Lord our God is the one and only God. And you must love Him with all your heart and soul and mind and strength." Mark 12:29, 30

Letter Focus

Tt, Vv, Hh

Tip of the Week

Remember to dot the *i*'s and cross the *t*'s after you finish a word. Two more lowercase letters require a second stroke after the word is written. They are *j* and *x*.

Extended Teaching

Remind students that sometimes increased speed in writing can produce sloppy results. Waiting to dot the *i*'s and *j*'s and cross the *t*'s and *x*'s after writing the whole word is not only more efficient, but is also essential to the flow of writing.

Point out that the lowercase *t* is a tall letter and should touch the top line.

For Discussion

How can you show God you love Him? List several ways your relationship with others reflects your love for God.

Lesson 19

Scripture Verse

"All who listen to My instructions and follow them are wise, like a man who builds his house on solid rock." Matthew 7:24

Letter Focus

Mm, Bb, Rr

Tip of the Week

In Cursive writing your letters should slant slightly — just as if they were blowing in a light wind. But remember, they must all slant the same way and the same amount!

Extended Teaching

Remind students that the capital *M* is a canestroke letter that is connected to the rest of the word. Ask if they know why the word *My* is capitalized in this verse? (It's a pronoun in a quote where Jesus is speaking — and we capitalize pronouns that refer to God and Jesus).

Ask students what letter group *B* and *R* belong to (forward oval). What other letter is in that group? (*P*)

For Discussion

What happens when things don't have good foundations? What is the "solid rock" our lives should be built on?

Lesson 20

Scripture Verse

"Don't always be wishing for what you don't have. For real life and real living are not related to how rich we are." Luke 12:15

Letter Focus

Dd, Ww, Nn

Tip of the Week

The letters *b, o, w*, and *v* all end with a connecting bridgestroke. Without the bridgestroke, the *v* will look like a *u*; the *o* like an *a*; the *b* like a *l*; and the *w* like three *i*'s you forgot to dot!

Extended Teaching

Have students practice bridgestroke *w* combinations: *wa*, *we*, *wh*, and *wi*.

Remind students that this week's verse shows that "real life" is not tied to how rich we are. Have students list some of the things that are very important to them, but that don't cost any money. (Note: This list is slightly different from the Discussion question.)

For Discussion

Do you need to be rich to be happy? List several things that don't take much money, but are still lots of fun!

 **Lesson 21**

Scripture Verse

"Anyone who takes care of a little child like this is caring for Me! And whoever cares for Me is caring for God who sent Me. Your care for others is the measure of your greatness." Luke 9:48

Letter Focus

Aa, Gg, Cc

Tip of the Week

Strive to be a **Five Star** student this week! (Student Worktext, page 6) What are your strong points?

Extended Teaching

Challenge students to verbalize the goals of the **Five Star** Student: alignment, slant, size, shape, and spacing.

Students need to practice looking for the best in each other. (This is a challenge because we live in a competitive society!) Model this behavior by using comments like, "This word is written right on the line," "Your slant makes your writing so easy to read," etc.

For Discussion

Make a list of some ways you can help younger children. Compare your list with a friend's. How are your lists similar? How are they different?

 **Lesson 22**

Scripture Verse

"Good salt is worthless if it loses its saltiness; it can't season anything. So don't lose your flavor! Live in peace with each other." Mark 9:50

Letter Focus

Pp, Ss, Ll

Tip of the Week

This week, make sure your *r*'s and *s*'s are distinctive. The strokes should be pointed, not rounded. When writing the *th*, remember that both letters are tall letters and should be the same height.

Extended Teaching

Ask students to locate a compound word (*anything*), a contraction (*can't, don't*), and several words with unique endings (*worthless, saltiness, loses*) in this week's verse.

Share stories of some "peacemakers" who have made a difference in society, (William Penn, Mother Teresa, Henry Kissinger, Martin Luther King Jr., etc.)

For Discussion

"Don't lose your flavor!" this verse says. What might that mean? How does it relate to "living in peace" with one another?

Lesson 23

Scripture Verse
"If you give, you will get! Your gift will return to you in full and overflowing measure, pressed down, shaken together to make room for more, and running over." Luke 6:38

Letter Focus
Ii, Yy, Uu

Tip of the Week
Look at the word gift. Notice that the *f* has open loops, but the *t* has none. Watch for the lowercase loop letters in this week's lesson.

Extended Teaching
Ask students to identify the letters with loops as they write this week. (upper loop: *b*, *e*, *f*, *h*, *k*, *l*; lower loop/tail letters: *f*, *g*, *j*, *p*, *q*, *y*, *z*). Show students that some letters appear in more than one group. (See Cursive Letter Group, page 234.)

Double letters provide an extra challenge in consistent letter formation. There are four in this verse.

For Discussion
List some ways you can give to those around you. Does giving always involve things? What about your time and energy?

Lesson 24

Scripture Verse
"Look at the birds! They don't worry about what to eat — they don't need to sow or reap or store up food — for your Heavenly Father feeds them. And you are far more valuable to Him than they are." Matthew 6:26

Letter Focus
Rr, Hh, Vv

Tip of the Week
Look for punctuation in this week's verse. An exclamation mark follows a word or words that show strong feeling; a dash indicates a pause. Watch for the period and semicolon, too.

Extended Teaching
Review the fact that while tall letter *h* is a loop letter, the tall letter *t* is a non-loop letter. Students should form them correctly, and make sure both letters touch the top line.

Remind students that God gives us many reasons to use exclamations. Ask them to think of at least three. (God loves me! What a neat day! I'm so blessed!)

For Discussion
What sort of things do you worry about? Can trusting God help you deal with your problems? Explain.

Scripture Verse

"When you are praying, first forgive anyone you are holding a grudge against, so that your Father in heaven will forgive you your sins too."
Mark 11:25

Letter Focus

Gg, Zz, Ff

Tip of the Week

The lowercase *z* begins with the same overstroke as the letters *m*, *n*, *v*, *x*, and *y*. Be sure to spend some time practicing this group of letters.

Extended Teaching

Encourage students to practice overstroke letters in sets of three. The lowercase letters *y* and *z* provide an extra challenge because they're both overstroke *and* tail letters.

Students will benefit from practicing the following tricky letter combinations: *ai*, *an*, *ar*, *at*, *av*, *ay*, *ol*, *oo*, and *or*.

For Discussion

When someone holds a grudge, how does it make them feel inside? If you're upset with someone, what might you do to change the situation?

Scripture Verse

"When you pray, go away by yourself, all alone, and shut the door behind you and pray to your Father secretly, and your Father, who knows your secrets, will reward you." Matthew 6:6

Letter Focus

Ww, Uu, Kk

Tip of the Week

The lowercase tall letters *h* and *k* can easily be mistaken for each other if not written clearly. This week, focus on writing these two important letters carefully.

Extended Teaching

Point out that this week's focus letters (*W*, *U*, *K*) are all canestroke capitals. The *U* and *K* both connect to the rest of the word.

Have students practice letter combinations with *w* and *u* (*wa*, *wi*, *wh*, *ua*, *un*, and *us*) to help reinforce the similarities and differences of these two letters. Remind students to be consistent with the size of letters, and fill space appropriately.

For Discussion

Why is prayer important? Are there different kinds of prayers? Explain.

Lesson 27

Scripture Verse
"The greatest love is shown when a person lays down his life for his friends; and you are My friends if you obey Me." John 15:13, 14

Letter Focus
Tt, Bb, Pp

Tip of the Week
What was the name of the town where Jesus was born? (Bethlehem — see Luke 2:11) You will write that name this week as you practice the capital *B*.

Extended Teaching
Point out that the capital *T* starts at the top line with a downstroke ending in a boatstroke. The *T* is a two-stroke capital letter. Other two-stroke capitals are *H*, *K*, and *X*.

Remind students that when they stick up for a classmate, they show they care. Say, "Don't let others be mistreated. Speak up!"

For Discussion
Jesus gave His life to save us. How does that make you feel? What does He ask us to do to show that we are His friends?

Lesson 28

Scripture Verse
"I have told you all this so that you will have peace of heart and mind. Here on earth you will have many trials and sorrows; but cheer up, for I have overcome the world." John 16:33

Letter Focus
Cc, Ll, Hh

Tip of the Week
Spacing your words and letters properly is as important to readability as is correct letter formation. As you write your words this week, be sure to leave a letter space between them.

Extended Teaching
Illustrate the necessity of proper spacing to your students by writing a morning message — without any spaces!

Ask students to think about the promise in this verse. Encourage students to share this week's Scripture Border Sheet with someone who could benefit from peace.

For Discussion
What kinds of "trials and sorrows" have you had this year? How has your relationship with God helped you through?

Scripture Verse
"No one lights a lamp and hides it! Instead, he puts it on a lampstand to give light to all who enter the room." Luke 11:33

Letter Focus
Nn, Mm, Oo

Tip of the Week
The capitals *M* and *N* are part of a much larger family of canestroke letters. (*H, K, M, N, U, V, W, X, Y,* and *Z*). Take time this week to practice these capital letters.

Extended Teaching
Ask students to discover which canestroke capitals connect to the rest of the word. If students are having trouble with canestroke letters, help them visualize the strokes by forming letters from pipe cleaners or clay.

Point out the differences between the *n* and *m*, focusing on the double and triple overstrokes.

For Discussion
What kind of light is this verse talking about? (a lamp, but also the "light" of God's love) How can you "hide" the light? List some ways to share God's love with others.

Scripture Verse
"A good man's speech reveals the rich treasures within him. An evil-hearted man is filled with venom, and his speech reveals it." Matthew 12:35

Letter Focus
Ss, Ee, Vv

Tip of the Week
Consistent letter size is very important. It helps make your writing readable! Take extra care this week to make sure the size of your letters is consistent.

Extended Teaching
As students focus on the *size* of letters this week, remind them to be aware of the top line, base line, and lower line as they write.

Ask students to define the word venom (poisonous fluid; malice or spite). Discuss how a person could have "venom" coming from his or her mouth.

For Discussion
How does the way you talk about others show what you're like inside? Give some examples. What does *your* speech say about *you*?

Scripture Verse

"I am giving a new commandment to you now — love each other just as much as I love you. Your strong love for each other will prove to the world that you are My disciples." John 13:34, 35

Letter Focus

Jj, Ii, Yy

Tip of the Week

Notice the similarities and differences between the lowercase *i* and *j*. Both are written with an upstroke, and are dotted after the word is written. But the *j* is a tail letter, and the *i* is not.

Extended Teaching

The capital letters *J* and *I* are upswing letters that begin like the capital *Q*. Remind students that these letters require practice to make the slant consistent. Also point out that the capital and lowercase *J* and *Y* are all tail letters.

Ask students what differences others might see in their behavior if they do what this verse suggests.

For Discussion

How does the way we treat each other impact what people think of Christians? List some ways you can show love for your friends.

Scripture Verse

"A good man produces good deeds from a good heart. And an evil man produces evil deeds from his hidden wickedness. Whatever is in the heart overflows into speech." Luke 6:45

Letter Focus

Dd, Qq, Ww

Tip of the Week

Time for a final **Five Star** evaluation. How has your handwriting improved this year? Continue to encourage others with your writing — both with the style *and* the message!

Extended Teaching

Students will benefit from a personal conference evaluating their growth in handwriting. Review samples of their writing using the **Five Star** evaluation to highlight improvement. Continue to be as positive as possible, looking for areas of strength.

Review positive experiences your students have had this year sharing their Scripture Border Sheets. Talk about the joy of helping others.

For Discussion

Choose two character traits we've discussed this year that you would like to improve during the summer. Don't forget to ask God to help you.

Scope & Sequence - Level D

Skills/letters emphasized in Student Worktext D are found in the following lessons.

Practice Letters

A
Capital: 1, 7, 16, 21
Lowercase: 1, 2, 7, 16, 21

B
Capital: 6, 19, 27
Lowercase: 4, 6, 19, 27

C
Capital: 2, 16, 21, 28
Lowercase: 2, 16, 21, 28

D
Capital: 4, 12, 20, 32
Lowercase: 2, 4, 12, 20, 32

E
Capital: 3, 17, 30
Lowercase: 3, 8, 17, 30

F
Capital: 2, 8, 17, 25
Lowercase: 2, 4, 8, 10, 17, 25

G
Capital: 1, 13, 21, 25
Lowercase: 1, 2, 10, 13, 21, 25

H
Capital: 3, 18, 24, 28, 29
Lowercase: 3, 4, 18, 24, 28

I
Capital: 4, 15, 23, 31
Lowercase: 4, 8, 15, 23, 30

J
Capital: 5, 9, 31
Lowercase: 5, 9, 31

K
Capital: 3, 15, 26, 29
Lowercase: 3, 4, 15, 26

L
Capital: 4, 13, 22, 28
Lowercase: 4, 13, 22, 28

M
Capital: 6, 19, 29
Lowercase: 6, 19, 25, 29

N
Capital: 8, 15, 20, 25, 29
Lowercase: 8, 15, 20, 25, 29

O
Capital: 8, 14, 17, 29
Lowercase: 2, 8, 14, 17, 29

P
Capital: 11, 13, 22, 27
Lowercase: 10, 11, 13, 22, 27

Q
Capital: 16, 32
Lowercase: 2, 16, 32

R
Capital: 7, 11, 19, 24
Lowercase: 7, 11, 19, 24

S
Capital: 2, 14, 22, 30
Lowercase: 2, 14, 22, 30

T
Capital: 5, 12, 18, 27
Lowercase: 4, 5, 12, 18, 27

U
Capital: 1, 23, 26, 29
Lowercase: 1, 23, 26

V
Capital: 9, 18, 24, 29, 30
Lowercase: 9, 18, 24, 25, 30

W
Capital: 9, 20, 26, 29
Lowercase: 9, 20, 26, 30

X
Capital: 5, 7, 11, 29
Lowercase: 5, 7, 11, 29

Y
Capital: 6, 14, 23, 29
Lowercase: 6, 10, 14, 23, 25

Z
Capital: 12, 25, 29
Lowercase: 12, 25

Cursive Terms

CAPITAL GROUPS
Boatstroke (B, F, G, I, S, T)
Canestroke (H, K, M, N, U, V, W, X, Y, Z)
Downstroke (D, L)
Forward oval (B, P, R)
Oval (A, C, E, O)
Tail (J, Y, Z)
Two/Three stroke (F, H, K, T, X)
Upswing (I, J, Q)

LOWERCASE GROUPS
Bridgestroke (b, o, v, v)
Loop (b, e, f, h, k, l)
Oval (a, c, d, g, o, p, q)
Overstroke (m, n, v, x, y, z)
Tail (f, g, j, p, q, y, z)
Tall (b, d, f, h, k, l, t)
Two-stroke (i, j, t, x)
Upstroke (i, j, p, r, s, t, u, w)

General Skills

IN EVERY VERSE
Letter formation
Connecting strokes
Number formation
Sentence structure
Punctuation
Capitalization

LETTER PRACTICE

Capital Letters
Boatstroke: 6, 27
Canestroke: 9, 15, 19, 29
Downstroke: 4
Forward oval: 11, 19
Oval: 8, 17
Tail: 12, 14, 31
Two-stroke: 27
Upswing: 16

Lowercase Letters
Bridgestroke: 6, 9, 20
Loop: 15, 23
Oval: 2, 17
Overstroke: 5, 12, 25, 29
Tail: 10, 16, 23
Tall: 4, 16, 22, 26
Two-stroke: 8, 13
Upstroke: 31

FIVE STAR SKILLS
Letter alignment: 13
Letter shape: 8, 11, 22
Letter size: 10, 14, 26, 30
Letter slant: 11, 19, 31
Letter spacing: 14, 17, 28

MECHANICS
Paper position: 9
Pencil position: 11
Posture: 9

OTHER PRACTICE
Connected capitals: 6, 10, 19, 29
Connecting stroke: 2, 4, 7
Loop/Non-loop: 4, 23
Manuscript review: 14
Name focus: 3, 15
Peer evaluation: 21
Self evaluation: 1, 32
Similar cap/lowercase: 17

Vocabulary List

This list is composed of all the practice words from Lessons 1-32 in Student Worktext D.

Aa
against
all
always
am
and
anyone
anything
anyway
apart
are
as
ask
asking
away

Bb
because
before
behind
believe
believes
Bethlehem
birds
blessed
blessing
branch
builds
but

Cc
can
care
cares
caring
cheer
child
citizen
come
comforter
commandment
criticize
criticized

Dd
darkness
deeds
dens
disciples
don't
door
dawn

Ee
earth
earthly
enemies
enter
eternal
even
evil-hearted
exact
exacting
exactly
except
extinguish

Ff
Father
feeds
filled
finding
first
flavor
follow
food
for
forgive
foxes
friends
from
fruit
fruitful

Gg
gave
getting
gift
gives
giving
God
God's
good
greatest
greater
greatness
grudge

Hh
happiness
hate
have
haven't
heart
heaven
Heavenly
here

hidden
Him
His
holding
Holy
home
honest
house
how

Ii
if
implore
in
into
instead
instructions
is

Jj
Jesus
John
just

Kk
keep
knock
know
knows

Ll
lamp
lampstand
large
lay
lays
life
Light
like
listen
little
live
living
looking
loses
love
loved
Luke

Mm
man
mankind
mans
many

matters
Matthew
Mark
me
means
measure
Messiah
mind
much
must
my

Nn
name
nests
never
no
not
nor

Oo
obey
one
only
opened
other
others
our
overcome
overflowing
overflows
own

Pp
path
peace
perish
person
place
pray
prayer
praying
pressed
produce
produces
prove

Qq
Quirinius
quail

Rr
reap
related

remember
return
responsibilities
reveals
reward
rich
rock
room
running

Ss
saltiness
season
secrets
secretly
seen
send
sent
severed
shaken
sheep
shepherd
shines
shown
shut
small
so
solid
son
soul
source
speech
spirit
store
strength
strong
stumbling

Tt
takes
than
the
they
this
through
to
together
told
treat
treasures
trials
truth

Uu
unless

Vv
valuable
venom
vine

Ww
way
welcomes
welcoming
what
whatever
when
who
whoever
wickedness
will
wise
wishing
with
within
won't
world
worry
worthless

Yy
yes
you
your
yourself

Zz
Zacharias

GENERAL LESSONS

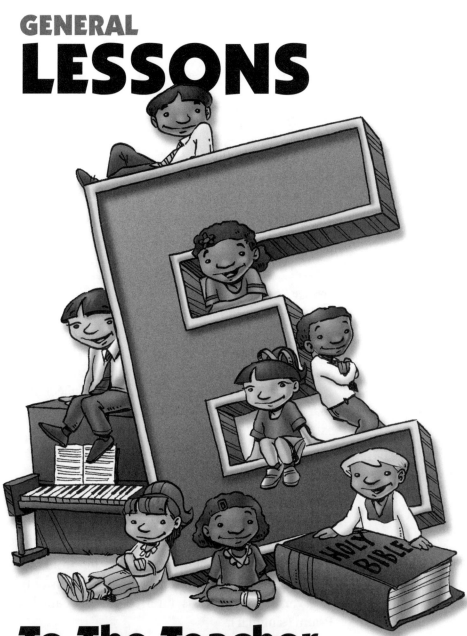

To The Teacher

Before beginning the daily lessons, have students review the following:

 The mechanics of handwriting
 (See **Proper Positioning**, page 10.)
 The format of the class
 (See **Weekly Lesson Format**, page 56.)
 The evaluation process
 (See **Tips on Grading**, page 57.)

It's also very important to have students write the alphabet (capital and lowercase letters) on a sheet of paper, then sign his or her name and date it. Use this sheet later to pinpoint areas of special need.

Most importantly, remember that as you acknowledge and reward progress, the learning process is greatly enhanced!

Scripture Verse
"All day long I'll praise and honor You, Oh God, for all that You have done for me." Psalm 71:8

Letter Focus
Aa, Ii, Gg

Tip of the Week
This year, focus on working carefully through each handwriting lesson. Rushing only creates bad habits! Use the **Five Star** evaluation (Student Worktext, page 6) to help you become a better writer.

Extended Teaching
Review the **Five Star** evaluation with your students (Teacher Guidebook, page 243; Student Worktext, page 6). Explain the grading procedure, and encourage students to set personal goals within these five areas.

Have each student write the alphabet (capital and lowercase) on a sheet of paper, adding their name and date at the top. File these papers as a starting point for future evaluation.

For Discussion
What are some ways you can praise or honor God? (singing, praying, caring for others, etc.) Make a list of some of the blessings that God has given you.

Scripture Verse
"Overlook my youthful sins, Oh, Lord! Look at me instead through eyes of mercy and forgiveness, through eyes of everlasting love and kindness." Psalm 25:6, 7

Letter Focus
Oo, Ll, Vv

Tip of the Week
Make certain your lowercase oval letters (*a, c, d, g, o, p, q*) touch both lines. Also, check the shape of each letter to make sure it's closed — except the *c*, of course!

Extended Teaching
Point out that the letter *o* is a bridgestroke letter. When the connecting stroke dips too far, it makes the *o* look like an *a*!

Remind students that these verses are from the Psalms (which means "songs") — so when only one verse or chapter is referred to, it's called a Psalm (singular).

For Discussion
Give an example of God's love and kindness. What are some ways you can share God's love with others? (answers will vary . . . focus on service and caring)

Scripture Verse
"Create in me a new, clean heart, Oh God, filled with clean thoughts and right desires... make me willing to obey You." Psalm 51:10, 12

Letter Focus
Cc, Dd, Ss

Tip of the Week
Notice how much easier it is to write when you sit up straight with both feet flat on the floor. Also, check to make sure your paper is going the same direction as your writing arm.

Extended Teaching
Remind students that a tight grip not only tires the hand, but makes writing smoothly more difficult. Make positive comments when you see students holding their pencils in a natural, relaxed manner.

Keeping the paper the same direction as the writing arm helps both left and right-handed writers (page 10).

For Discussion
Rewrite this verse in your own words, making it into a personal commitment. Why not share it with God tonight when you pray?

Scripture Verse
"Every morning tell Him, 'Thank You for Your kindness,' and every evening rejoice in all His faithfulness... You have done so much for me... I sing for joy." Psalm 92:2, 4

Letter Focus
Ee, Kk, Yy

Tip of the Week
There are many different kinds of punctuation in this week's Scripture. Watch for the period, ellipses, and quotation marks. What other type of punctuation can you find? (comma, colon)

Extended Teaching
Remind students that every Scripture reference will contain a colon. This separates the numbers so the verse can be found.

Point out that while the capital *E, K,* and *Y* this week connect to the rest of the word, only about half the capitals letters do. Remind students to check the alphabet chart for correct formation.

For Discussion
How much time do you spend talking to your best friend each day? Be sure to take some special time to talk to God each day, too!

Scripture Verse
"I am always thinking of the Lord; and because He is so near, I never need to stumble or to fall. Heart, body, and soul are filled with joy." Psalm 16:8, 9

Letter Focus
Nn, Mm, Ff

Tip of the Week
This Scripture contains the tail letters *f*, *g*, *j*, and *y*. Write them on practice paper (in groups of three) to work on your connecting strokes. Make certain the tails touch the bottom line.

Extended Teaching
Though not found in this verse, the *y*, *q*, and *z* are also tail letters. Encourage students to practice them as part of this letter group.

The boatstroke capital *F* is the only three-stroke capital letter. Remind students that boatstroke capitals are not connected to the rest of the word.

For Discussion
List some ways that "thinking of the Lord" can make a person joyful (answers will vary). How can this affect your attitude when things go wrong? (problems are easier to handle with God's help; we're able to trust things will get better; we have a clearer perspective; etc.)

Scripture Verse
"Just tell me what to do and I will do it, Lord. As long as I live I'll wholeheartedly obey." Psalm 119:33, 34

Letter Focus
Jj, Ii, Qq

Tip of the Week
This week's capital letters (*J*, *I*, and *Q*) all begin with an upswing. It takes practice to write them all with the same slant. Check to see how much better you're doing by the end of the week.

Extended Teaching
Students will benefit from extra practice of the upswing capitals. It's challenging to write them smoothly and with the correct slant. Remind students these letters all begin at the same position.

Point out the similarities of the *i* and *j*. Both are upstroke and two-stroke letters. Remind students that the dot is added after the word is written.

For Discussion
How does showing obedience to God relate to your relationship with your parents? (See Exodus 20:12.) List some ways you can show this kind of obedience (doing chores cheerfully, helping without being asked, etc.).

Scripture Verse
"Be delighted with the Lord. Then He will give you all your heart's desires. Commit everything you do to the Lord. Trust Him to help you do it and He will." Psalm 37:4, 5

Letter Focus
Bb, Tt, Cc

Tip of the Week
Many letters are never delivered because the name and address are unreadable. Don't let it happen to you! Watch the size and shape of your letters as you write this week.

Extended Teaching
Remind students all numbers are written with one stroke, except the number *4*. Also, numbers for Scripture Verses are the same size as capital letters.

Make your handwriting suggestions on the grading form or weekly practice sheet — not the Scripture Border Sheet. This way students can share their verse with others each week.

For Discussion
What does "commit" mean in this Scripture Verse? (give, dedicate, etc.) Look at James 1:5. How is it similar to the last half of this verse. (God can help us if we trust Him.)

Scripture Verse
"Oh my people, trust Him all the time. Pour out your longings before Him, for He can help!" Psalm 62:8

Letter Focus
Pp, Hh, Oo

Tip of the Week
The forward oval capitals *B*, *P*, and *R* all begin the same way. As you practice them this week, watch for their similarities and differences.

Extended Teaching
Due to the unusual connecting stroke on the *p*, your students may benefit from added practice of specific letter combinations. Here are some important combinations for them to practice: *pa*, *pe*, *pr*, *pi*, and *pl*.

Remind students that the capital letters *C* and *H* are connected to the rest of the word. Have them check the letter formation chart to see which letters are connected.

For Discussion
Does God always answer our prayers with "yes?" (No, He doesn't.) What other answers might God give? ("no" or "wait a while") Why? (God has all knowledge and keeps our best interests in mind.) How does "trust" fit into this picture? (We must believe that God knows what is best for us.)

Lesson 9

Scripture Verse
"Your throne is founded on two strong pillars — the one is Justice and the other Righteousness." Psalm 89:14

Letter Focus
Rr, Uu, Jj

Tip of the Week
Work on your writing slant this week. You can check to see if the slant is consistent by drawing a line (top to bottom) through each letter. If your slant is correct, the lines will be parallel.

Extended Teaching
If you notice that a student is having particular difficulty with writing slant, check the position of their writing paper. It's much easier to maintain a consistent slant if the paper is going the same direction as the writing arm.

Remind students that their name is the most important word they write. Stress size and legibility of letters.

For Discussion
Look up the definitions for "justice" and "righteousness." How are they similar? How are they different? (Similar = both mean "moral rightness" Different = justice carries the connotation of fairness and equality; righteousness denotes being guiltless. Students will obviously express these concepts in their own words.)

Lesson 10

Scripture Verse
"My protection and success come from God alone. He is my refuge, a Rock where no enemy can reach me." Psalm 62:7

Letter Focus
Mm, Ee, Aa

Tip of the Week
The canestroke capital letters are *H, K, M, N, U, V, W, X,* and *Y.* Although they all begin the same they are very different. Can you match the letters that are the most similar? (*M, N; U, V;* and *W, H,* and *K*)

Extended Teaching
Challenge students to sort the canestroke letters into smaller, similar groups (*M* and *N; U, V,* and *W; H* and *K*). Because some students benefit from practice of similar letters, the resource section of this Teacher Guidebook includes a Cursive Letter Group Chart (page 234).

Remind students that the *m* and *n* are two overstroke letters that can easily be mistaken for each other.

For Discussion
What does the word "refuge" mean in this verse? (a place of safety) List some ways that God protects us everyday. (answers will vary)

Scripture Verse

"Nothing is perfect except Your words. Oh, how I love them. I think about them all day long. They make me wiser than my enemies, because they are my constant guide." Psalm 119:96-98

Letter Focus

Nn, Xx, Ss

Tip of the Week

For speed and smoothness in writing, remember to cross the *x* or *t* after the word is written (This week's word *except* gives you double practice!) Be sure the *t* touches the top line.

Extended Teaching

Manuscript handwriting is a life skill. In order to help maintain this skill, have students practice the verse once this week in Manuscript. Remind students their Manuscript letters should fill the spaces and be rounded in formation.

The capital *X* is a two-stroke capital. Ask students to identify other two- or three-stroke capitals (*F, H, K, T*).

For Discussion

What kind of wisdom can be found in God's Word? (guiding principles; advice for daily living; eternal truths; etc.) List at least three principles from Scripture that apply to your daily life (honesty, generosity, kindness, loyalty, etc.).

Scripture Verse

"How I praise you! I will bless you as long as I live, lifting up my hands to you in prayer. At last I shall be fully satisfied; I will praise you with great joy." Psalm 63:3-5

Letter Focus

Hh, Rr, Ff

Tip of the Week

If you've ever ridden a skateboard, you know how important it is to stay balanced. This week, make certain your letters are balanced on the lines. This is called "letter alignment."

Extended Teaching

The *h* and *f* are both loop letters. You may wish to have students practice the entire family of lowercase loop letters: *b, e, f, h, k,* and *l*.

Any letter practiced in a group of three will provide connecting stroke practice as well as a review of letter formation.

For Discussion

List several ways that you can praise God (singing, praying, caring for others, etc.). This week's verse says that doing these things can be satisfying. Explain (we feel good when we do good things; love fills our hearts; etc.).

Lesson 13

Scripture Verse
"Keep me far from every wrong; help me, undeserving as I am, to obey Your laws, for I have chosen to do right." Psalm 119:29, 30

Letter Focus
Kk, Ww, Bb

Tip of the Week
The lowercase *b, o, v,* and *w* have a connecting bridgestroke that does not dip to the line. Written correctly, this stroke helps prevent misreading of words. Practice it carefully.

Extended Teaching
Remind students that bridgestroke letter combinations may require extra work to write legibly. Helpful combinations to practice from this verse include: *ob, om, on, ou, ov, ve, vi,* and *wr.*

Look for proper spacing in students' writing and encourage them by commending their progress.

For Discussion
Some of God's laws are similar to the laws where we live. Give some examples. (don't steal; don't kill; etc.) Why is it important to obey laws? (makes a safer, better world, etc.)

Lesson 14

Scripture Verse
"Unless the Lord builds a house, the builders' work is useless. Unless the Lord protects a city, sentries do no good." Psalm 127:1

Letter Focus
Uu, Qq, Ii

Tip of the Week
As you write the word *quality* this week, remember that God wants you to always do your very best. What two letters in the word *quality* always go together? (*q* and *u*)

Extended Teaching
Because the letter *q* isn't used frequently, have students brainstorm *qu* words to practice (*quack, quart, quail, quick, quite,* etc.).

Ask students to guess what a sentry does, based on context clues in the verse. (A sentry is a soldier who stands guard.)

For Discussion
What does this verse mean when it says, "Unless the Lord builds a house, the builders' work is useless?" (Our plans are useless unless they include God.) Does God build houses? Explain. (This question provides an excellent opportunity to discuss analogies and figures of speech.)

Scripture Verse

"Let the sea in all its vastness roar with praise! Let the earth and all those living on it shout, 'Glory to the Lord.'" Psalm 98:7

Letter Focus

Vv, Gg, Oo

Tip of the Week

Remember, good posture makes a difference in the quality of your writing. For the best results, make certain you are sitting up straight, and that your feet are both flat on the floor.

Extended Teaching

This is a great week for students to check their letter size as they write the lowercase oval letters *a, c, d, g,* and *o.*

Have students explain how they think the sea can "roar with praise."

For Discussion

Compare this verse to Proverbs 6:6. What other lessons might we learn from watching nature? (Ants: Hard work usually pays off; Bees: Use your talents to help others; etc.)

Scripture Verse

"Your kindness and love are as vast as the heavens. Your faithfulness is higher than the skies." Psalm 57:10

Letter Focus

Yy, Ee, Kk

Tip of the Week

Y, J, and *Z* are the only capital tail letters. For extra practice, copy them onto practice paper, making sure their tails extend to the bottom line. What do these letters have in common with the *E* and *K*? (All these capital letters are joined to the rest of the word.)

Extended Teaching

Emphasize the *th* combination this week. Point out that both are tall letters, and both touch the top line.

For extra practice of tall letters, the word *faithfulness* is excellent!

For Discussion

God says His love is "as vast as the heavens." How would you describe your love for God? How about your parents? Your friends? Your enemies? (Answers will vary.)

Lesson 17

Scripture Verse
"What a God He is! How perfect in every way! All His promises prove true. He is a shield for everyone who hides behind Him." Psalm 18:30

Letter Focus
Ww, Pp, Nn

Tip of the Week
Pay close attention to your letter spacing. If your letters are too close together, thentheywillbehardtoread. See what we mean?

Extended Teaching
It's helpful for students to occasionally grade their own handwriting using the **Five Star** evaluation form. Encourage them to circle their best letters, and choose one area for improvement.

Have students practice the lowercase tail letters *p* and *q*. Challenge them to find similarities and differences in these letters.

For Discussion
What does this verse mean when it says God is our shield? (various answers relating to God's protection) List some ways that your relationship with God can shield you from evil (focuses the mind on positive things; knowing right from wrong; etc.).

Lesson 18

Scripture Verse
"There I will go to the altar of God my exceeding joy, and praise Him with my harp. Oh God — my God!" Psalm 43:4

Letter Focus
Xx, Zz, Rr

Tip of the Week
This week we have two bonus words. To discover them, look up Psalm 64:9. Here's a hint: This verse should help you realize how amazing God is!

Extended Teaching
Psalms 64:9 says, "Then everyone shall stand in awe and confess the greatness of the miracles of God; at last they will realize what amazing things He does."

Point out that the capital *X* is a two-stroke letter. There are four (*H, K, J,* and *X*). The capital *F* is a three-stroke capital.

For Discussion
There are many ways we can praise God. Make a list of some of your favorites.

Scripture Verse

"Don't be impatient. Wait for the Lord, and He will come and save you! Be brave, stouthearted and courageous. Yes, wait and He will help you." Psalm 27:14

Letter Focus

Dd, Bb, Mm

Tip of the Week

Time to be a **Five Star** student! As you write your letters this week, pay close attention to all five areas.

Extended Teaching

Discuss different ways of sharing Scripture Verses (page 58). Don't let your students miss this opportunity to think of others!

Encourage students to think of opposite words for brave, stouthearted, and courageous (cowardly, fearful, etc.). This comparison activity will help them better understand the meaning of this verse.

For Discussion

The words brave and courageous usually refer to action. Why does this verse use these words for waiting? (waiting is not easy) Why is waiting so hard sometimes? (inaction can be stressful; not sure of what will happen; too much time to worry; etc.)

Scripture Verse

"Let everyone bless God and sing His praises, for He holds our lives in His hands. And He holds our feet to the path." Psalm 66:8, 9

Letter Focus

Ll, Hh, Aa

Tip of the Week

There are lots of lowercase tall letters this week (*b, d, f, h, k, l,* and *t*). Some have loops, and some do not. Make certain you practice them correctly, and that all tall letters touch the top line.

Extended Teaching

Point out that tall letters are the same height as capital letters. Also, remind students that not all tall letters are loop letters.

Remember to look for each student's best work. Make positive comments like, "good posture," "good letter size," "your handwriting is really improving," etc.

For Discussion

What do you think the word "path" means in this verse? (the correct course for our lives) List some ways that a relationship with God keeps us on this path. (Answers will vary.)

Scripture Verse

"God's laws are pure, eternal, just. They are more desirable than gold. They are sweeter than honey dripping from a honeycomb." Psalm 19:9, 10

Letter Focus

Gg, Jj, Tt

Tip of the Week

Focus on the dotted letters *j* and *i* this week. Think of five words that contain either *j* or *i* and write them on practice paper (*joy*, *reject*, *mine*, *pride*, etc.). Remember to dot these letters after you finish the word.

Extended Teaching

Students may benefit from practicing words that contain both the *j* and *i* (*rejoice*, *join*, and *justify*).

Honeycomb is available at many grocery stores. Students will enjoy seeing the interior shape of the honeycomb, or even a taste of this ancient delicacy.

For Discussion

How does your relationship with God affect how you relate to His laws? (If we love God, we will obey Him — see John 14:15.) How can a law be "sweet?" (It's fun to do something that pleases someone we love.)

Scripture Verse

"Show me the path where I should go, Oh Lord; point out the right road for me to walk. Lead me; teach me; for You are the God Who gives me salvation. I have no hope except in You." Psalm 25:4, 5

Letter Focus

Ss, Vv, Xx

Tip of the Week

When you drive a car, you must keep all four tires on the road. When you write a word, you must keep all the letters on the line. Pay close attention to letter alignment this week.

Extended Teaching

Have students practice this week's focus letters in groups of three. Each of these letters presents a unique challenge: *s* = upstroke; *v* = bridgestroke; *x* = two-stroke letter. This activity helps students improve their connecting strokes and refine their letter formation.

This would be a good week to reinforce Manuscript writing practice. (See "Extended Teaching," Lesson 11.)

For Discussion

Scripture and nature are sometimes referred to as "God's two books." How does God use these things to teach us? Give some examples. (Answers will vary.)

Scripture Verse

"Quick, Lord, answer me — for I have prayed. Listen when I cry to You for help!" Psalm 141:1

Letter Focus

Qq, Yy, Ll

Tip of the Week

This week, each capital letter begins with a different stroke. Imagine someone who has never written before. How would you tell them how to write each of these capital letters?

Extended Teaching

Draw students' attention to the starting stroke of the focus capitals (the upswing *Q*; downstroke *L*; and the canestroke *Y*).

Students will benefit from identifying other capitals in the capital groups (page 235).

For Discussion

Describe an answer to prayer that happened to you or someone you know. What kind of other answers might God use? (Answers will vary — see also Lesson 8.)

Scripture Verse

"Those who trust in the Lord are steady as Mount Zion, unmoved by any circumstance."
Psalm 125:1

Letter Focus

Zz, Uu, Mm

Tip of the Week

If you have trouble holding your hand steady as you write, you may be holding your pencil too tightly. Focus on the *un* and *um* combinations this week, as well as the lowercase overstroke letters.

Extended Teaching

The overstroke letter group includes the letters *m*, *n*, *v*, *w*, *x*, *y*, and *z*. Remind students that the capital *Z* is the only overstroke capital. It's also a tail capital — as is the *J* and *Y*.

As you stress similarities and differences of letters, it serves to establish visual brain imaging. If students can't see the formation in their minds, they will have trouble writing it.

For Discussion

List some unexpected circumstances you (or someone you know) has had to face. How can trusting God help us in such situations? (The more we trust God, the easier it is to deal with uncertainty since we know God is in control.)

Scripture Verse

"Friendship with God is reserved for those who reverence Him. With them alone He shares the secrets of His promises." Psalm 25:14

Letter Focus

Ff, Ww, Cc

Tip of the Week

As you practice the boatstroke capital *F*, think of other capital letters that end with this same stroke. Also, notice that boatstroke capitals never connect to the rest of the word.

Extended Teaching

Ask students to tell how boatstroke letters might have gotten that name. Change a capital *L* into a simple rowboat and sail shape to illustrate.

Ask students to explain how the words friendship, reserved, and reverence are tied together in this Scripture. Is friendship a reward or an undeserved benefit?

For Discussion

Why would God reserve his "secrets" for those who reverence Him? (They are the ones who are close and listening to Him.) List some ways that we can show reverence for God (reading Scripture; prayer; being kind to others; etc.).

Scripture Verse

"Trust in the Lord instead. Be kind and good to others; then you will live safely here in the land and prosper, feeding in safety." Psalm 37:3

Letter Focus

Tt, Nn, Rr

Tip of the Week

There are a couple of tricky combinations this week. Remember that the lowercase *r* and *s* are not rounded, but are always written with distinct, sharp points.

Extended Teaching

Remind students that there are a large number of upstroke letters: *e, i, j, p, r, s, t, u,* and *w*. But all of these (except the letter *j*) are found in this verse! It provides excellent upstroke practice.

Make a conscious effort this week to make specific positive remarks to students as they're writing. ("good spacing of letters," "good posture," "excellent hand position," etc.)

For Discussion

List several ways you can show kindness to each of the following: your parents, your friends, your classmates, and the elderly. (Answers will vary.)

Scripture Verse

"But as for me, I will sing each morning about Your power and mercy. For You have been my high tower of refuge, a place of safety in the day of my distress." Psalm 59:16

Letter Focus

Bb, Yy, Dd

Tip of the Week

Remember, your name is the most important word you write! Always write it with care. (That way, you will be sure to get credit for all those great papers you're turning in!)

Extended Teaching

While everyone's signature is unique, caution students to use good handwriting guidelines when they write their name. Have them pay special attention to the size and shape of the letters.

Remind students to write the *u*, *w*, *m*, and *n* carefully. They'll quickly discover why each of these letters is a unique challenge!

For Discussion

What does this verse mean when it says God is our "high tower of refuge?" (various answers relating to safety) Look at your list from Lesson 10. What else would you add?

Scripture Verse

"Jehovah Himself is caring for you! He is your defender. He protects you day and night. He keeps you from all evil, and preserves your life." Psalm 121:5-7

Letter Focus

Jj, Ii, Pp

Tip of the Week

As you write your *e*'s and *i*'s this week, notice that one needs a small loop and the other doesn't. These two letters create many spelling errors when they are not written carefully and correctly.

Extended Teaching

Remind students to watch the slant of their letters as they write this week. Slant does not have to be identical to the model, but it should be consistent.

The capital and lowercase *Cc* are look-alikes. Ask students to identify other look-alikes (*Aa, Oo, Xx, Yy*).

For Discussion

Continue the discussion of God's protection from last week.

Scripture Verse

"Come, everyone, and clap for joy! Shout triumphant praises to the Lord! For the Lord, the God above all gods, is awesome beyond words; He is the great King of all the earth." Psalm 47:1, 2

Letter Focus

Cc, Ss, Kk

Tip of the Week

If your hand gets tired from writing, you may be holding your pencil too tightly! Also, to keep your slant consistent, make certain your paper is at the same angle as your writing arm.

Extended Teaching

Point out the five punctuation marks used in this Scripture: exclamation marks, commas, a semicolon, a colon, and a period.

Using the Psalmist David as an example, encourage students to write praise to God in their own words.

For Discussion

How do people react when their team makes a touchdown? (excited, cheering, etc.) In what way does this relate to this week's verse? (Answers will vary.)

Scripture Verse

"Who may stand before the Lord? Only those with pure hands and hearts, who do not practice dishonesty and lying." Psalm 24:3, 4

Letter Focus

Ww, Oo, Ll

Tip of the Week

Watch your lowercase letters this week. Make certain your tall letters touch the top line; your tail letters touch the bottom line; and your oval letters fill the space completely.

Letter size is very important. By this time students should recognize the different letter groups and the placement of each letter. As you mention a letter group, let students point out what letters belong in that group (page 234).

Extended Teaching

Discuss with students how honesty is important in their lives.

For Discussion

What kinds of problems are created by telling lies? (feelings hurt, relationships damaged, etc.) Are there other ways to be dishonest besides lying? Explain (taking advantage of someone; cheating; lying by omission; etc.).

Scripture Verse
"For all God's words are right, and everything He does is worthy of our trust. He loves whatever is just and good; the earth is filled with His tender love." Psalm 33:4, 5

Letter Focus
Ff, Ee, Hh

Tip of the Week
The oval capital letters *C* and *E* start with the same stroke, which begins just below the top line. Can you think of some words describing the characteristics of God that begin with these two letters? (compassionate, caring, eternal, everlasting, etc.)

Extended Teaching
Ask students to carefully study the lowercase *f*, *e*, and *h* — then describe the similarities and differences. (Similarities: all loop, all begin with upstroke, *f* and *h* are tall letters. Differences: size, *f* has tail, etc.).

Remind students that the pronouns that are used for God are capitalized.

For Discussion
To really trust someone you have to get to know them, and they have to be trustworthy. How does that relate to this verse? (We can't really know God unless we take time out for Him. Also, God is infinitely trustworthy. We can depend on Him to keep His promises.)

Scripture Verse
"Teach us to number our days and recognize how few they are; help us to spend them as we should." Psalm 90:12

Letter Focus
Tt, Zz, Dd

Tip of the Week
Time for a final **Five Star** evaluation. Compare your writing from the beginning of the year with this lesson. Remember, with God's help, you can use your writing to make a difference in the world!

Extended Teaching
As you do a final evaluation of each student's progress, be sure to compare their work with the paper you filed at the beginning of the year. (See Lesson 1, "Extended Teaching," part 2, page 184.)

Encourage students to continue applying the lessons they've learned in handwriting this year, and to continue sharing God's Word with those around them!

For Discussion
List some good ways to spend time each day. (Answers will vary — focus on positive, helpful behaviors.) In what way are these different from wasteful activities? How can you apply these ideas this summer? (Answers will vary.)

Scope & Sequence - Level E

Skills/letters emphasized in Student Worktext E are found in the following lessons.

Practice Letters

A
Capital: 1, 10, 20
Lowercase: 1, 2, 10, 15, 20

B
Capital: 7, 8, 13, 19, 27
Lowercase: 7, 13, 19, 20, 27

C
Capital: 3, 7, 25, 29, 31
Lowercase: 2, 3, 7, 25, 29

D
Capital: 3, 19, 27, 32
Lowercase: 2, 3, 19, 20, 27, 32

E
Capital: 4, 10, 16, 31
Lowercase: 4, 10, 16, 28, 31

F
Capital: 5, 12, 18, 25, 31
Lowercase: 5, 12, 20, 25, 31

G
Capital: 1, 15, 21
Lowercase: 1, 2, 5, 15, 21

H
Capital: 8, 10, 12, 18, 20, 31
Lowercase: 8, 12, 20, 31

I
Capital: 1, 6, 14, 28
Lowercase: 1, 6, 14, 21, 28

J
Capital: 6, 9, 16, 21, 28
Lowercase: 5, 6, 9, 21, 26, 28

K
Capital: 4, 10, 13, 16, 18, 29
Lowercase: 4, 13, 16, 20, 29

L
Capital: 2, 20, 23, 30
Lowercase: 2, 20, 23, 30

M
Capital: 5, 10, 19, 24
Lowercase: 5, 10, 19, 24

N
Capital: 5, 10, 11, 17, 26
Lowercase: 5, 11, 17, 24, 26

O
Capital: 2, 8, 15, 30
Lowercase: 2, 8, 13, 15, 30

P
Capital: 8, 17, 28
Lowercase: 5, 8, 17, 28

Q
Capital: 6, 14, 23
Lowercase: 2, 5, 6, 14, 23

R
Capital: 8, 9, 12, 18, 26
Lowercase: 9, 12, 18, 26

S
Capital: 3, 11, 22, 29
Lowercase: 3, 11, 22, 26, 29

T
Capital: 7, 18, 21, 26, 32
Lowercase: 7, 11, 21, 26, 32

U
Capital: 9, 10, 14, 24
Lowercase: 9, 14, 24, 26

V
Capital: 2, 10, 15, 22
Lowercase: 2, 13, 15, 22, 24

W
Capital: 10, 13, 17, 25, 30
Lowercase: 13, 17, 24, 25, 30

X
Capital: 10, 11, 18, 22
Lowercase: 11, 18, 22, 24

Y
Capital: 4, 10, 16, 23, 27
Lowercase: 4, 5, 16, 23, 24, 27

Z
Capital: 16, 18, 24, 32
Lowercase: 5, 18, 24, 32

Cursive Terms

CAPITAL GROUPS
Boatstroke (B, F, G, I, S, T)
Canestroke (H, K, M, N, U, V, W, X, Y, Z)
Downstroke (D, L)
Forward oval (B, P, R)
Oval (A, C, E, O)
Tail (J, Y, Z)
Two/Three stroke (F, H, K, T, X)
Upswing (I, J, Q)

LOWERCASE GROUPS
Bridgestroke (b, o, v, v)
Loop (b, e, f, h, k, l)
Oval (a, c, d, g, o, p, q)
Overstroke (m, n, v, x, y, z)
Tail (f, g, j, p, q, y, z)
Tall (b, d, f, h, k, l, t)
Two-stroke (i, j, t, x)
Upstroke (i, j, p, r, s, t, u, w)

General Skills

IN EVERY VERSE
Letter formation
Connecting strokes
Number formation
Sentence structure
Punctuation
Capitalization

LETTER PRACTICE
Capital Letters
Boatstroke: 25
Canestroke: 10, 23
Forward oval: 8
Oval: 31
Tail: 16, 24
Two-stroke: 5, 11, 18, 25
Upswing: 6, 23

Lowercase Letters
Bridgestrokes: 2, 13, 22
Loop: 12
Oval: 2
Overstroke: 10, 24
Tail: 5, 17
Tall: 16, 20, 30
Two-stroke: 6, 21
Upstroke: 26

FIVE STAR SKILLS
Letter alignment: 12, 22
Letter shape: 2, 7, 26
Letter size: 2, 5, 7, 20, 30
Letter slant: 6, 9, 28
Letter spacing: 13, 17

MECHANICS
Paper position: 3, 9, 29
Pencil position: 3, 24, 29
Posture: 3, 15

OTHER PRACTICE
Beginning point: 23
Combinations:
(qu): 14
(ex): 11
Connected capitals: 4, 8, 16
Context clues: 14
Loop/Non-loop (i, e): 20, 28
Name focus: 9, 27
Peer evaluation: 19
Self evaluation: 1, 17, 32
Similar cap/lowercase: 31

Vocabulary List

This list is composed of all the practice words from Lessons 1-32 in Student Worktext E.

Aa
about
all
alone
altar
always
am
amazing
and
any
are
as
awesome

Bb
be
been
before
behind
beyond
bless
brave
builders
builds
but

Cc
caring
chosen
circumstance
city
clap
clean
come
commit
constant
courageous
create
cry

Dd
day
days
defender
delighted
desirable
desires
dishonesty
distress
done
don't
dripping

Ee
earth
enemies
enemy
eternal
evening
everlasting
every
everything
evil
exceeding
except
eyes

Ff
faithfulness
fall
far
feeding
feet
few
filled
for
forgiveness
founded
friendship
fully

Gg
give
gives
glory
God
God's
gold
great
guide

Hh
hands
harp
have
he
hearts
heart's
heavens
help
here
hides
high
higher

him
himself
his
holds
honeycomb
honor
house
how

Ii
I
I'll
impatient
instead

Jj
Jehovah
joy
joyful
just
justice

Kk
keep
kind
King
kindness

Ll
land
last
laws
lead
let
lifting
listen
live
lives
living
long
longings
Lord
love
lying

Mm
mercy
morning
mount
my

Nn
near
never
new
night
nothing
number

Oo
obey
oh
on
one
only
others
out
overlook

Pp
path
people
perfect
pillars
point
pour
power
practice
praise
praises
Psalm
prayed
prayer
preserves
promises
prosper
protection
protects
prove

Qq
quality
quick
quickly
quietly

Rr
reach
realize
recognize
refuge
rejoice

reserved
reverence
right
righteousness
road
roar
rock

Ss
safely
safety
salvation
satisfied
save
sea
secrets
sentries
shall
shares
should
shout
show
sing
sins
skies
sky
spend
stand
steady
stouthearted
strong
stumble
success
sweeter

Tt
teach
tell
tender
than
thank
that
them
then
there
they
think
thinking
those
thoughts
throne

through
tower
triumphant
true
trust
two

Uu
undeserving
unless
unmoved
useless

Vv
vast
vastness
very

Ww
wait
what
whatever
when
where
who
wholeheartedly
will
willing
wiser
with
words
work
worthy
wrong

Yy
yes
you
your
youthful

Zz
Zion

A Reason for Handwriting

Cursive F Worktext

With Scripture Verses & Outreach

GENERAL
LESSONS

To The Teacher

Before beginning the daily lessons, have students review the following:

The mechanics of handwriting
(See **Proper Positioning**, page 10.)
The format of the class
(See **Weekly Lesson Format**, page 56.)
The evaluation process
(See **Tips on Grading**, page 57.)

It's also very important to have students write the alphabet (capital and lowercase letters) on a sheet of paper, then sign his or her name and date it. Use this sheet later to pinpoint areas of special need.

Most importantly, remember that as you acknowledge and reward progress, the learning process is greatly enhanced!

Scripture Verse

"Love forgets mistakes; nagging about them parts the best of friends. A true friend is always loyal, and a brother is born to help in time of need."
Proverbs 17:9, 17

Letter Focus

A a, U u, N n

Tip of the Week

A good goal for this year is to improve your handwriting as you share God's Word with others. Review the **Five Star** evaluation (Student Worktext, page 6) with your teacher to see how you measure up.

Extended Teaching

Review the **Five Star** evaluation with your students (page 243). Explain your grading procedure and encourage students to set personal goals within these five areas.

File a sample of each student's writing to serve as a starting point for future evaluation. Use either this week's Day Four practice — or have students write the complete alphabet (capital and lowercase). Be sure to date the sample.

For Discussion

"List the characteristics of a good friend." (loyal, trustworthy, supportive, etc.) "What things on this list describe you?" (Answers will vary.) "How could you be a better friend?" (Notice when others are happy or sad, say kind words to others, etc.)

Scripture Verse

"Despise God's Word and find yourself in trouble. Obey it and succeed. The advice of a wise man reflects like water from a mountain spring."
Proverbs 13:13, 14

Letter Focus

D d, G g, W w

Tip of the Week

Make sure your lowercase *e*'s and *i*'s are easily distinguishable. Poorly written, these two letters account for many spelling errors.

Extended Teaching

To enhance understanding of this verse, ask students to define the word "despise" (to scorn, to regard with extreme dislike).

Remind students that some lowercase letters have loops and some do not. Have them compare the loop letters *b, e, f, h, k,* and *l* with the non-loop letters *d, i,* and *t.* This exercise will be especially helpful for visual learners.

For Discussion

"List some ways you can share God's Word with others." (using Scripture as you write letters, sharing Scripture Border Sheets, reading Scripture to elderly friends, etc.) "How can this help you succeed in life?" (make me sensitive to other's needs, teach me lasting principles, etc.)

Scripture Verse

"How does a man become wise? The first step is to trust and reverence the Lord! Only fools refuse to be taught. Listen to your father and mother." Proverbs 1:7, 8

Letter Focus

Hh, Tt, Ll

Tip of the Week

For a car to drive smoothly, its wheels must be in proper alignment. Smooth handwriting requires proper alignment, too. Make sure your letters are on the line, not above or below it.

Extended Teaching

Using the board (or overhead projector), write an exaggerated example of letters above and below the line. This will quickly illustrate correct and incorrect alignment.

Breaking the word *reverence* into parts offers excellent *e* connecting stroke practice: *re • ve • er • en • ce*.

Draw attention to punctuation in this verse.

For Discussion

"How do we learn to trust someone?" (get to know them) "What does trusting God really mean?" (Answers will vary. For Discussion: Point out that bungee-jumping takes a certain kind of trust. Even walking down the street takes a kind of trust! Ask students how trusting in God compares to these.)

Scripture Verse

"The Lord despises every kind of cheating. The character of even a child can be known by the way he acts — whether what he does is pure and right." Proverbs 20:10, 11

Letter Focus

Cc, Ee, Rr

Tip of the Week

Your name is the most important word you write. Write it with care on every paper you turn in. Even though your signature is unique, you should avoid unnecessary tails and frills.

Extended Teaching

For extra name practice, suggest students write their name as if someone was looking for a person who'd inherited a great estate, and who could only be identified by their signature.

Remind students that God's followers have a great inheritance — eternal life! (Fortunately God knows all of us by our hearts, not our handwriting!)

For Discussion

"How do your actions reflect your character?" (kind hearts produce kind deeds) "Give at least two examples." (doing a task without being asked, being honest even when no one is looking, etc.)

Scripture Verse

"Just as a father punishes a son he delights in to make him better, so the Lord corrects you." Proverbs 3:12

Letter Focus

Jj, Mm, Yy

Tip of the Week

The capital letters *J*, *Y*, and *M* fill the whole letter space. Make sure these letters touch the top line, and descend to the lower base line.

Extended Teaching

Show students how the tail letters *j* and *y* extend to the lower line. Then challenge students to identify the other tail letters: *f*, *g*, *p*, *q*, and *z*.

Remind students that the capital letters *J*, *Y*, and *Z* are all connected to the rest of the word.

For Discussion

"Are there bad ways to punish someone?" (critical, mean) "Are there good ways?" (firm, but caring) "Discuss the difference." (Read Hebrews 12:5-8 aloud. Remind students that rules help teach self-control. Use a household rule as an illustration.)

Scripture Verse

"It is an honor for a man to stay out of a fight. Only fools insist on quarreling." Proverbs 20:3

Letter Focus

Ii, Oo, Qq

Tip of the Week

The capitals *I* and *Q* are both upswing letters, just like the capital *J*. As you practice these letters this week, try to use the same slant for each one.

Extended Teaching

Students will benefit from practicing the *I* and *Q*. It will take some practice to write each smoothly.

While the *O* and *Q* have similar shapes, they begin and end at different points on the line. These two letters show the importance of beginning letters at the correct point.

For Discussion

"Is fighting always a physical thing?" (some fights are with words) "List some good techniques for avoiding a fight." (walk away; try to see the other person's point of view; don't be overly sensitive)

Scripture Verse
"For the reverence and fear of God are basic to all wisdom. Knowing God results in every other kind of understanding." Proverbs 9:10

Letter Focus
Ff, Bb, Kk

Tip of the Week
This week, check the size of your letters. Using consistent size will make your letters look great, and your handwriting much easier to read.

Extended Teaching
Encourage students to keep letters a consistent, readable size. This age group has a tendency to begin using smaller letters.

This would be a good verse for students to write in Manuscript (either for practice or on a Scripture Border Sheet). Remind students that Manuscript handwriting is a life skill, and must be maintained.

For Discussion
"What does the word 'fear' mean in this verse?" (respect, awe) "How does knowing God result in deeper understanding?" (God is the source of knowledge. As we understand God better, our understanding of life expands.)

Scripture Verse
"Telling lies about someone is as harmful as hitting him with an axe, or wounding him with a sword, or shooting him with a sharp arrow." Proverbs 25:18

Letter Focus
Tt, Xx, Ss

Tip of the Week
This week's focus letters are the 'boatstroke' capitals *T* and *S*. Boatstroke capitals are not joined to the rest of the word. Can you identify other boatstroke capitals? (*B, F, G, I*)

Extended Teaching
Remind students that the capital *X* is one of four two-stroke capital letters. The others are *H*, *K*, and *T*.

The lowercase *x* is also a two-stroke letter. The words *except*, *excellent*, and *exit* are great *x* practice words because each word contains at least one other letter requiring a second stroke after the word is written.

For Discussion
"How are lies and criticism of others harmful?" (lies can ruin reputations, etc. — see Ephesians 4:25) "What is the opposite approach?" (praise and encouragement — see Ephesians 4:29)

 **Lesson 9**

Scripture Verse

"It is better to get your hands dirty — and eat, than to be too proud to work and starve. Hard work means prosperity. Only a fool idles away his time."
Proverbs 12:9, 11

Letter Focus

Aa, Pp, Vv

Tip of the Week

Bridges connect one bank of the river to the other. "Bridgestrokes" help us connect one part of a word to another. This week's bridgestroke letters are *b, o, v,* and *w*.

Extended Teaching

Extra practice of the bridgestroke letter combinations from this verse (*be, ou, oo, or, wa, wo, ve*) would be beneficial.

Challenge your students to be creative in coloring their Scripture Border Sheets.

For Discussion

"What are some ways people foolishly idle away their time?" (watching TV, playing video games, etc.) "Name some situations where hard work can really pay off." (improved grades, cleaner environment, etc.)

 **Lesson 10**

Scripture Verse

"Take a lesson from the ants, you lazy fellow. Learn from their ways and be wise! They labor hard all summer, gathering food for the winter."
Proverbs 6:6, 8

Letter Focus

Zz, Tt, Ll

Tip of the Week

As you practice the capital and lowercase *z* this week, watch for their similarities and differences. Can you identify other similar letter pairs? (*Aa, Cc, Oo, Uu, Vv, Ww, Xx,* and *Yy*)

Extended Teaching

The lower case *z* is an overstroke letter in a group that includes *m, n, v, y, x,* and *z*. Talking about and emphasizing similarities such as these can be very helpful to both auditory and visual learners.

One book in the Old Testament was written by the prophet Zechariah. Challenge your students to use a Bible Dictionary to discover other names beginning with *Z*.

For Discussion

"What did Solomon mean when he told us to learn from the ants?" (Hard work usually pays off.) "What are some other lessons we can learn from nature?" (Answers will vary. Example: Bees all have special talents   worker, scout, nurse. So do people!)

Scripture Verse
"From a wise mind comes careful and persuasive speech. Kind words are like honey — enjoyable and healthful." Proverbs 16:23, 24

Letter Focus
Ff, Pp, Kk

Tip of the Week
Posture and paper position make a difference. Make sure your feet are flat on the floor, and your back is straight. Lean slightly forward, with your paper slanted in the direction of your writing arm.

Extended Teaching
Point out that *f* and *k* are loop letters. Other loop letters include *b, e, h,* and *l*.

Encourage students to practice correct number formation. Numbers are written with one stroke — with the exception of the number *4*.

For Discussion
"List some ways we can make our words 'like honey'." (appreciation words, praise words, polite words) "Make an extra effort to talk softly and kindly this week." Ask students, "What is the difference between appropriate 'honey-coated' words and 'smooth talking?'" (Clue: motivation)

Scripture Verse
"Your own soul is nourished when you are kind; it is destroyed when you are cruel . . . the good man's reward lasts forever." Proverbs 11:17, 18

Letter Focus
Yy, Nn, Rr

Tip of the Week
Here's a way to check your letter slant: Draw a line through the downstrokes. If your slant is consistent, the lines will be parallel. How does *your* slant measure up? (Although writing slant may vary slightly from student to student, each student's individual slant needs to be consistent.)

Extended Teaching
In addition to the *Y* and *N*, extra practice of the other canestroke capitals (*H, K, M, U, V, W,* and *X*) can be beneficial.

Choose two teams and ask them to write down proper names or towns or people that begin with these canestroke capitals. The Bible Dictionary is a good source for names of places and people.

For Discussion
"Discuss the concept of 'random acts of kindness.' Watch for such opportunities at school this week. Remember, your kind act is a secret! Don't let anyone know!"

Scripture Verse

"A soft answer turns away wrath, but harsh words cause quarrels. Gentle words cause life and health: griping brings discouragement." Proverbs 15:1, 4

Letter Focus

Cc, Gg, Qq

Tip of the Week

This week's verse contains all the lowercase oval letters (*a, c, d, g, o, p,* and *q*). Make sure they are well rounded, and that the oval portion fills the letter space.

Extended Teaching

Point out that the oval capital groups includes the letter *C* as well as *A, E,* and *O*.

While *p* is an oval letter, it does not begin with an oval stroke. The *p* and *q* both have tails, but they are written with a different beginning and ending stroke. By contrast, the *c* is left open.

For Discussion

"Think of a situation where there were critical or harsh words. Now imagine that same scene with positive, kind words. Describe the difference between the two." (Answers will vary.)

Scripture Verse

"Everyone enjoys giving good advice, and how wonderful it is to be able to say the right thing at the right time! The road of the godly leads upward." Proverbs 15:23, 24

Letter Focus

Ee, Jj, Oo

Tip of the Week

How you hold your pencil when you write is very important! If your wrist gets tired, you may be holding your pencil too tightly. Move your wrist in a circular motion to relax your hand.

Extended Teaching

When students grip their pencils too tightly, it not only tires their wrists, but often results in very heavy writing. Watch for students who stop and shake their hand after writing. Encourage a more relaxed grip.

Practice wrist-relaxing exercises. Have students shake their hands from the wrist in a rag doll manner, or have them rotate their wrists in a circular motion.

For Discussion

"Can you think of a story or situation where someone said 'the right thing at the right time?' Describe it." (Answers will vary.)

Scripture Verse

"It is better to be slow-tempered than famous; it is better to have self-control than to control an army." Proverbs 16:32

Letter Focus

Ss, Uu, Vv

Tip of the Week

Putting a hyphen between two words can modify their meaning. Look at this week's hyphenated words. What is the meaning of each separate word? How does the hyphen change the meaning? (slow-tempered, self-control, etc.)

Extended Teaching

Point out the similarities and differences between the lowercase *v*, *u*, and *w*. Remind students that upstroke letters *u* and *w* can easily be misread if not written correctly. Ask students to identify and write the other upstroke letters (*i*, *j*, *p*, *r*, *s*, *t*).

Point out that the capitals *S* and *G* begin with the same upswing stroke.

For Discussion

"List some situations that might give an opportunity to demonstrate self-control." (Possible answers could relate to anger, temptation, personal issues, etc.) "How can we learn to become slow-tempered?" (Think of a good general response ahead of time, ask God to help you control your temper, etc.)

Scripture Verse

"A happy face means a glad heart; a sad face means a breaking heart. When a man is gloomy, everything seems to go wrong; when he is cheerful everything seems right!" Proverbs 15:13, 15

Letter Focus

Ww, Cc, Yy

Tip of the Week

Punctuation often changes the meaning of a sentence. This week's verse contains many types of punctuation. Can you name and correctly use each type? (semicolon, period, comma, exclamation point, colon)

Extended Teaching

Use the following example to expand on the Lesson Tip: "Today is Tuesday. This simple sentence changes greatly with punctuation. Replace the period with a question mark, and it appears that you're not sure what day it is! Replace it with an explanation mark, and then it becomes a special day you've been waiting for — perhaps a birthday! What a difference!"

For Discussion

"What does the phrase 'look on the bright side' mean? How can our outlook affect our attitude?" (We tend to find what we're looking for, if we're negative it can make others respond negatively, etc.)

Scripture Verse
"Timely advice is as lovely as golden apples in a silver basket. Be patient and you will finally win, for a soft tongue can break hard bones."
Proverbs 25:11, 15

Letter Focus
Bb, Pp, Rr

Tip of the Week
The capital *B*, *P*, and *R* all have the same forward oval stroke. Focus on making this common stroke the same as you write each letter.

Extended Teaching
Remind students that boatstroke capitals do not connect to the rest of the word — like the capital *B* in this lesson.

Point out that the letter *P* is used in every lesson this year since the Scripture Verses are all from the book of Proverbs.

For Discussion
Someone once said, "Sometimes when you win, you lose!" Ask the students what they think this might mean. (Example: winning an argument, but losing a friend.)

Scripture Verse
"Don't talk so much. You keep putting your foot in your mouth. Be sensible and turn off the flow . . . The words of fools are a dime a dozen."
Proverbs 10:19, 20

Letter Focus
Dd, Ff, Zz

Tip of the Week
All the lowercase tall letters are contained in this verse. Make sure that these letters all touch the top line. Also, notice that two of these letters are written without loops. (*d* and *t*)

Extended Teaching
In addition to this week's verse, students may benefit from reading other texts about the tongue. See Proverbs 12:18 and James 3:4, 5.

Have students critique their own writing, looking specifically at letter size and how letters fill the space.

For Discussion
"Do others think you talk too much, or not enough? What do your parents and friends think? What are some ways we can regulate our speech?" (Answers will vary — See Ecclesiastes 3:1, 7.)

Scripture Verse

"Telling the truth gives a man great satisfaction, and hard work returns many blessings to him. Truth stands the test of time; lies are soon exposed." Proverbs 12:14, 19

Letter Focus

Tt, Xx, Aa

Tip of the Week

For more efficient writing, remember to dot the *i*'s and cross the *t*'s and *x*'s *after* you've written the entire word. This will make your writing smoother.

Extended Teaching

The focus letter *A* is an oval capital. Other letters to practice in this letter group are *C, E,* and *O*. Ask students how these capitals are alike and different.

A great way to practice connecting strokes is by having students write any lowercase letter in groups of three. (*aaa, xxx,* etc.)

For Discussion

"Can you 'tell the truth' even without speaking? What do your actions say? Give examples." (Kind, gentle actions tell others "the truth" about God's character, etc.)

Scripture Verse

"If you want a long and satisfying life, closely follow My instructions. Never forget to be truthful and kind. Hold these virtues tightly. Write them deep within your heart." Proverbs 3:2, 3

Letter Focus

Nn, Hh, Kk

Tip of the Week

Critique a classmate's paper this week, using the **Five Star** evaluation (letter alignment, shape, size, slant, and spacing). Be sure your critique is kind and constructive.

Extended Teaching

All this week's focus capitals are canestroke letters. Remind students that the cane needs to be leaning slightly!

In this week's verse, the capital letters *M* and *N* connect to the rest of the word; the *I, P,* and *W* do not.

Point out that the lowercase *h* and *k* can be easily confused if not written correctly.

For Discussion

"List some ways you can show kindness to your friends . . . your family . . . your neighbors. How does being kind make you feel inside?" (Answers will vary.)

Lesson 21

Scripture Verse
"It is hard to stop a quarrel once it starts, so don't let it begin. The Lord despises those who say that bad is good, and good is bad." Proverbs 17:14, 15

Letter Focus
Ii, Qq, Oo

Tip of the Week
What two letters almost always go together? (*q* and *u*) As you practice the *qu* combination this week, think of other words that use this combination.

Extended Teaching
Since the capital *Q* is not often used, students may benefit from extra practice of words like: *Quincy*, *Quebec*, *Queens*.

Point out that the same upswing beginning stroke is part of the *I* and *Q*. This verse also contains the lowercase oval letters: *a, c, d, g, o,* and *q*. The shape of these letters determines their readability.

For Discussion
"What are some ways to stop a quarrel from beginning?" (See also Lesson 6.) "In what way can our character help prevent quarrels?" (harder to quarrel with someone who demonstrates gentleness, goodness, patience, etc.)

Lesson 22

Scripture Verse
"A cheerful heart does good like medicine, but a broken spirit makes one sick." Proverbs 17:22

Letter Focus
Ss, Mm, Uu

Tip of the Week
Focus on letter spacing and letter size this week. Consistency in these two skills helps give your handwriting a balanced look, and makes it easier to read.

Extended Teaching
Encourage students to practice this week's verse in Manuscript (printing). Challenge them to print like a computer — consistent letters, spacing, and size.

Students may practice the letter combinations *er, ar, ir,* and *or*. These combinations are challenging due to the loop/non-loop contrast, as well as the points on the letter *r*.

For Discussion
"What are some outward signs of a cheerful heart? A broken spirit? How should we respond when we see these signs in others?" (If you think a friend is depressed or in trouble, don't be afraid to ask for help, etc.)

Scripture Verse

"If you want favor with both God and man, and a reputation for good judgment and common sense, then trust the Lord completely; don't ever trust yourself." Proverbs 3:4, 5

Letter Focus

Ee, Zz, Cc

Tip of the Week

The capital letters *E*, *Z*, and *C* are our focus this week. Think of the name of a person or place that begins with each of these letters. (Esther, Ethiopia, Zarephath, Zeri, Christ, Cyprus, etc.) Just for fun, practice writing these names, as well as others.

Extended Teaching

Remind students that the *z* is an overstroke letter. Other letters to practice from this group are: *m*, *n*, *v*, *x*, and *y*.

Students may enjoy consulting a Bible dictionary to find the names of people and places beginning with the letters *E*, *Z*, and *C*. Note that these three capitals are connected to the rest of the word.

For Discussion

"In order to really trust someone, you have to know them very well. What are some of the ways we can get to know God better?" (Read about God, spend time in prayer, spend time in nature, fellowship with others who know God, etc.)

Scripture Verse

"If you must choose, take a good name rather than great riches; for to be held in loving esteem is better than silver and gold." Proverbs 22:1

Letter Focus

Ll, Rr, Hh

Tip of the Week

This verse contains all the lowercase loop letters. As you write the words, make certain you only place loops where they belong. Also, review your posture and paper position this week.

Extended Teaching

Remind students that their writing paper should be slanted the same direction as their writing arm. (See page 10.)

Encourage students to rewrite the verse of the week in their own words. (Example: "If I had to choose between being rich or having a good reputation, I'd have to admit that a good name is more important.")

For Discussion

"How do our actions affect what others think of us? Does our relationship with God impact our behavior? In what way?" (Answers will vary. For discussion: "What does this phrase mean — Your actions speak louder than your words?")

Scripture Verse
"A mirror reflects a man's face, but what he is really like is shown by the kind of friends he chooses."
Proverbs 27:19

Letter Focus
Bb, Ss, Yy

Tip of the Week
To drive a car properly, you have to keep it between the lines! Handwriting alignment is a lot like that. Take extra care this week to keep your letters and words between the lines.

Extended Teaching
This verse contains several bridgestroke letter combinations. Students will find it beneficial to practice these. They are *bu*, *or*, *os*, *ov*, *ve*, *wh*, and *wn*.

Remind students that the letters *r* and *s* are written with distinctive points.

For Discussion
"Think about your closest friends. What are they really like? How is this similar or different from what you'd like to become?" (Answers will vary.)

Scripture Verse
"Wisdom is a tree of life to those who eat her fruit; happy is the man who keeps on eating it."
Proverbs 3:18

Letter Focus
Pp, Dd, Xx

Tip of the Week
Few verses contain *x* words, yet the *x* is still an important letter to practice! Proverbs 4:8, 9 is similar to this week's verse, so we borrowed an *x* word from it for our practice this week.

Extended Teaching
Ask your students to compare Proverbs 4:8, 9 with this week's verse. It says "If you exalt wisdom, she will exalt you. Hold her fast and she will lead you to great honor."

Remind students that the tail letters *p* and *f* both contain loops that extend to the lower line.

For Discussion
"List some ways we can 'eat' wisdom." (following good advice; applying what we read; looking for ways to improve; etc.) "What is the difference between wisdom and knowledge?" (Knowledge means knowing or being aware of something; collecting facts . . . wisdom implies using those facts wisely; using good judgment.)

Scripture Verse

"Don't be conceited, sure of your own wisdom. Instead, trust and reverence the Lord, and turn your back on evil; when you do that, then you will be given renewed health and vitality."
Proverbs 3:7, 8

Letter Focus

Ii, Nn, Vv

Tip of the Week

The overstroke is easy to identify in letters like *n* and *m*. Watch for other overstroke letters as you practice this week. (The *n*, *m*, *v*, and *y* are in this verse. The *x* and *z* are not.)

Extended Teaching

Ask your students to define the word *vitality* (exuberant physical and mental strength; capacity for survival or endurance; power to live or grow).

Have students rewrite the verse using words from the definition to better understand the verse. (example: ". . . you will be given renewed health and exuberant physical and mental strength.")

For Discussion

"Proverbs 16:18 offers additional insight into this topic. Describe its similarities to this week's verse." (Pride, conceit, and haughtiness are similar traits that detract from a healthy body and mind. For discussion: "When we fall down, the only direction to look is up!")

Scripture Verse

"We can justify our every deed but God looks at our motives. God is more pleased when we are just and fair than when we give Him gifts."
Proverbs 21:2, 3

Letter Focus

Ww, Jj, Mm

Tip of the Week

This verse contains the lowercase tail letters: *f*, *g*, *j*, *p*, and *y*. As you write, make certain that you extend all these letters to the lower line.

Extended Teaching

The words *justify* and *exit* each contain three two-stroke letters. Remind students that the second stroke is added after the word is written.

This week, have your students practice the verse once in Manuscript, and once in Cursive. Remember, Manuscript handwriting is a life skill!

For Discussion

"Can a person do something good for the wrong reasons? (being good just to impress or get a reward) Why do our motives matter, anyway?" (Answers will vary. For discussion: Read I Samuel 16:7 to see what God says about this topic.)

 Lesson 29

Scripture Verse

"Follow My advice . . . always keep it in mind and stick to it. Obey Me and live! Guard My words as your most precious possession." Proverbs 7:1, 2

Letter Focus

Ff, Oo, Uu

Tip of the Week

As you near the end of this year of handwriting, don't forget the importance of good posture! Your posture has a direct impact on the consistency of letter and word slant.

Extended Teaching

Show students the double letters *ee*, *ll*, and *ss* in this verse. Encourage students to keep these letters consistent in slant.

This week's verse also contains several types of punctuation. Review the use and purpose of ellipses (to show words are omitted), as well as the exclamation mark, the semicolon, and the colon.

For Discussion

"Name some specific advice from God that you can put into practice this week." (Honor your father and mother; don't put other gods before me; love your neighbor as yourself; etc. Philippians 4:6, Romans 12:9-11.) "In what way can we guard God's Word?" (Show it respect; take it seriously; protect its reputation by living in harmony with it; etc.)

 Lesson 30

Scripture Verse

"Look straight ahead; don't even turn your head to look. Watch your step. Stick to the path and be safe. Don't sidetrack; pull back your foot from danger." Proverbs 4:25, 27

Letter Focus

Ll, Kk, Aa

Tip of the Week

Poor handwriting can cause some letters to be mistaken for others. This week our focus is on the *h* and *k*. Other letters easily mistaken for each other include *e-i*, *a-o*, *m-n*, and *y-z*.

Extended Teaching

Students needing help with easy-to-mistake letters may practice the following words: *hike, hymn, Bible, share, zephyr,* and *yoke.*

Remind students that the capital *L* is written with a downstroke. Tell them to watch for a similar stroke in the capital *D*. This suggestion is especially helpful for visual learners.

For Discussion

"List some common things that might distract us from looking straight ahead and following God's path." (TV, video games, bad eating habits, poor choice of friends, etc.) "How can we deal with these distractions. Be specific." (Answers will vary.)

Lesson 31

Scripture Verse
"I would have you learn this great fact: that a life of doing right is the wisest life there is. If you live that kind of life, you'll not limp or stumble as you run." Proverbs 4:11, 12

Letter Focus
Ii, Mm, Dd

Tip of the Week
Remember, your name is the most important word you write. It should always be clear and legible. (Someday when you're famous, we want to be able to read your signature!)

Extended Teaching
Show students the signatures at the bottom of the "Declaration of Independence"— especially John Hancock's. (You can find a copy in most encyclopedias or online.) Discuss the historical difference these signatures made.

Have your students write a "statement of purpose." (Example: "I agree to pick up three pieces of trash a day.") Have your students sign this document, then post it.

For Discussion
"List some attributes of right living." (happier, healthier, etc.) "Name at least two good habits that you'd like to develop before next school year." (Answers will vary. Suggest reading I Corinthians 13:4-7.)

Lesson 32

Scripture Verse
"When a man is trying to please God, God makes even his worst enemies to be at peace with him." Proverbs 16:7

Letter Focus
Ww, Gg, Ee

Tip of the Week
This final handwriting lesson is a good time to use the **Five Star** evaluation once more. Compare your writing from the beginning of the year with your writing today. Evaluate your progress. (Show each student his/her handwriting sample you collected at the beginning of the year.)

Extended Teaching
For a final evaluation, have students write the alphabet (capital and lowercase) as a comparison with earlier handwriting samples.

If possible have individual evaluation sessions with each student. Focus on the positive areas of growth in their handwriting this year.

For Discussion
"Choose two character traits we've discussed this year that you'd like to improve this summer. Don't forget to ask God to help you."

Scope & Sequence - Level F

Skills/letters emphasized in Student Worktext F are found in the following lessons.

Practice Letters

A
Capital: 1, 9, 19, 30
Lowercase: 1, 9, 13, 19, 30

B
Capital: 7, 8, 17, 25
Lowercase: 7, 8, 17, 18, 25

C
Capital: 4, 13, 16, 23
Lowercase: 4, 13, 16, 23

D
Capital: 2, 18, 26, 31
Lowercase: 2, 13, 18, 26, 31

E
Capital: 4, 14, 23, 32
Lowercase: 2, 4, 14, 23, 32

F
Capital: 7, 8, 11, 18, 29
Lowercase: 7, 11, 18, 24, 28, 29

G
Capital: 2, 8, 13, 32
Lowercase: 2, 13, 28, 32

H
Capital: 3, 20, 24
Lowercase: 3, 18, 20, 24, 30

I
Capital: 6, 8, 21, 27, 31
Lowercase: 2, 6, 19, 21, 27, 31

J
Capital: 5, 6, 14, 28
Lowercase: 5, 14, 19, 28

K
Capital: 7, 11, 20, 30
Lowercase: 7, 11, 18, 20, 24, 30

L
Capital: 3, 10, 24, 30
Lowercase: 3, 10, 18, 24, 30

M
Capital: 5, 22, 28, 31
Lowercase: 5, 22, 27, 28, 31

N
Capital: 1, 12, 20, 27
Lowercase: 1, 12, 20, 27

O
Capital: 6, 14, 21, 29
Lowercase: 6, 13, 14, 21, 29

P
Capital: 9, 11, 17, 26
Lowercase: 9, 11, 17, 26, 28

Q
Capital: 6, 13, 21
Lowercase: 6, 13, 21

R
Capital: 4, 12, 17, 24
Lowercase: 4, 12, 17, 24

S
Capital: 8, 15, 22, 25
Lowercase: 8, 15, 22, 25

T
Capital: 3, 8, 10, 19
Lowercase: 3, 8, 10, 18, 19

U
Capital: 1, 15, 22, 29
Lowercase: 1, 15, 22, 29

V
Capital: 9, 15, 27
Lowercase: 9, 15, 27

W
Capital: 2, 16, 28, 32
Lowercase: 2, 9, 16, 28, 32

X
Capital: 8, 19, 26
Lowercase: 8, 19, 26, 27

Y
Capital: 5, 12, 16, 25
Lowercase: 5, 12, 16, 25, 27, 28

Z
Capital: 5, 10, 18, 23
Lowercase: 10, 18, 23, 27

Cursive Terms

CAPITAL GROUPS
Boatstroke (B, F, G, I, S, T)
Canestroke (H, K, M, N, U, V, W, X, Y, Z)
Downstroke (D, L)
Forward oval (B, P, R)
Oval (A, C, E, O)
Tail (J, Y, Z)
Two/Three stroke (F, H, K, T, X)
Upswing (I, J, Q)

LOWERCASE GROUPS
Bridgestroke (b, o, v, v)
Loop (b, e, f, h, k, l)
Oval (a, c, d, g, o, p, q)
Overstroke (m, n, v, x, y, z)
Tail (f, g, j, p, q, y, z)
Tall (b, d, f, h, k, l, t)
Two-stroke (i, j, t, x)
Upstroke (i, j, p, r, s, t, u, w)

General Skills

IN EVERY VERSE
Letter formation
Connecting strokes
Number formation
Sentence structure
Punctuation
Capitalization

LETTER PRACTICE
Capital Letters
Boatstroke: 8
Canestroke: 12, 20
Downstroke: 29
Forward oval: 17
Oval: 13, 21
Tail: 5, 10
Upswing: 6:15

Lowercase Letters
Bridgestrokes: 9
Loop: 11, 24
Oval: 13, 21
Overstroke: 10, 23, 27
Tail: 5, 28
Tall: 18, 30
Two-stroke: 8, 19, 26, 28
Upstroke: 15

FIVE STAR SKILLS
Letter alignment: 3, 25
Letter shape: 2, 5, 13, 24, 26
Letter size: 5, 7, 13, 18, 22
Letter slant: 6, 12, 29
Letter spacing: 22

OTHER PRACTICE
Combinations
(qu): 21
(ex): 26
Connected capitals:
(C, E, Z): 23
(M, N): 20
(R): 17
Hyphenated words: 15
Loop/Non-loop
(i, e): 2
Name focus: 4, 31
Peer evaluation: 20
Self evaluation: 1, 18, 32
Similar cap/lowercase: 10

Vocabulary List

This list is composed of all the practice words from Lessons 1-32 in Student Worktext F.

Aa
about
acts
advice
ahead
always
and
answer
ants
apples
are
army
away
axe

Bb
back
bad
basic
basket
be
begin
better
blessings
bones
born
break
breaking
brings
broken
brother
but

Cc
careful
cause
character
cheating
cheerful
child
come
choose
chooses
common
completely
conceited
control
corrects
cruel

Dd
deed
delights
despise
despises

destroyed
dime
dirty
discouragement
does
doing
don't
dozen

Ee
eating
enemies
enjoyable
enjoys
esteem
even
ever
every
everyone
everything
evil
exalt
expose

Ff
face
fact
fair
famous
father
fear
fellow
fight
find
first
flow
follow
fools
foot
for
forever
friend
friends
from
fruit

Gg
gathering
gentle
gifts
given
gives
giving
glad
gloomy

God
godly
God's
gold
good
great
griping
guard

Hh
hands
happy
hard
harmful
harsh
have
health
healthful
heart
held
him
hitting
hold
honor
how

Ii
idles
insist
instructions
is
it

Jj
judgment
just
justify

Kk
keep
keeps
kind
knowing

Ll
lazy
learn
lesson
life
like
limp
listen
live
look
Lord

loving
loyal

Mm
make
man
many
means
medicine
mirror
more
mother
motives
mountain
must

Nn
nagging
need
never
nourished

Oo
obey
once
only
out
own

Pp
path
patient
peace
persuasive
please
pleased
possession
precious
prosperity
Proverbs
pull
punishes
pure
putting

Qq
quarrel
quarreling
quarrels

Rr
rather
really
reflects
renewed

reputation
results
reverence
reward
riches
right
road
run

Ss
safe
satisfaction
satisfying
seems
self
self-control
sense
sensible
sharp
shooting
shown
sick
sidetrack
silver
slow
slow-tempered
soft
son
soul
speech
spirit
spring
starts
starve
stay
step
stop
straight
stumble
succeed
sword

Tt
take
taught
telling
test
than
the
those
tightly
time
tongue
tree
trouble

true
trust
truth
truthful
trying
turn

Uu
upward
understanding

Vv
vitality

Ww
want
watch
water
ways
we
what
when
whether
who
will
winter
wisdom
wisest
with
within
wonderful
word
words
work
worst
would
wounding
wrong

Yy
you
you'll
your

Zz
Zion

Read This First!

This Appendix contains charts, lists, suggested activities, and other tools to enhance the teaching of the **A Reason For Handwriting**® Curriculum.

Please note: Except for the Black Line Masters section (page 237), all material in this Teacher Guidebook is copyright protected and may not be photocopied or duplicated in any form.

APPENDIX

Detailed Descriptions of
Manuscript Letters

The lowercase a starts at the two o'clock position, goes up/around in a circle, then up to the Ceiling and straight down to the Floor. Don't lift your pencil, and make sure the circle touches the Ceiling and Floor.

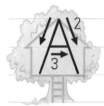

The capital A has three strokes. The first stroke starts at the Roofline and slants down left to the Floor. Return to the starting point and slant down right to the Floor. The third stroke connects the first two at the Ceiling.

The A stands for the Ark and the animals in it. Read the story in your favorite Bible story book, then draw an Ark and some animals. There should be seven of some animals, and two of others. Make sure to leave room for all of them in your picture!

The lowercase b starts at the Roofline and goes straight down to the Floor, then circles up/around right, touching the Ceiling and the Floor. Don't lift your pencil.

The capital B has two strokes. Start at the Roofline and go straight down to the Floor. Lift your pencil. Return to the starting point and go around/down to the Ceiling, then around/down to the Floor.

B begins a very special word: Bible. Write it several times. Notice that this word has both a capital and a lowercase b in it. Just for fun, count how many Bibles there are in your classroom.

The lowercase c begins at the two o'clock position, and circles up/around. It ends at the four o'clock position. Be sure the circle touches the Ceiling and Floor.

The capital C is made exactly like the lowercase c — only bigger! Make sure it touches the Roofline at the top and the Floor at the bottom.

The c begins a word we use a lot: come. "Come here." "Come help me!" Do you know how to ask someone to come without saying a word, just by using your hands? See how many people you can "talk" to without saying a word.

The lowercase d is like an a except the stick goes straight up to the Roofline, then back down to the Floor. Don't lift your pencil, and make sure the circle touches the Ceiling and Floor.

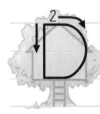

The capital D has two strokes. Start at the Roofline and go straight down to the Floor. Back at the starting point, go out/around and back down to the Floor.

The word dove starts with d. Draw a dove. Keep your eyes open wide today, and maybe you can find a real feather to glue on your drawing!

The lowercase e starts with a straight line in the middle of the meeting room (left to right), then circles up/around and ends at the four o'clock position. Don't lift your pencil, and make sure the circle touches the Ceiling and Floor.

The capital E has three strokes. Start at the Roofline, go straight down to the Floor, then straight right. Return to the starting point and make two short strokes to the right — one at the Roofline, and a shorter one at the Ceiling.

Just for fun, write a lot of e's on a page, then add faces and hair to each one. Do your e's look like a bunch of people talking to each other?

The lowercase f starts in the attic with a canestroke. Circle up/around, then straight down to the Floor. Lift your pencil and make a cross at the Ceiling.

The capital F is like an E without the bottom stroke. Start at the Roofline and go straight down to the Floor. Return to the starting point and make two short strokes to the right — one at the Roofline, and a shorter one at the Ceiling.

The word fruit begins with f. Name some different kinds of fruit you like. Draw a basket. Fill it with different kinds of fruit.

The lowercase g starts at the two o'clock position, goes up/around in a circle, then up to the Ceiling and down to the Ground with a monkey tail to the left. Don't lift your pencil. Make sure the circle touches the Ceiling and Floor.

The capital G is made just like a capital C, but continue the circle up to the Ceiling, then go straight to the left. Don't lift your pencil.

The word go begins with a g. Can you spell it? Write the word several times. Then draw a traffic signal showing a green light.

The lowercase h starts at the Roofline and goes straight down to the Floor, then back up to the Ceiling, circle over, and back down to the Floor.

The capital H has three strokes. The first stroke starts at the Roofline and goes straight down to the Floor. Make the second stroke parallel to the first. The third stroke connects the first two at the Ceiling.

The word heart begins with an h. Draw several hearts in many sizes and colors. Start with a big heart, then draw smaller and smaller ones inside.

The lowercase i starts at the Ceiling and goes straight down to the Floor. Lift your pencil, then place the dot in the middle of the attic.

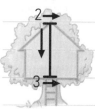

The capital I has three strokes. It begins at the Roofline and goes straight down to the Floor. Finish with a short line from left to right across the top, then across the bottom.

The ibex is a wild goat. Have someone help you find out where the ibex lives and what kind of horns it has. Try looking for it in the dictionary or an encyclopedia. God created lots of unusual animals for us to enjoy!

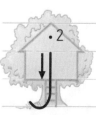

The lowercase j begins at the Ceiling and goes straight down the ladder to the Ground with a monkey tail to the left. Lift your pencil and place the dot in the middle of the attic.

The capital J begins at the Roofline and goes straight down to the middle of the meeting room, curves left touching the Floor, then curves back up to the middle of the meeting room.

The word jump starts with j. Can you jump for joy? See how many times you can jump rope without missing or stopping.

The lowercase k starts with a stroke from the Roofline straight down to the Floor. Lift your pencil. Now start at the Ceiling and slant left/slant right and end at the Floor.

The capital K begins with a stroke from the Roofline to the Floor. The second stroke starts at the Roofline, slants left to touch the first line at the Ceiling, then slants right down to the Floor.

K is for the Kingdom where we all want to live someday. Revelation 21:16-21 describes it. Can you imagine how beautiful it will be? Draw a picture that shows some of the gold and the precious jewels that are there.

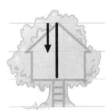

The lowercase l is one of the easiest letters! Begin at the Roofline and go straight down to the Floor. That's it!

The capital L starts at the Roofline and goes down to the Floor. Turn right when you reach the Floor to make a leg for it to stand on. Don't pick up your pencil.

The word light begins with an l. The Scriptures talk about our being lights that cannot be hidden. What are some ways that people can be lights? (Discuss this with students.) Now draw a picture of some kind of light.

The lowercase m begins at the Ceiling, and goes straight down to the Floor, then circles up/around/down, up/around/down. Make sure your humps touch the Ceiling, and don't lift your pencil.

The capital M starts with a stroke from the Roofline straight down to the Floor. Return to the starting point, then angle right down to the Floor, angle right up to Roofline, then straight down to the Floor.

The word Mom begins with an M. Draw a picture for your Mom to thank her for something she's done for you this week.

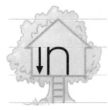

The lowercase n begins with a stroke from the Ceiling straight down to the Floor, then up/around/down, and back to the Floor. Don't lift your pencil.

The capital N starts with a stroke from the Roofline straight down to the Floor. Return to the starting point and angle right down to the Floor, then straight up to the Roofline.

The word nice begins with an n. Why not try to be especially nice today? Do something helpful for someone — but don't tell anyone you did it!

The lowercase o starts at the two o'clock position and circles up/around and back to the start. Be sure it touches the Ceiling and the Floor.

The capital O is exactly like the lowercase o, only bigger! It circles up/around and back to the start. Be sure it touches the Roofline and the Floor.

Open your eyes wide. Do they remind you of o's? Draw your eyes. (You may need to look in a mirror to see what color they are.) Now design a pair of glasses that you might like to wear.

The lowercase p starts with a stroke from the Ceiling straight down to the Ground, then back up and circle around. Don't lift your pencil until you're finished.

The capital P begins with a stroke from the Roofline to the Floor. Return to the starting point and circle around and down to the Ceiling.

The word pet begins with a p. Draw a picture of your pet, or an animal you would like to have for a pet. If your pet is wild, be sure you draw a cage, too!

The lowercase q starts at the two o'clock position, goes up/around in a circle, then up to the Ceiling and down to the Ground with a monkey tail to the right. Don't lift your pencil. Make sure the circle touches the Ceiling and Floor.

The capital Q is made exactly like a capital O, but you add a short slanting line in the bottom right corner. Be sure the circle touches the Roofline and the Floor.

The title Queen begins with the letter Q. Find the story of brave Queen Esther in Scripture. Imagine how beautiful Esther's crown must have been. Draw a crown fit for a queen.

The lowercase r begins with a stroke from the Ceiling to the Floor, then back up and over to the two o'clock position.

The capital R begins with a stroke from the Roofline to the Floor. Return to the starting point, and curve around and down to the Ceiling, then angle right down to the Floor.

The word rainbow begins with an r. See if you can find a Scripture story that talks about a rainbow. Draw a rainbow. Make sure your colors are in the right order. (Primary rainbow colors, from inside to outside, are violet, blue, green, yellow, orange, and red.)

The lowercase letter s is a double curve letter. It begins at the two o'clock position, curves up to the left, then curves to the right in the middle of the meeting room, then back to the left, stopping at the eight o'clock position.

The capital S is just like the lowercase s, only larger! Be sure it touches the Roofline and the Floor!

The word song begins with an s. Sometime today, sing a special song to someone who is really special!

The lowercase t starts with a stroke from the Roofline straight down to the Floor. Lift your pencil, and then make a cross at the Ceiling from left to right.

The capital T starts with a stroke from the Roofline straight down to the Floor. Lift your pencil, then make a cross at the Roofline from left to right.

The word thankful begins with t. There are so many things that we can be thankful for! Draw a picture of at least three things that you are thankful for.

The lowercase u begins at the Ceiling. Go straight down toward the Floor, curve around and back up to the Ceiling, then straight down to end at the Floor.

The capital U is just like the lowercase u, only bigger! Start at the Roofline and go straight down toward the Floor, curve around and back up to the roof, then straight down to end at the Floor.

The word umbrella begins with u. Draw a picture of yourself under an umbrella. Are you staying dry? Then you should be smiling!

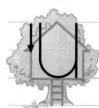

The lowercase v stays inside the meeting room. It starts at the Ceiling and slants down right to the Floor, then slants up right to the Ceiling. Make sure you don't lift your pencil!

The capital V is just like the lowercase v, only bigger! The stroke is just the same except it starts and ends at the Roofline: slant down/slant up. Make sure you don't lift your pencil.

The word vine begins with v. Jesus talks about the vine in one of His parables. Design a vine, making it cover as much of the page as you can. If you wish, you can draw a few birds or bugs hiding in the vine, too!

The lowercase w is made with one long stroke. Starting at the Ceiling, slant down right to the Floor, slant up to the Ceiling, slant down to the Floor, and slant up to the Ceiling.

The capital W is just like the lowercase w, only bigger! Starting at the Roofline, slant down right to the Floor, slant up to the Roofline, slant down to the Floor, and slant up to the Roofline. Don't lift your pencil!

The word worm begins with w. Find out why worms are useful to gardeners. Make a "worm" by wrapping a pipe-cleaner around a pencil, then carefully pulling the pencil free. Tie a string to it, and you have a pet to pull around!

Both strokes in the lowercase x start at the Ceiling and end at the Floor. The first stroke slants down from left to right. The second slants down from right to left.

The capital X is just like the lowercase x, only bigger! Make sure that both strokes go from the Roofline to the Floor, and cross at the Ceiling.

Not many words *begin* with x, but the word exit has an x as the second letter. Draw an exit sign that you could put by the door leading out of the classroom or your room at home.

The first stroke of the y slants right from the Ceiling down to the Floor. The second slants left from the Ceiling down to the Ground — touching the first at the Floor.

Begin the capital Y by making a lowercase v in the attic. Make sure it touches the Roofline and the Ceiling. The second stroke goes from the bottom of the v straight down to the Floor.

A y word that we use often is yes. Practice writing this word, then talk about questions that should have "yes" answers.

The lowercase z is a one-stroke letter starting at Ceiling. Make a line straight right, slant left down to the Floor, then make a line straight right.

The capital Z is just like the lowercase z, only bigger! Use the same zigzag stroke — straight right/slant down/ straight right. Remember it must touch the Roofline and the Floor.

The word zoo begins with a z. Draw a picture of a zoo animal that begins with the letter z. Here's a hint: It's an animal looks like a horse with stripes! (zebra)

Letter Groups

Children often enjoy discovering the similarities and differences between letters — much like sorting buttons by size, color, or shape. This activity helps children form clear mental models of letters and strokes, leading to more accurate letter formation and better handwriting.

As you explore the following groups with your students, be sure to remind them that some letters have multiple characteristics, and so can be included in more than one group. (A good example is the lowercase b.)

CAPITAL GROUPS
Circle (C, G, O, Q)
Curve (J, S, U)
Downstroke (B, D, E, F, H, I, J, K, L, M, N, P, R, T, U)
Forward curve (B, D, P, R)
Single stroke (C, G, J, L, O, S, U, V, W, Z)
Slantstroke (A, K, M, N, V, W, X, Y, Z)
Two-stroke (B, D, K, M, N, P, Q, R, T, X)
Three-stroke (A, E, F, H, I)

LOWERCASE GROUPS
Circle (a, b, c, d, e, g, o, p, q)
Curve (h, m, n, r, s, u)
Downstroke (b, f, h, i, j, k, l, m, n, p, r, t)
Slantstroke (k, v, w, x, y, z)
Tail (g, j, p, q, y)
Tall (b, d, f, h, k, l, t)
Two-stroke (f, i, j, k, t, x, y)

Letter Formation Charts

Manuscript Letter Formation

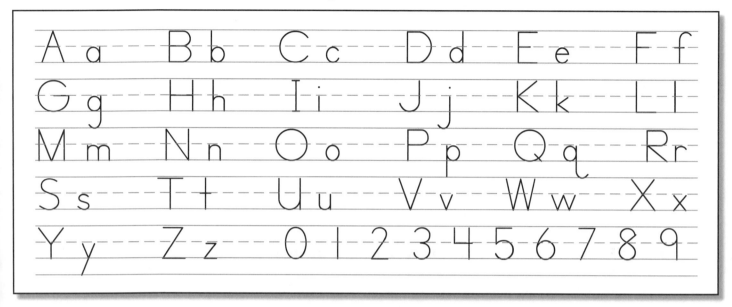

Cursive Letter Formation

How & When to Use the Transition Worktext

Manuscript is a skill needed for a lifetime!

A child learns to read using a Manuscript alphabet. Most all books are published in Manuscript. Computer screens display in Manuscript. Job application forms ask you to print in Manuscript. Traffic direction signs, street signs, and store signs almost always use Manuscript. That's why it is so important for a child to master Manuscript skills. Then, it's time to transition into Cursive.

The Transition Student Worktext is designed to offer maximum flexibility in making the transition from Manuscript to Cursive handwriting. Extra Manuscript Lessons and extra Cursive Lessons allow you to begin the transition process according to individual student readiness!

Please note: No option uses ALL the pages in the Transition Student Worktext!

Pages in the Transition Worktext are perforated so teachers can easily remove unused lessons if desired before the school year begins. Extra pages can be filed for later use in individual remediation.

OPTION 1: Transition to Cursive at the Beginning of 3rd grade.

This is the traditional and researched-based, best method for teaching Handwriting! It allows the maximum time for small motor skills development. Students begin 3rd grade with 9 weeks of special Transition practice, followed by 27 weeks of Cursive writing.

Note: Lesson pages 9-74 are optional—for use with students who may not have had two, full years of Manuscript practice.

1st nine weeks: use pages 77-122	**3rd nine weeks:** use pages 143-160
2nd nine weeks: use pages 125-142	**4th nine weeks:** use pages 161-178

Using this option, the correct curriculum sequencing would be:

1st grade	- Manuscript A Worktext		4th grade	- Cursive D Worktext
2nd grade	- Manuscript B Worktext		5th grade	- Cursive E Worktext
3rd grade	- Transition Worktext		6th grade	- Cursive F Worktext

OPTION 2: Transition at the start of the fourth 9 weeks of 2nd grade.

This method allows for 27 weeks of Manuscript writing, followed by 9 weeks of special Transition practice. Its primary advantage is extra time for small motor skills development.

Note: If extra Manuscript review is needed, begin with the Practice Lessons on page 9 and omit pages 53-56.

> **1st nine weeks:** use pages 21-38   **3rd nine weeks:** use pages 57-74
> **2nd nine weeks:** use pages 39-56   **4th nine weeks:** use pages 77-122
>   Omit pages 123-178

Using this option, the correct curriculum sequencing would be:

1st grade	- Manuscript A Worktext	4th grade	- Cursive D Worktext
2nd grade	- Transition Worktext	5th grade	- Cursive E Worktext
3rd grade	- Cursive C Worktext	6th grade	- Cursive F Worktext

OPTION 3: Transition at the start of the third 9 weeks of 2nd grade.

This method allows for 18 weeks of Manuscript writing, 9 weeks of special Transition practice, and 9 weeks of Cursive practice. For most students, this timing correlates well with the development of small motor skills.

Note: If extra Manuscript review is needed, begin with the Practice Lessons on page 9 and omit pages 53-56.

> **1st nine weeks:** use pages 21-38   **3rd nine weeks:** use pages 77-122
> **2nd nine weeks:** use pages 39-56   **4th nine weeks:** use pages 123-142
>   Omit pages 57-74, 143-178

Using this option, the correct curriculum sequencing would be:

1st grade	- Manuscript A Worktext	4th grade	- Cursive D Worktext
2nd grade	- Transition Worktext	5th grade	- Cursive E Worktext
3rd grade	- Cursive C Worktext	6th grade	- Cursive F Worktext

Cursive Letter Chart

Many letters in Cursive writing use similar patterns in their formation. **Cursive Letter Chart** help focus attention on these similarities, enhancing the understanding of letter formation. These groupings are also helpful for introducing new letters, and for providing direction in continued practice. (Please note that most letters have features that apply to more than one group.)

The following descriptions help identify similar characteristics of LOWERCASE Cursive letters:

Oval Letters

Upstroke Letters

Loop Letters

Tail Letters

Tall Letters

Overstroke Letters

Bridgestroke Letters

Two-Stroke Letters

The following descriptions help identify similar characteristics of CAPITAL Cursive letters:

Oval Capitals

A C E O

Forward Oval Capitals

B P R

Boatstroke Capitals

B F G I S T

Canestroke Capitals

H K M N U V W X Y

Upswing Capitals

I J Q

Tail Capitals

J Y Z

Downstroke Capitals

L D

Two- and Three-Stroke Capitals

F H K T X

Extended Activities

As students become more proficient at Cursive writing, these activities can be used to expand their opportunities for enjoyable and challenging writing practice.

The Rest of the Story

Some students (especially older, more mature ones) may wish to do further research about the Verse of the Week. Challenge them to be "reporters," and to come up with "the rest of the story." Using a Bible Commentary or other religious reference book, students can quickly discover the author of that particular book of Scripture, and often find interesting background information about the specific verse.

Results of student research may be shared in a short speech — or you may wish to have students produce a written report that summarizes their findings.

The Writing Center

Develop a writing center where students can create "special messages." This activity offers yet another creative outlet for students to continually improve their handwriting. Special messages might include:

- Letters to family members
- Special occasion cards
- Thank-you notes
- Pen-pal messages
- Birthday cards
- Greeting cards
- Invitations
- Posters
- Letters to friends

Encourage students to come up with even more ideas for this activity. You can stock the writing center with items like:

- construction paper
- wallpaper sample books
- yarn or thread
- glue
- bright-colored ribbons
- wrapping paper remnants
- old greeting cards
- scissors
- felt-tip pens
- tape

Include suggested messages, inspirational poems, and additional Scripture verses that students can incorporate into their creations.

Integrated Curriculum

Tie handwriting class into other core curricula. Every Student Worktext in **Handwriting** has a corresponding Vocabulary List which can be used as a basis for further practice. Ask students to write a sentence using each word from the list. The words may also be used as bonus spelling words or as the basis for a spelling bee.

Other Suggestions

It's amazing how creative students can be when given the chance! Brainstorm with your class about other extended activities they might enjoy. We'd love to hear your creative ideas. (And, maybe we'll even include them in a future edition of this Teacher Guidebook!) Here's our address:

Concerned Communications, LLC
PO Box 1000
Siloam Springs, AR 72761
www.AReasonFor.com

BLACK LINE MASTERS

PLEASE
PHOTOCOPY!*

The following pages contain Black Line Masters for use with the **A Reason For Handwriting®** curriculum. Please feel free to photocopy these pages.*

Here are some suggested uses:

Getting Ready To Write! (page 239) makes a great mini-poster.

Treehouse Practice Sheet (page 241) allows your students more room for letter formation practice. Feel free to make multiple copies of this page for students who need additional practice. This practice sheet also includes a diagram of the Treehouse, so you may demonstrate and reinforce specific letter placement as needed.

Five Star Evaluation Examples (pages 242-243) Help illustrate various points of the **Five Star** grading system (see page 57).

Watch Out for These Troublemakers (page 245) shows samples of common mistakes in student handwriting. It can be made into a poster to help show students problems to avoid.

Getting Ready To Write!

1 Be Comfortable. Clear other books and papers off your desk. Sit well back in the chair with your feet flat on the floor. Your eyes should not be too close to the paper — 10 to 15 inches is ideal.

2 Hold your pencil correctly (about a half inch above the sharpened part).

3 Keep your wrist straight, allowing your arm to move freely.

4 Place your writing paper at an angle. (It should be in line with your writing arm.)

5 Work to make your letters the right size. Remember that all small letters should come to the middle dotted line. Capitals should all be the same size — from the top line to the bottom line.

6 Have a good attitude. Be positive about handwriting.

7 Take enough time to write neatly. Your handwriting makes a statement about you!

8 Practice doing your very best.

The Treehouse

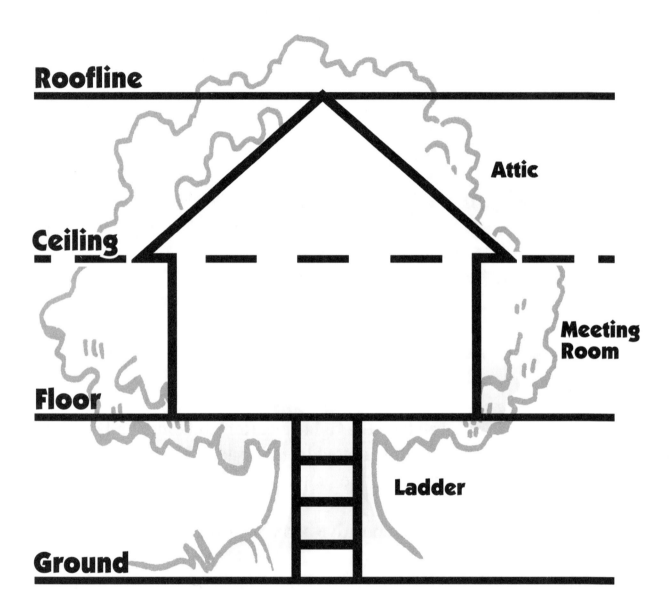

Roofline

Attic

Ceiling

Meeting Room

Floor

Ladder

Ground

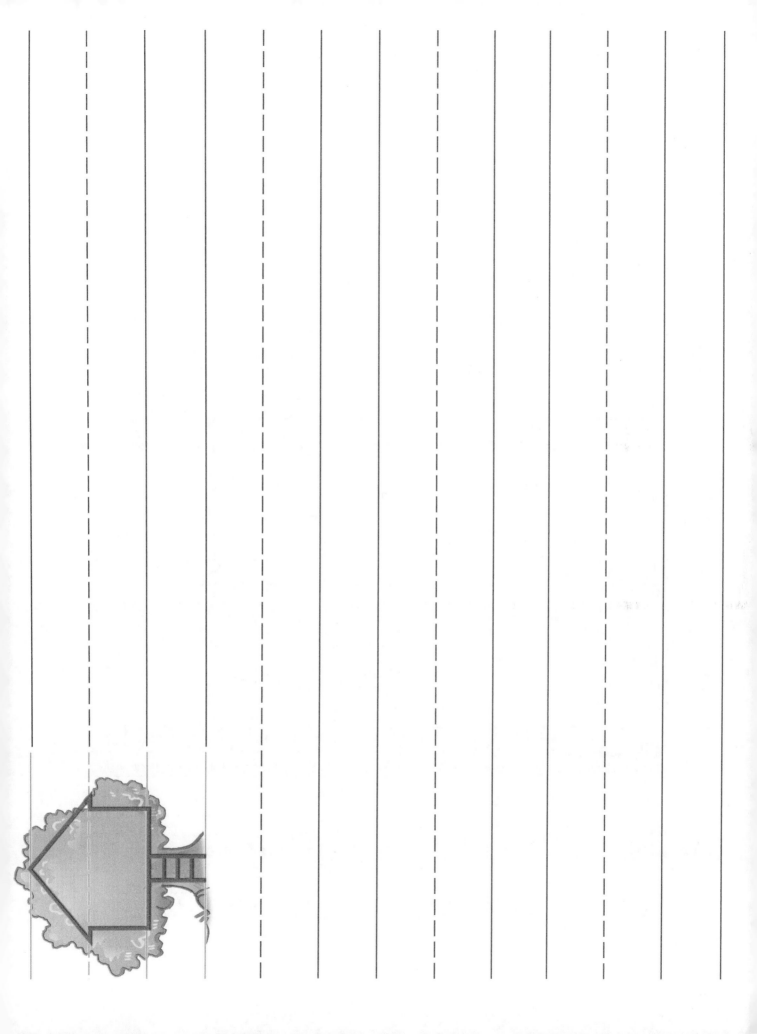

Manuscript Examples

Example 1
Alignment

Improved Form

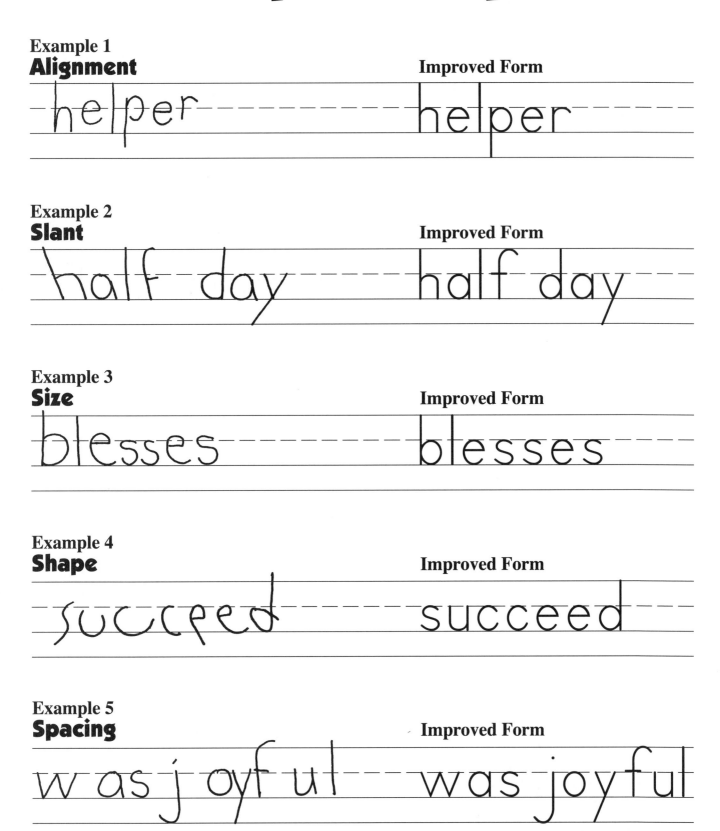

Example 2
Slant

Improved Form

Example 3
Size

Improved Form

Example 4
Shape

Improved Form

Example 5
Spacing

Improved Form

FIVE STAR
Cursive Examples

Example 1
Alignment

Improved Form

willing helper   *willing helper*

Example 2
Slant

Improved Form

half a day   *half a day*

Example 3
Size

Improved Form

blesses   *blesses*

Example 4
Shape

Improved Form

succeed   *succeed*

Example 5
Spacing

Improved Form

was joyful   *was joyful*

PRACTICING
Connecting Strokes

To strengthen connecting strokes, write each letter in groups of three.

h   *hhh*

c   *ccc*

g   *ggg*

j   *jjj*

r   *rrr*

u   *uuu*

w   *www*

m   *mmm*

n   *nnn*

v   *vvv*

y   *yyy*

WATCH OUT FOR THESE
Troublemakers

Letter	Problem	Improved Form
a	*a a u*	*a*
b	*b*	*b*
c	*c c*	*c*
d	*d d*	*d*
e	*e e*	*e*
g	*g g*	*g*
h	*h k*	*h*
i	*i i*	*i*
l	*l l*	*l*
m	*m m*	*m*
n	*n n*	*n*
q	*q q*	*q*
r	*r r*	*r*
t	*t t*	*t*
u	*u*	*u*

Handwriting Evaluation Form

• Two points possible for each •

Alignment
Letters/words sit on the line _____

Slant
Letters have the same slant _____

Size
Capital & lowercase letters
are the correct size _____

Shape
Letters are shaped correctly
and neatly _____

Spacing
Letters and words are
spaced correctly _____

Total _____

Handwriting Evaluation Form

• Two points possible for each •

Alignment
Letters/words sit on the line _____

Slant
Letters have the same slant _____

Size
Capital & lowercase letters
are the correct size _____

Shape
Letters are shaped correctly
and neatly _____

Spacing
Letters and words are
spaced correctly _____

Total _____

Handwriting Evaluation Form

• Two points possible for each •

Alignment
Letters/words sit on the line _____

Slant
Letters have the same slant _____

Size
Capital & lowercase letters
are the correct size _____

Shape
Letters are shaped correctly
and neatly _____

Spacing
Letters and words are
spaced correctly _____

Total _____

Handwriting Evaluation Form

• Two points possible for each •

Alignment
Letters/words sit on the line _____

Slant
Letters have the same slant _____

Size
Capital & lowercase letters
are the correct size _____

Shape
Letters are shaped correctly
and neatly _____

Spacing
Letters and words are
spaced correctly _____

Total _____

View All Curricula, Download Samples, and See More at:
www.AReasonFor.com